PLATO

Robert W. Hall
Professor of Philosophy, University of Vermont

London
GEORGE ALLEN & UNWIN
Boston   Sydney

**George Allen & Unwin (Publishers) Ltd,
40 Museum Street, London WC1A 1LU, UK**

George Allen & Unwin (Publishers) Ltd,
Park Lane, Hemel Hempstead, Herts HP2 4TE, UK

Allen & Unwin Inc.,
9 Winchester Terrace, Winchester, Mass 01890, USA

George Allen & Unwin Australia Pty Ltd,
8 Napier Street, North Sydney, NSW 2060, Australia

First published in 1981

By the same author:

Plato and the Individual (The Hague: Nijhoff, 1963)
Studies Religious Philosophy, editor (New York: Van Nostrand, 1969)

British Library Cataloguing in Publication Data

Hall, Robert W.
  Plato.—(Political thinkers; 9)
1. Plato—Political science
I. Title   II. Series
320.5'092'4   JC71
ISBN 0-04-320145-8
ISBN 0-04-320146-6 Pbk

Library of Congress Cataloging in Publication Data
Hall, Robert William.
  Plato.
(Political thinkers; 9)
Bibliography: p.
Includes index.
1. Plato—Political science. I. Title.   II. Series.
JC71.P6H34   321'.07   81-10943
ISBN 0-04-320145-8   AACR2
ISBN 0-04-320146-6 (pbk.)

Set in 10 on 11 point Plantin by Gilbert Composing Services
and printed in Great Britain
by Biddles Ltd, Guildford, Surrey

CONTENTS

Dedication
To my wife, Mary, and our children, Christopher, Jonathan, Pamela, Timothy, Jennifer and Nicholas, with love and affection

PREFACE

This study does not deal with the political thought of the historical Socrates as found in the *Apology* and *Crito*. References to Socrates are usually to the Platonic Socrates who as Plato's spokesman may reflect views that agree with those of the historical Socrates.

I am grateful to Professor Geraint Parry of the University of Manchester for his careful reading of my manuscript and for his helpful comments. Leslie Weiger and Carolyn Besaw provided expert secretarial assistance in deciphering a recalcitrant text, for which I am deeply indebted. The editors of the *Journal of the History of Philosophy* have kindly granted permission for me to use portions of my article 'Plato's political analogy: fallacy or analogy' (vol. XII, no. 4, 1974). Finally, I wish to thank the Institutional Grants Committee of the University of Vermont for its support of research resulting in this book.

Chapter 1

The Athenian Democracy

Plato was born in 427 BC into a noble and wealthy family, a circumstance usually guaranteeing a successful career in politics. He did not play the expected political role, however, because of his dislike of prevailing conditions in Athens. Prior to his birth Athens had evolved into a powerful democratic state with a bustling economy and a continually increasing trade. The principal factor in the rise of Athens was her navy, which was the largest and strongest in the Greek world. For glory and profit Athens gradually transformed the defensive Delian League of Greek states into her empire. A desire for more power, more influence and more trade brought Athens into a collision course with the land-based power of Sparta in 431 BC in the great Peloponnesian war. The Spartans were naturally conservative and content with the *status quo*, but they finally became alarmed at the seemingly endless Athenian thirst for power and expansion and decided on war to curb Athens' growth (Thucyd., I, 23, 6). (For a different view that takes issue with this standard interpretation cf. de Ste. Croix, 1972, esp. pp. 290–2.)

Plato saw the war and Athens' eventual defeat in 404 BC as a sign of her inadequacy to meet the political, moral and spiritual needs of the people. What Plato viewed as a decline in values was due to the cynicism and desire for immediate gratification that was, in part, brought on by the sufferings and deprivations the Athenians experienced in the war. But it was also attributed to earlier movements of thought that presented a world view that was 'scientific' or naturalistic in providing explanations of the nature of the world and its processes that avoided any reference to teleology or the action of the gods. Plato believed such a naturalistic world view was responsible for the development of a moral relativism that denied any absolute or unchanging standards of morality and society. Society was based not on nature, but on an implicit recognition by men that organized social existence was necessary for their survival and advancement. The prevalence of these views around him and the decline of values they caused was a prime factor in Plato's development as a political and moral thinker.

Plato's exposure to Socrates was a second influence that shaped his life from his youth. Plato took up the search for universal moral values which Socrates never succeeded in finding. The execution of Socrates in 399 by the restored democracy, like the excesses of the Thirty after the Peloponnesian war, had much to do with Plato's decision not to undertake the political career which beckoned him as a wealthy and well-born youth. Instead he turned inward to speculation and developed in the dialogues the theory of forms, that notion of an eternal intelligible world which contained within it certain unchanging and perfect moral and political ideals which could serve as models. To implement his educational and political goals, Plato founded his famous academy while he was still fairly young in the early years of the fourth century. Enduring for some 900 years, the academy was a center for the training of future political leaders of the cities of Greece. During the last two of his three visits to Sicily, Plato attempted to reproduce his ideals in Syracuse; he was unsuccessful because of the refusal of Dionysus, the tyrant of Syracuse, to follow his advice. Plato died in 347 BC.

The customary division of Plato's dialogues is threefold. The early dialogues reflect more of the thought of the historical Socrates and are exercises in elenchus or refutation. The middle group of dramatic dialogues presents Socrates as the chief speaker but their content goes beyond the interests and concerns of the historical Socrates. Finally in the late dialogues the dramatic element largely disappears, and the chief speaker is someone other than Socrates. The late dialogues are occupied chiefly with critical discussion of method and a painstaking and subtle analysis of logical and epistemological problems; as well as, in the case of the *Politicus* and the *Laws,* an extensive analysis of political and constitutional matters.

Although for him there was no clear-cut distinction between theory and practice, Plato's political development can be said to reflect more of a practical rather than a theoretical concern. His founding of the academy, his attempts to put into practice his ideals in Syracuse despite his realization that given the circumstances they probably would not succeed, his profound study of Greek institutions and his proposals for reform as manifested in his political dialogues in the critical as well as constructive aspects surely suggest the necessity of a radical political and social change. It is to that change that Plato dedicated himself in his dialogues.

The *Laws* did not merely continue traditional political institutions but sought to give them a new meaning and direction based on the *Republic's* view of the true nature of reality of the state, and of the individual soul. By this further development of the Socratic concern for care or tendance of the soul, Plato saw the soul's moral well-being as distinct from that of the polis, but dependent upon it for its realization. As a complement to his treatment of the *Republic's* ideal polis as a means of exploration of the justice of the individual and as an embodiment of the principles of the best state, Plato provides us with an implementation of his ideal of the best state and of the moral individual in the practical polis of the *Laws.* Whether we consider the ideal polis of the *Republic* or the practical state of the *Laws,* we can see that Plato's constant preoccupation is developing that kind of society which will bring about what he, and of course the Athenians as well, had always considered the principal goals of the state: freedom, unity or friendship among its citizens, and wisdom. .

At various stages of its constitutional development, the Athenian state displayed these principles in different ways. Athens' role in bringing about the Peloponnesian war, the defeat, the moral and spiritual decline during the war years into the fourth century, the political factionalism and abuse of political power, the prominence of convention as the basis of justice and the state, the doctrine that might is right, and the wanton individualism that cared only about the good of the self and not the common good of the community, all these factors as perceived by Plato indicated to him that something was seriously wrong in the implementation of these principles in a democratic Athens. But before considering how these principles fared in the democratic state, some mention should be made of its important institutions and the significance of Athens' commitment to the maintenance and expansion of her empire.

Aristotle's comment that the demos or people relished acting as a monarch (*Pol.*, 1313b 37–8) was an accurate description of the Athenian radical democracy of the late fifth and fourth centuries. The people had complete sway over the selection of their leaders and all important powers of the state. All male citizens over 18 belonged to the assembly which had final control over all important decisions concerning domestic and foreign affairs. The people selected from their number by lot the members of the other important constitutional bodies such as the council of 500 or the courts. By majority vote in assembly (through the showing of hands) they elected the ten generals or strategoi who were to be their military leaders, and in some cases, their political leaders for a year (and longer if the people re-elected them for additional year terms). Memberships in all these bodies as well as almost all the magistracies was open to all citizens 30 years old or older regardless of their economic and social background. The term of all offices was one year and allowed for rotation of the people in governmental offices to obtain a maximum of popular participation in the state. All successful candidates had to pass a scrutiny not of their fitness for office, but of the legitimacy of their citizenship and of their observance of various civic and familial duties. Outgoing officials underwent a searching examination, usually in the courts, of the performance of their duties. Any citizen had a right to question the record of any official during his term of office and after.

The assembly worked in concert with the council of 500, which primarily served as a clearing house for matters to be put before the assembly. But even here the assembly was able to modify whatever the council sent to it for consideration or to suggest and act on its own agenda. The power of the people was clearly demonstrated in the courts manned by hundreds of citizens. Many political careers were advanced or blighted because of the nature of the litigation brought before the courts of the people. The courts became the arenas of rivalry for power with the better orator usually winning the day. The judgment of people was final; no appeal from their verdict was possible. The people were the absolute power, 'for the masters of the judicial verdicts became masters of the state' (Bonner and Smith, 1968, p. 378).

Plato's position on the Athenian democracy of the late fifth century and the fourth can be better understood if we briefly consider some aspects of Thucydides' account of the relation between the radical democracy and the development of Athenian imperialism. For it is the spirit and character of the Athenian people that precipitated the move towards imperialism and determined the character of Athenian domestic life and politics (Grene, 65, pp. 31–2).

Thucydides in his *History* separated moral from political judgments. If, for example, he seemed to express moral disapproval of the desire for power and pleonexia, getting more than what is fitting or what is one's due, he did not let that moral judgment cloud his intellectual appraisal of its political success. He accepted the fact that the Athenians were naturally interested in practical action and in the winning of power as well as for fame, honors, renown (de Romilly, 1963, p. 79). A leader like Pericles had as an idealized goal in the quest for empire that of glory, but the ordinary individual displayed simply a lust for power, along with a lesser degree of lust for material possessions. Thucydides believed that the Athenians' actions reflected a fundamental law of human nature: the principle of force that the stronger rule over the weaker (de Romilly, 1963, pp. 336–43).

For Thucydides the exercise of power according to this law had a built in tendency towards hybris or excess. Within his political analysis of imperialism, Thucydides distinguished between a moderate, well-reasoned and thought out pleonexia as in the case of Pericles, and an immoderate, senseless pleonexia that reflected hybris, domination of reason by the passions or emotions as with Cleon or Alcibiades (de Romilly, 1963, pp. 60–1). As long as Pericles was in power, all was well with Athens, and the success of her imperialistic policy was assured.

The application of the principle of pleonexia after the death of Pericles is illustrated in two well-known incidents related by Thucydides. The Athenian decision to spare the inhabitants of Mytilene, a subject ally that had revolted against Athenian rule, was based not on any moral considerations, but on its expediency for preserving the Athenian empire (III, 44, 2–3). Again in the famous Melian dialogue, the Athenians demanded that despite its desire to remain neutral, the island state 'obey the Athenians like the rest of the islanders' (V, 84, 2). Athens' demand was in accordance with nature. Both gods and men agreed that men 'by a necessity of their nature wherever they have power . . . always rule' (V, 105), an application of the law of force. Spurning the Athenian demand, the Melians went to war and were defeated. The men were put to death and the women and children became slaves.

The implication of Thucydides' 'law of force' (de Romilly, 1963, p. 338) was that might, if wisely and temperately exercised, was justified if not right according to the way things were in the world. Plato's entire political philosophy took issue with Thucydides' political realism that the quest for power could be judicious and moderate. He sharply questioned whether the rule of the strong was justified because it was successful. Plato probably did not know Thucydides' *History* (de Romilly, 1963, pp. 364–5) but the idea that the strongest should rule the weaker was a characteristic view of his times to which many Athenians and some Sophists subscribed.

For Plato, Pericles and the other so-called great statesmen of Athens, Themistocles, Miltiades and Cimon may have been able to apply the law of force with better results than their successors in the fourth century and also have been more skilled in providing the people with harbors, naval fleets, magnificent public and religious buildings (*Gorg.*, 517a–19a). But still they were giving the people what they wanted, not what was good for them (*Gorg.*, 502d–e). True statesmen would transform their desires and make them want to become moral. But this would require knowledge that they did not have.

While Thucydides may not have seen any necessary connection between Athenian democracy and imperialism, it seems clear that Plato found more than an incidental correlation. Of course for him all existing forms of government revealed the desire for gain (*Rep.*, 548a ff.). Democracy evolved into a tyranny characterized by a single overmastering passion. Although in its constitution Athens was not a tyranny, to Plato the people and its leaders seemed gripped by the desire of pleonexia in both private and public affairs.

In addition to its promulgation of the law of force, of the legitimate rule of the strong over the weak, Thucydide's *History* relates how a 'greater lawlessness' (II, 53, 1) rose through the terrible effects of the plague that devastated Athens and the cynicism bred by the war and its sufferings; people ignored earlier religious and moral restraints on self-indulgence. Pleasure was always taken as it came. With a person's life in constant jeopardy whether he was pious or impious, personal gratification and self-interest might as well take precedence over obedience to the law, piety towards the gods or concern for the good of the community. This notion of 'seizing the day' became a persistent attitude in Athenian popular opinion down to Plato's time (Thucyd., II, 53, 2–4; Plato, *Rep.*, 560–1; Isocrates, *Areop.*, 20; Hammond, 1976, p. 167).

Another continuing feature in the fourth-century democracy noted by Thucydides in his *History* was the pervasiveness of factionalism in all of the Greek states. Political factions were formed in the various states not to act in accordance with the established laws for the common good, but the factions acted against the laws solely to gain personal advantage and power (III, 82–4). The instability and divisiveness of such factional strife continued in Athens well into the fourth century and discouraged many able individuals, including Plato, from participating in politics (Hammond, 1976, pp. 234–5).

While to some of Plato's contemporaries and to many of us today, Athens in the late fifth and fourth centuries may have seemed to be a free, united state ruled generally by wise leaders chosen by the people, Plato's view in the dialogues was much more skeptical. The principles of freedom, unity and fellow feeling and wisdom so crucial to the development of the polis from Solonian times seemed in the radical democracy to pass dialectically into their opposites. (For a different modern assessment cf. Jones, 1957.)

The people were free in the most important sense of freedom for the Greek states. They were autonomous and free from domination by other states. Freedom in the radical democracy also meant the political freedom extended to all citizens so that in theory any citizen could serve with pay in almost any governmental position. Such freedom meant freedom of speech especially in the assembly, although at times individuals who differed from the opinions of the majority would be fearful of revealing disagreement that might be thought disloyal to the state (Thucyd., VI, 24, 4; Isoc., *On the Peace*, 3–8). But despite the existence theoretically of complete political freedom, the people could elect their important leaders such as the generals only from members of the great and wealthy families of Athens.

Only individuals with the right family and social connections could belong to a sort of social and political club called a philoi whose support was usually the only way for the politically ambitious to attain power. But the demos, the moderately well-to-do or the poor could not fully play the political role the democratic constitution allowed them since they had none of the obvious advantages enjoyed by the politically ambitious aristocrat. Even the poorest citizen was guaranteed a 'voice in his city's affairs', but 'to make that voice heard, coordination, prestige, and influence were very important' (Connor, 1971, p. 29).

Pericles became the father of a new breed of statesman. Although he was a member of one of the great families of Athens, Pericles saw the political advantage of taking the people as his ally. Others after him followed his lead, especially those who had wealth but no important familial connections. New words appeared to express this courting of the people or demos, 'philodemos', love of the people, and 'polisphilia', love of the state (Connor, pp. 99–108). An individual ambitious to become a leader of the people now had to be proficient in rhetoric. Through his rhetorical skills in the assembly and other public forums, he would gain the necessary popular support either to be elected as general or to be influential in important decisions. Training in rhetoric was costly, so that usually only wealthy individuals could attain the necessary proficiency in speech to vie for political leadership. Political success was tenuous and depended on the politician's continuing ability to retain his following among the people. Failure to do so could lead to loss of face or office, or both. A politician relying on rhetoric could also be bested at his own game by an opponent more skilled in the art of persuasion.

Obviously the people were sovereign. They were also free politically to choose whomever they wished to lead them. But their choice was the most persuasive orator who was not necessarily an able statesman by Athenian standards. Although such a leader could persuade the people to select him, in turn he was led by them to satisfy their desires and inclinations. What Thucydides wrote about the successors of Pericles applies equally well to the fourth-century Athenian politicians who 'striving each to be first, were ready to surrender to the people even the conduct of public affairs to suit their whims' (II, 65, 10-11). Even a Pericles who led the people and resisted their tendency to ill-considered action was himself led by a nobler version of what was driving the citizens, the desire for empire, power and influence. He may have differed with his citizens about the means to fulfill this desire, but like them he was mastered by it.

Meeting as a crowd in the assembly or courts, the people did not always maintain a sense of personal responsibility that should go along with political freedom and power. Thucydides has noted that collectively the people at times were able to exert no self-control, were changeable and subject to fits of enthusiasm and depression (II, 65, 4; IV, 28, 3; VI, 63, 2; de Romilly, 1963, p. 330). As a writer hostile to the Athenian democracy observed, in a crowd like the assembly the people could always blame others if some matter that they passed on turned out badly. It was always easy to evade responsibility for the assembly's action by blaming whoever introduced the proposal or maintaining that it was agreed on by a few who went against the common interest (Frisch, 1942, p. 29; Thucyd., VIII, 1, 1-2). The people had the power to make new laws or override existing laws of long standing by decree and thus avoid the more lengthy and intricate process of initiating legislation. Constitutional safeguards against the abuse of such decree-making power were not always effective (Hignett, 1952, pp. 209-10).

Despite their unfettered political sovereignty the people were bound over to those politicians who could most persuasively assure them of their continued ability to enjoy such satisfactions and pleasures. The freedom of the people, then, came to be understood by Plato as slavery to the desire for power, pleonexia and self-gratification. If the people were free to choose their leaders, they chose those they thought would best fulfill their strongest desires.

The democratic constitution of fourth-century Athens did bring a political unity of sorts to the state. Political equality existed as all citizens were eligible for almost all of the offices of the state. Pay already was given to the people for governmental service to encourage the less well-to-do to participate in governance. Beginning before 389 BC citizens were paid for attendance at the assembly to encourage their greater participation. Real political unity and fellow feeling, however, were never fully established. For social and economic equality were never as completely realized as political equality. Athens was spared the anarchy that afflicted her neighbors, but she was split into factions of the rich and the poor, townspeople and the country residents. The poor and the townspeople were ready for any foreign adventure that might enable them to recover some of the material prosperity that had been lost in the dissolution of the Athenian empire (Mossé, 1973, pp. 12–17). But the rich dreaded such a move for the burden of military costs, especially building and equipping a navy for such ventures, would largely fall on them. Residents of the country had suffered heavily from the pillaging and laying waste of their land in the Peloponnesian war. Political factions representing these groups were constantly vying for political power. Stability in the external character of the democratic constitution was not matched by political and social stability.

The individual in the late fifth- and fourth-century Athens was more concerned with his own welfare and that of his relatives and friends than with the common good of society (Adkins, 1960, p. 231). The sense of fellow feeling and loyalty to the community that had characterized the Athenians during the Persian wars of the previous century was disappearing (Hammond, 1976, p. 238). The rise of professionalism in Athenian life eroded the apparent political unity of the democratic constitution. Some governmental functions, especially those dealing with finance, became so specialized and technical that experts were required on a relatively permanent basis (Mossé, pp. 25–7). In the previous century the generals were both political and military leaders. But in the fourth century the generals were usually only military leaders due to the complexity of warfare. Military costs were heavy, especially since Athenian armies were composed of mercenaries. The separation of the political from the military function of the generalship meant that the generals had a difficult time in acquiring adequate funds for their campaigns. They either had to resort to their own ingenuity in raising the money or depend on their colleagues or friends in the assembly for financial support.

The orators became the political leaders of the people. The term applied to such orators, 'demagogue', initially had a neutral meaning, 'leader of the people'. But as some of the orator politicians abused their power 'demagogue' gradually took on its usual pejorative connotation in the definition suggested by Aristotle, 'flatterer of the people'. Although it is certainly exaggerated, Isocrates' comment on the ability of some of these orator statesmen is revealing:

We pretend that we are the wisest of the Hellenes, but we employ the kind of advisers whom no one could fail to despise, and we place these very same men in control of all our public interests to whom no one could entrust a single one of his private affairs. (*On the Peace*, 52-3)

Regardless of their abilities as statesmen, politically ambitious Athenians with oratorical skills were able to gain the confidence and support of the people. Orators exercised considerable power in the political affairs of fourth-century Athens and it was prudent behavior for the prominent and politically ambitious to cultivate the friendship of orators who could make or break a man's career (Isocrates, *Antid.*, 136-71). Such power made the careers and even lives of those in important offices uncertain. Litigation involving political cases was heavy (Mossé, p. 29). Important individuals seldom lived out their lives without experiencing prosecution, exile, a heavy fine or a death sentence (Field, 1930, p. 111). Political life was unstable and during the fourth century it did not usually attract men who could most effectively lead the state.

Democratic Athens, then, in the fourth century had an outward facade of political unity that barely covered beneath it the antagonism of different factions, especially the rich and the poor, a concern for the individual over the community and an increasing specialization of government that required experts. In contrast to the older democracy of the fifth century and its political imperialism, the fourth-century democratic state contained 'only the dry bones clad in whatever rags and shreds of political propaganda happen to fit' (Grene, p. 34).

The breakdown of the close relationship between religion and the state also affected the sense of community in the polis. Religion was an intimate part of state functions. The socialized institutions and rites of religion, especially the frequent religious festivals supported by the state, gave a sense of fellow feeling among the citizens that contributed to unity. At least outwardly, citizens were expected to show reverence and piety towards the gods of the city and to participate in family religious observances of birth, marriage and death. The citizens traditionally regarded the gods as the basis of the state and its laws.

The unravelling of the intimate relationship between religion and the state was already occurring before the fourth century. The 'nature philosophers' of the fifth century questioned the anthropomorphic character of the gods and attempted to give only scientific explanations of the world and its events. Another influence separating religion from the state was the related rise of the notion that the basis of the state and its laws was not divine but came from convention or agreement among men that they would be better off in observing laws. Religious views such as Orphism emphasized a spiritual well-being of the individual and his soul that was personal and had nothing to do with the state. Finally, another form of personal religion, the family religion, was on the wane. The rites of the family religion were conducted at shrines in the political districts or demes in the country. During the Peloponnesian war these areas were abandoned for some time as the inhabitants either fought or went into Athens. The stability of the family depended on the strength of this family religion. A lessening of respect for parents and for marriage by the youth accompanied the weakening of the family religion (Hammond, 1959, p. 434).

Except for the brief oligarchic rule of the 400 in 411 and the tyranny of the Thirty in 404, the people of democratic Athens were the absolute rulers of the state. Wisdom resided in their judgment as well as the judgment of the leaders they chose to represent them. The people in the early years of the democracy were in a sense wise in choosing as their leaders Themistocles, Miltiades, Cimon and Pericles. For these leaders knew what means to use to realize the goals they shared with the people: the security, glory and advancement of Athenian interests in preserving and expanding her empire. Many of the judgments the Athenian people made under the direction of these leaders could be considered sound and moderate in achieving their goal of pleonexia. But after the death of Pericles the important decisions they reached under different leaders at times reflected a lack of sound judgment and a pleonexia associated with hybris. The unwisdom of the people and their leaders was evident in the many grave mistakes made during the Peloponnesian war. According to Thucydides, even up to the last the Athenians could have won if they had known how to make the right choices (II, 65; IV, 108; VII, 28; de Romilly, 1963, p. 317). But mastered by hybris, their reason and that of their leaders were dominated by the emotions so that they could not avoid serious errors which resulted in their defeat.

In fourth-century Athens down to the death of Plato, the people and their leaders on the whole showed a lack of knowledge of how to achieve their ultimate goal of restoring Athens to a position of eminence (Hammond, 1976, p. 222) but fourth-century Athens did have some able leaders although not much is known about them. Whatever effective policies men like Callistratus and Timotheus may have proposed, such as the second Athenian confederation, they were frustrated either by factionalism or by the short term of office of the leaders of the people. No politician was of sufficient stature to be elected year after year as Pericles was. There was no continuity of effective leadership for the development of coherent and comprehensive foreign and domestic policies (Field, 1930, p. 109). The principal problem plaguing the Athenian leaders of the fourth century was financial. The state treasury had to pay considerable amounts of money annually to the many thousands of citizens who participated in governmental affairs. Equipping and maintaining a navy as well as supporting an army of mercenaries was particularly expensive. Finally, the custom of payment of money to the poor in the fifth century for admission to state festivals and activities evolved in the fourth century into regular disbursals to the people from the theoric fund which ate up much of the state's surplus revenue.

A primary goal of both the people and their leaders of fourth-century Athens was to reassert Athenian power and influence in the Greek world. Towards this end Athens played a principal role in the formation of the second Athenian confederation (387/7), a defensive alliance of Greek states directed against possible Spartan aggression. Athens agreed to certain safeguards for her allies that would prevent the confederation from being turned into another Athenian empire. But eventually the Athenian leaders, responding to popular opinion, adopted policies that suggested to her allies a rebirth of Athenian imperialism (Hammond, 1976, p. 222). Fearing such a turn of events, some of her allies revolted in 357 and defeated Athens in 355 in what was called the 'social war' and gained their autonomy in the peace settlement of 354. The defeat of Athens ended her dream of renewed influence and power in the Greek world, a dream that was irrevocably ended by the rise of Macedonia (Hammond, 1959, pp. 513-16).

With power at their disposal the people and leaders of Athens after Pericles' death did in Plato's words 'whatever they think best', but they 'did nothing that they wish' (*Gorg.*, 467d). They wished for pleonexia, for empire, for the glory and renown of their city. But as events showed they did not know how to use the means they had to reach their goals. Ignorance made their power useless.

In a more profound sense, according to Plato, even those who were wise in the sense of knowing how to use the appropriate means to reach their end of pleonexia were ignorant of the true goals of the state and of the individual. This kind of wisdom had not been seen earlier in the development of the Athenian state. But the wisdom of knowing how to attain its ends that the Athenian state had displayed in the judgments of the people and its leaders like Solon, Cleisthenes, Themistocles and Pericles measured by the failures of Athenian policy turned into the ignorance of the people and their statesmen in the waning years of the fifth century and in the fourth century.

Despite sympathy with Plato's position, Morrow (1962, pp. 131-2) has stressed that fourth-century Athenian democracy was far from being in a hopeless condition. Although it was riven by factionalism, anarchy did not prevail. Honest and sometimes able politicians did exist. Athens experienced an economic resurgence and regained for a time something of her former influence and prestige in her leadership of the second Athenian confederation. The rich were not exploited by the poor in a wholesale way in the assembly and the courts. Constitutional checks did exist in the assembly against illegal procedures.

Mitigating circumstances such as these would not affect Plato's estimate of contemporary Athenian democracy. Nor, as we have seen, was he at all impressed by the achievements of the Periclean democracy. No reform of the existing society and its institutions could arrest the 'dry rot' (Skemp, trans. *Statesman*, 1957, p. 74, n. 29) underlying the foundations of the state as laid down by Solon. The crisis in political and moral values gripping the radical democracy stemmed from the disposition of the Athenian character to pleonexia, to always getting more. As individuals and as political leaders the Athenians justified the rule of the strong over the weak as legitimate and a fact to be accepted as the way of the world. Given the natural disposition of the Athenians, such a principle was almost a law of nature, like the dominance of the lion over other animals.

This positivistic outlook denied any purpose or teleology in the world. Legitimacy seemed to be measured by the universality of whatever occurred. Closely allied to this naturalistic world outlook was the distinction between law or convention (nomos) and nature (physis). The state and its laws had no natural basis but were the result of an agreement or convention among men.

To deal with what he considered as moral and spiritual rot Plato confronted the one-world naturalism prevalent in his day with his dualism between appearance and reality. The real world of nature was not the physical world around us. It was a changeless, intelligible world of reality and value. The nature of things was not necessarily to be found in the way they behaved in this world of appearance. Their real nature could be discovered only from their archetypes in this timeless real world. Teleology or purpose came into this world from the world of universal and eternal reality and value. The true nature of things in this real world prescribed how they should be approximated by their copies in this world of appearance.

Plato's rejection of the physical world around us as the only reality thus entailed the denial of the distinction between nature and law. For nature as he conceived it, the world of timeless values, the world of forms, provided norms or standards that were to be implemented in the state, its laws and institutions and in man as well. Both man and the state could be transformed through realizing the potentialities of their true nature. Only those with knowledge of the world of forms and of how to implement its values in the institutions and men of this world would be able to effect such a transformation.

Chapter 2

The Controversy of Convention or Nature as the Basis of the State

The development of the Athenian polis and the decline of its democratic constitution in the late fifth and early fourth centuries provide an account of the society that Plato was attempting to reform in his political dialogues. Underlying that society was a conception of nomos or law that Plato felt was the basis of the society's malaise. This view saw law, both written and unwritten, as a matter of convention. The people of the society agreed to be governed by certain rules. The only sanction for such rule was that it had been agreed upon by the citizens, and it could be changed at their subsequent pleasure. This conception of law became possible beginning in the second half of the fifth century BC because of the presocratic philosophers or physiologoi (Vlastos, 1975, pp. 1–22).

The physiologoi had secularized the universe and all that was within it. They removed from the cosmic scene the Homeric gods and their allied divine forces. The world as a whole was physis, whatever is, and there was in physis no place for the gods. Secondly, the universe did not owe its existence to divine intervention. The initial attempts by some of the presocratics like Thales or Anaximenes to find a universal substance from which all else in the universe was derived evolved into explaining, as Heraclitus for example attempted to do, the unvarying principles which governed the operation of the universe. Common to these speculative thinkers was the assumption that all that took place in the universe was interaction among its parts which had the same physis or nature. Anaxagoras attempted to propose mind or an intelligent principle as underlying the workings of the universe, but he reduced such a principle to mechanical operation immanent within the world. The order of the universe was imposed by physis itself and did not come from a source outside it.

The attempts of some of the earlier presocratics like Heraclitus and Anaximander to find common principles which applied to both the physical world and the moral and political world of man were jettisoned by the later atomistic philosophers, Democritus and Leucippus, who removed from physis any relationship to human values. Values could only be human and agreed upon by convention among men. Democritus

affirmed the separation of nomos from physis: 'by convention [nomos]
are sweet and bitter, hot and cold, by convention is colour: in truth are
atoms and the void' (Kirk and Raven, 1957, p. 422).

Nomos meant what was traditional or accepted, custom or habit. It
retained this connotation in the fifth century when nomos also began to
be used of legislated or enacted law, law as written or codified. In early
Greek thought justice or dike made nomos authoritative. Since dike
either as a personification or abstraction was divine or had divine power,
it provided a divine sanction to laws. But with the secularization of the
universe by the physiologoi the gods and their divine helpmates were
banished from the universe once and for all. Nothing remained to replace
the normative basis of the divine dike as a criterion for the validity of law.
Instead, law as set down in Athens by the sovereign people determined
what justice was (Morrow, 1948, p. 22). Cut loose from any absolute basis
law could be whatever the people or its leaders with their approval
thought to be most expedient. On such a basis did the Athenians decide
the fate of Mytilene and Melos. The ability of the Athenian demos to pass
decrees without the usual legislative procedures that had force of law and
could nullify existing laws testified to how variable and precarious the
rule of law had become both in fact and in theory.

The important distinction between nomos and physis as it governed
the development of Greek political thought in the second half of the fifth
century and thereafter was probably introduced by the physicist
Archelaus. He 'laid down that there were two causes of growth or
becoming; heat and cold; that living things were produced from slime;
and that what is just and what is base depends not on nature but upon
convention' (Diog. Laert., 2, 16). The implications of this distinction
between convention and nature articulate the problem of political
thought that Plato grappled with throughout those dialogues concerned
with the basis of society and of the state.

The Sophists who developed the influential political distinction
between law and nature, or nomos and physis (Heinimann, *Nomos und
Physis*, 1945), appeared on the scene in the latter half of the fifth century
BC. They answered a need for knowledge in many diverse subjects. The
growing complexity of life in the Greek city-states generated a demand
for technical knowledge because of the growth of business,
manufacturing and trade. Political leaders had to acquire the necessary
knowledge and skill to deal effectively with the economic, social and
political problems arising from the increase in all forms of commercial
activity. Sophists who specialized in rhetoric and the political arts were in
particular demand in democratic cities like Athens. The way to
political power in a democracy for those not gifted with wealth and
aristocratic birth, and even for those blessed with these qualities, was a
quick wit and ready tongue which could sway the opinion, heart and votes
of the demos. The Sophists usually resided in no particular

city, and traveled extensively, teaching to whoever could pay their fee.

Until recently, the Sophists have appeared in a rather unflattering light, perhaps because of Plato's unflagging attack on their positions. He detested their demand for payment for lessons, and scorned their moral and epistemological relativism, best summed up in Protagoras' dictum, 'man is the measure of all things'. Recent attempts to counter the attack of such influential and prestigious thinkers as Plato and Aristotle have presented a more favorable view of the Sophists and their humanism (Havelock, 1957; Guthrie, 1971, pp. 10–13).

There are four positions on the nature of law which are of particular importance in understanding what Plato's political thought was combatting, and they all turn on the separation of law from nature. They are presented by Protagoras, Thrasymachus, Glaucon and Callicles. They all represent a view of law as convention, but each has a special focus that Plato is trying to combat.

There is no sense of an opposition between law and nature in Protagoras' views as presented in the *Protagoras* and the *Theaetetus*. Plato's account of Protagoras' views is probably historically accurate (Guthrie, 1971, p. 266). Although the virtues which law brings about are not inherent in man he has a capacity to realize them under the proper conditions. Protagoras believed man's nature, talents and dispositions could best be organized and developed through the civilizing influence of society with its determination of what was right by the laws or conventions it had established.

There is a fundamental incoherence in Protagoras' account of how man actually entered into society and developed a sense of the social virtues. What seems clear, however, is that these qualities are not in man by nature. This is implied by the myth devised by Protagoras to show how man was created and how he developed into a social being (*Prot.*, 320c–8d). Initially men were fashioned by the gods from earth and fire and different mixtures of both elements within the earth. While they were still under the earth, Prometheus bestowed upon them knowledge of the arts of Hephaestus and Athene, as well as fire because Prometheus' brother, Epimetheus, had used up all the other qualities available to him on creatures other than man. And at this time, Protagoras explicitly notes, man did not have political wisdom, for that was in Zeus' possession, although man had the means for taking care of his physical needs.

Although Protagoras says because man had a share in divinity, he was the only animal kindred to the gods, Protagoras is not claiming that man's nature is in any sense divine or other than natural. In addition to having a conception of the gods and erecting altars and likenesses of them, man invented language, and was able to construct houses, make clothes and till the fields. At this stage of development men lived isolated lives and individually were no match for the beasts that were prowling about. So men forsook isolation and banded together in cities or settlements (poleis) because of 'the desire of collective living and of self preservation'. Gifted with the technical arts, men in the poleis still did not have the art of political wisdom, so that, while perhaps safe from the beasts, men were not safe from each other (322a–b).

To avoid the extinction of mankind, Zeus, through his winged messenger, Hermes, gave to all individuals dike and aidos. Dike was a sense of justice, and obedience to the laws of the state, and aidos meant reverence or conscience, a lively concern for one's responsibility for one's fellow members of society (Loenen, 1940, pp. 6–7). Unlike the technical arts which were intentionally distributed each to only a few men, dike and aidos Zeus ordered to be distributed to all individuals; presumably they were distributed in varying degrees, but even the least degree would be sufficient for one's loyalty to the polis. The individual without any sense of dike or aidos was to be put to death as an outcast and pariah of society (322c–d).

Although Protagoras depicted aidos and dike as gifts of Zeus, it is doubtful that as an empiricist he seriously believed in the existence of the gods. At most, he took an agnostic position concerning their existence.

As to the gods, I have no means of knowing either that they exist or that they do not exist. For many are the obstacles that impede knowledge, both the obscurity of the question and the shortness of human life. (Diog. Laert., 9, 51–2)

The acquisition of aidos and dike by men through the intervention of Zeus suggests that unlike the technical arts, they were not natural or innate in man. They were not part of physis in the sense that they constituted the nature of man; and Protagoras had no other concept of physis. Yet, if he did not really believe in the gods, the problem remained of making sense of the statement in the myth that Zeus gave aidos and dike to men for their self-preservation. Some have suggested that while the arts and knowledge of fire are part of man's natural endowment, aidos and dike must be acquired through 'time, bitter experience, and necessity' (Guthrie, 1971, p. 66). They are concepts that men acquire only through historical and evolutionary development, a commonplace assumption in theories of human progress current around Protagoras' time (Guthrie, 1971, pp. 60–3). An innate disposition towards dike and aidos is claimed as part of the natural man which finally flowers into the sense of aidos and dike that make society possible and bring about friendship and unity.

The problem which the historical account of the evolution of virtue in *Protagoras* must deal with is how can the natural man, even if he has a disposition towards aidos and dike, ever make the transition to man as the citizen who has realized in himself aidos and dike which make him a social being.

Protagoras postulates virtue as a condition of social life; at the same time he represents it as a product, through teaching, of social life. This is a standing problem for sociological realists and behaviouristic theories of ethics. Protagoras' answer, if not satisfying, is clear and consistent. Men, before societies existed, were unable to form societies, because they lacked what they could learn only from and through societies. Accordingly, divine intervention was required to enable the process to start. (Kerferd, 1953, p. 45 [cf. Guthrie, 1957, p. 92])

But clearly in view of Protagoras' agnosticism, if not atheism, divine intervention as an empirical statement of the way in which man developed historically could not be accepted. Protagoras' use of myth and the gods here seems to be a device to avoid spelling out the nature of the transition from man's natural condition to his civilized or social condition, perhaps because the precise way in which the transition occurs is not capable of consistent statement even apart from the myth.

To what extent were the principles of law and morality universal or relative for Protagoras (Versényi, 1963, pp. 30–4; Moser and Kustas, 1966, pp. 111–15; Guthrie, 1971, pp. 164–75)? Universal principles are those principles that are always present in societies although they may be realized in different ways. What appears as relative may on further examination turn out not to be so. In the famous passage in the history of Herodotus which contrasts the custom among the Indians of eating their parents with that of the Greeks in burning them, members of each group professed horror at the practices of the other (3, 38). But both groups were trying, in different ways, to honor their parents so that in fact they were advocating the same principle (Guthrie, 1971, p. 16, n. 2). Although there may be universal principles, they should be distinguished from absolute principles, especially those of Plato. Absolute ideas or the forms are intrinsically valuable, because they are what is most real; the same, of course, would hold of their closest approximations in this world. The universal principles, however, are always valuable for an end. Respect for parents, for example, is useful for maintaining the stability of the family, which, in turn, is necessary for a healthy society.

Aidos and dike which Zeus gave to all peoples 'to be the ordering principle of cities and the uniting bonds of friendship' (322c) obviously are universal. The existence of societies presupposed these two principles. But there was in Protagoras' great speech the implication that, apart from these two principles which were the necessary conditions for the existence of society, other principles, laws written and unwritten, and moral principles were relative to the society. Their validity depended on their acceptance by a majority of the community under the leadership of the type of man Protagoras professed himself to be, and whom he claimed to be able to produce through his art. Such principles were handed down through the semi-automatic educational process (Havelock, 1957, p. 178) and are presented both as traditional and authoritative in Protagoras' account.

> Education and admonition commence in the first years of childhood, and last to the very end of life. Mother and nurse and father and tutor are vying with one another about the improvement of the child as soon as ever he is able to understand what is being said to him; he cannot say or do anything without their setting forth to him that this is just and that unjust; this is noble, that is base; this is pious, that is impious; do this and don't do that. (325c–d)

Children were given examples from the poets as to what sorts of actions they must do or avoid. As they grew into adults, they were compelled 'to learn the laws and live after the pattern which they furnish, and not after their own fancies' and were punished as a deterrent for disobedience to the laws (326c–d). What society regarded as right was handed down in its poetry and art, its customs and traditions, its written and unwritten laws. The written laws constituted the positive law that had been agreed to by the people and indicated what kinds of actions the society wanted to encourage or discourage by the use of sanctions. But as the mood of the society changed, so did the moral values and the positive law which, in part, reflected them.

The changing character of Greek society reflected this relativity in the nature of the polis and its laws. The cities of Greece at different times were monarchies, aristocracies or oligarchies, democracies and tyrannies, all with different basic constitutions, laws and moral values. The constitution of Athens herself showed this relativity in its historical development.

Poetry that was studied as a means of moral instruction, as Protagoras indicated, displayed the values that were prevalent at the time. Writings of Solon, Aeschylus and Euripides reflected the trend in Athens towards democracy in the political and legal sphere. But the poetry of these authors was substantially different in its concept of arete or excellence from that, for example, of Homer or Theognis. Consequently, the education which the youth received, even if it did include the poetry of the past, would emphasize the more democratic and egalitarian aspects of contemporary poetry.

This is quite in keeping with a statement from one of Plato's later dialogues where Protagoras is reputed to have said, 'for I hold that whatever practices seem right and laudable to any particular state are so for that State, as long as it holds by them' (*Theaet.*, 167c). Here is a succinct statement that whatever is accepted as law or custom is right, if not true or beneficial, for the particular state concerned. It clearly showed that both law and morality were positive, that they were not to be judged by any other criterion than what seemed right to the particular society. Of course, all of these 'practices' were presumably adopted from the standpoint of their maintaining dike and aidos and their tendency to bring about the well-being of the society. But, again, there is no reason why different societies had to have the same concept of well-being. With an agricultural economy run by serfs, Sparta's notion of well-being was the preservation of courage and honor. At the same time Athens had as its goal the development of commerce, manufacturing and empire. While it may be true, trivially so, that something like aidos and dike were necessary for all societies to exist, laws and customs did differ from state to state and, at times, in the same state itself.

Although Protagoras recognized a distinction between nature and law, or physis and nomos, he did not consider them as opposed but as complementary. By nature man is not moral, but is disposed to morality and law. To fulfill his natural wants and needs, to develop his knowledge of the arts and crafts, man must become a social being governed by aidos and dike as ordering principles along with the 'uniting bond of friendship'. Although dike and aidos were universal for all societies, the law and morality within the society were relative and depended on the predominant climate of opinion which could be influenced by the wise man who saw a better way. That better way was based on maintaining order and friendship, but also on gaining what was thought to be profitable for the society at the time.

Thrasymachus was both a historical figure and a major character in the *Republic*, whose position gives the argument about law another direction. The challenge Thrasymachus hurled at Socrates in the *Republic* (338a–44c) through his definition or description of justice as the interest of the stronger was really to show that nomos was a strategem whereby the stronger benefited from the weaker. In no sense did Thrasymachus view justice as isonomia, as equality of all individuals before the law. We should not expect Thrasymachus to give a completely cogent and logical account of his position. Plato portrayed him as impulsive and headstrong, not altogether clear in his pronouncements; Thrasymachus intended to be shock-provoking rather than thought-provoking.

The law, for Thrasymachus, was solely a device whereby the stronger, in this case the rulers, could gain what was to their interest through the obedience of the subjects to the laws which the rulers laid down. In obeying the laws the subjects acted justly. But since the rulers made the laws for their own benefit and for the harm of their subjects, if the subjects acted justly they would be acting to their own detriment. The rulers' legal manipulations were in accordance with the desire for pleonexia, for getting more than their due. Thrasymachus uses this notion of injustice as pleonexia as a criterion of individual action that was a sign of arete or virtue. He presented injustice as a fact of life, not only among the rulers of state but also among individuals, especially in relation to their business dealings. A man who could successfully carry off his attempt at pleonexia was always better than the just man who abided by the law. Here the influence of the Thucydidean concept—of the place of pleonexia in human affairs is apparent. The only real measure of excellence among states or individuals was the success of their attempts at pleonexia. The successful achievement of pleonexia by rulers resulted not only in their own advantage but in the esteem and respect of the people. Thrasymachus also argued that for the individual injustice was a mark of excellence or virtue for it meant that he was more intelligent, stronger and happier than his victims.

Glaucon, who historically was Plato's half brother, and a character in the *Republic*, attempted to strengthen Thrasymachus' position. Glaucon's account of the origin of society (*Rep.*, 357a–62b), which he offered not as his own but in support of Thrasymachus' point of view, portrayed, perhaps more realistically than Protagoras' account, the way in which men entered into society. It depicted the entrance into society as the result of an implicit social contract, as a necessary compromise between the best of all situations, to deal with others for one's own advantage, and to be dealt with in such a fashion by others equally bent on their own well-being: 'this is the genesis and essential nature of justice–a compromise between the best, which is to do wrong with impunity, and the worst, which is to be wronged and be impotent to get one's revenge' (359a).

Glaucon presented the passage from the individual existence of men to society as the result of their prudence. Man realized that each individual would be better off under laws which protected one against the hostile assaults of others, always, of course, on the condition that one so protected would equally refrain from such acts towards others. No individual in the presocial society was strong enough to lord it over others, hence in society they were all equal before the law.

In the version of the origin of society related by Glaucon, men's nature did not change in society. Men still nursed their own egoistic aims, but more circumspectly, because of the danger of punishment. They refrained from doing wrong not because society made men moral or social beings, but because they feared punishment. In acting according to law or convention men did so unwillingly (359b). Given the opportunity to commit injustice with impunity, that is, to act against the law for one's own advantage, the so-called just man would act like the unjust, for his own profit. This is the point Glaucon makes by his tale of the Ring of Gyges, a fabled ring which makes its wearer invisible and able to accomplish the most heinous crimes with impunity (359d–60b). Physis in the guise of the selfish, grasping, covetous individual remained in society even while the individual was ruled externally by nomos, an artificial restraint. Obedience to nomos never became a part of the individual's nature. The desire for gain always flared up whenever the individual could accomplish his illegal aims safely. If he did not have the Ring of Gyges, still the individual could find ways to give the appearance of obeying the law, and have the reality of injustice as a means for realizing his egoistic and unlawful goals.

If we take Thrasymachus' doctrine that justice is the interest of the stronger over that of the weaker generally, not merely as the relation of the ruler to his subjects, we can see that a similar view prevails in Glaucon's version of society. In whatever way possible the stronger, because of legal or customary domination of the weaker, exploit the weaker under the appearance of lawfulness. Thrasymachus, as we saw, in no way advocated open violation of the law, unless one became the tyrant and could flout it without fear of retaliation.

Glaucon and Adeimantus made the point that in society the way commended by practically everyone was to live in apparent obedience to nomos or convention, but in reality to follow physis wherever possible, when it could be done without suffering retaliation (365a-d). This sentiment, of course, agreed completely with Thrasymachus' tirade. It stressed that advantage was to be secured only by following nature, that following the laws of the state was not for its own sake, but only for the appearance of justice. Thrasymachus' position seemed to be that obedience to law was but a sign of the simpleton and the weak, unless the outward show of conventional legality was supplemented by the inward drive towards pleonexia, getting more than one's share, and to all that would satisfy one's desires. Society in no way altered man's nature or physis. Through external conformity to law, it presented an additional way in which the unjust individual could accomplish safely his own egoistic and antisocial purposes if he was not a tyrant.

The last point of view is that of Callicles, a major character in the *Gorgias* whose historical reality is uncertain. The antithetical contrast between physis and nomos was passionately upheld by Callicles who can be taken as the spokesman of those who maintained according to Glaucon that unjust action was natural and to be exalted, just action was conventional and to be scorned. Law and justice arose from the impotence of the many weak to be strong and to get what they wanted from their neighbor. They resorted to laws to mask their weakness, and huddled together with their equally weak colleagues to seek protection against the naturally strong.

I can quite imagine that the manufacturers of laws and conventions are the weak, the majority, in fact. It is for themselves and their own advantage that they make their laws and distribute their praises and their censures. It is to frighten men who are stronger than they and able to enforce superiority that they keep declaring, to prevent aggrandizement, that this is ugly and unjust, that injustice consists in seeking to get the better of one's neighbor. They are quite content ...

to be on equal terms with others since they are themselves inferior. (*Gorg.*, 483b–c).

When Callicles claimed that 'nature herself reveals it to be only just and proper that the better man should lord it over his inferior', he included, despite a later disclaimer, physical strength as meaning, at least in part, the better. For, continued Callicles, 'this is the true state of affairs, not only in other animals (where physical strength is the criterion of the "better") but also in whole states and communities'. As he commented, 'this is, in fact how justice is determined: the stronger shall rule and have the advantage over his inferior'. On such a principle, claimed Callicles, did Xerxes invade Greece, and, it may be added, did Athens claim mastery over Melos during the Peloponnesian war. When men act according to their own strength they are acting in accord with natural justice, as well as with the law of nature (483d–e).

As if to emphasize his break with the Protagorean account of the education of youth to obedience to law and convention especially through the reading of the great poets and their moral exhortations, Callicles sneeringly referred to the process whereby society took out the claws and the will to power of the naturally strong so as to 'mold the natures of the best and strongest among us, raising them from infancy by the incantations of a charmed voice, as men do lion cubs; we enslave them by repeating again and again that equality is morality and only this is beautiful and just' (483e–4a).

Yet, rhapsodized Callicles, some lofty individual may appear who can trample these conventions and 'unnatural' legislation into the ground, 'our slave will stand forth revealed as our master and the light of natural justice will shine forth' (484a). But Callicles had not really thought through the implications of his position until Socrates showed him that the logic of his claim justified the existing laws as right by nature. For if the many weak were strong enough to compel the few strong to obey the laws and conventions, then, indeed, that was just or right by the law of nature as Callicles had stated it. In this case, convention was by nature. Shifting his ground, Callicles claimed that Socrates had purposely misunderstood him. What he really meant was that the stronger or better were the more intelligent in politics and statecraft. Here Callicles differed from Thrasymachus' apparent recognition that although the political leader is the crowning example of justice as the interest of the stronger, exploitation of the weaker by the stronger can exist in many different instances of such a relationship. But Callicles generally confined the superior solely to a few outstanding individuals in the political sphere. He would, however, apply it to the individual as well, in the sense of living life to its fullest, immoderately and without measure.

Although Callicles' program for the ascendancy of the natural man did not explicitly affirm that he assume the appearance of conventional justice and the reality of injustice or justice according to nature, it did go in for a heavy dosage of adopting the conventional ways. Callicles stressed to Socrates that as an adult he should shun philosophy so that he could 'taste the experiences which man must have if he's going to be a gentleman and have the world look up to him' (484c–d). Apparently our natural man, for Callicles, must really resemble those whom he professes to scorn as hidebound by convention. For Callicles, a man who wished to make his mark in the world should not, like the philosophers, 'know nothing about state laws and regulations' and be 'equally ignorant of the conversational standards that we have to adopt in dealing with our fellow men at home and abroad' (484d). In fact, in stressing the disadvantages of philosophy for the natural individual, Callicles claimed that although philosophy is a pleasant sign of good breeding, and appropriate for a child, it is ridiculous and unmanly for an adult to practice philosophy. Not knowing the law and conventions, the philosophers as exemplified by Socrates would be an easy prey for any accuser. Callicles earnestly entreated Socrates to 'take up the fine art of business', to forsake philosophy for something that would give him a reputation for 'good sense'. And, finally, Callicles recommended that Socrates imitate the pillars of society, the establishment itself: 'You must emulate, not those whose very reputations are paltry, but men of substance and high repute and everything else that is good' (486d).

Although his advice to Socrates to become a good, solid citizen may appear in conflict with his earlier praise of the lawless individual, in fact it was but a stage in the rise of the extraordinary man. Obviously Callicles exhorted the lofty individual to obey all laws and ordinances, attain all offices and honors, and win an influential and powerful place in the state as a means to winning total power and becoming a tyrant. Then the natural man would be revealed and would act according to the laws of nature in his never-ending quest for aggrandizement and personal satisfaction. Callicles himself seemed in the early stages of such a project. Socrates noted that Callicles was ever ready to follow the whims of the demos in the assembly (481e). For it was through currying favor with the assembly, by anticipating and satisfying its whims and desires that the aspiring tyrant in Athens or a city like it could gain power in accordance with law, and then seize absolute power. Only then would the tyrant, the slave turned master, sweep aside laws and conventions as lies and nonsense, unfurl the banner of the law of nature and reveal himself as the stronger and better and more intelligent who deserved to rule as he wills and for his own gratification.

Nomos, or convention, then, according to Callicles, was but a fabrication, a device of the weak to attempt to force the notion of equality down the throats of all, including the naturally better. Physis alone, and actions and laws based on it, had sole claim for validity. Still, laws and customs could be used expeditiously by the aspiring tyrant, and when absolute power was attained be contemptuously dismissed as not in accord with the laws of nature. Thus the distinction between nomos and physis applied to the political sphere had disastrous results which were implicit in the distinction and became a device to be used by the natural man to gain power in the polis. Once power was attained, the man acting according to nature would act in a lawless way to gain continual satisfaction of his desires.

Plato's opposition to the sophistic conception of nomos and its role in the polis required more than a refutation of its political and ethical consequences. For spawning the sophistic conception was the separation by the presocratics of the operations of the physical universe from those of man's political and ethical universe (Strauss, 1953, pp. 93–5). Man's own physis, as the aggregate of empirically observed, stable, human characteristics, that allowed for Protagoras a reasonable expectation of man's behavior, to Plato was an unsatisfactory basis for law and society. Plato distrusted the custom, habit, unwritten and written laws that arose primarily from empirical observation of the physical world around us, the world, as we shall see, of impermanence, of 'what is and what is not' (*Rep.*, 478d).

More unsatisfactory was Callicles' selection of some characteristics displayed in the natural and human worlds and constituting for him man's physis, the drive for excessive satisfaction of desires and appetites and the principle that might, physical and mental, was right and justified the rule of others by those naturally endowed with it (Jaeger, 1947, pp. 364–72). What Plato was searching for was an account of the universe that would explain not only how its elements operated singly and in relationship with one another, but why the operations of the elements were always for the best and how they were united by goodness.

Through Socrates' account in the *Phaedo* of his own philosophical development Plato must have also expressed his own search for such a transcendent, explanatory basis for the unity of what is and what ought to be (96a–9c). Reviewing the achievements of the presocratics, Socrates concluded:

> As for a power which keeps things disposed at any given moment in the best possible way, they neither look for it nor believe that it has any supernatural force. They imagine that they will someday find a more mighty and immortal and all-sustaining Atlas and they do not think that anything is really bound together by goodness or moral obligation. (*Phaedo*, 99b–c)

An important stage in the development of such a power is Plato's use of the Pythagorean principle of geometrical equality to give an account of a principle underlying the physical and human universe which accounts for the order and harmony of both. Addressing Callicles, Socrates affirmed that wise men say . . . that heaven and earth, gods and men, are held together by the principles of sharing, by friendship and order, by self-control and justice; that . . . is the reason they call the universe 'cosmos', and not disorder or licentiousness. Clever though you are, you seem not to have paid enough attention to these matters; it has in fact, escaped you what a mighty power is exercised, both among men and gods, by geometrical equality. (*Gorg.*, 507e–8a)

Plato is here developing a cosmic principle to unify the physical universe with the moral by predicating of the cosmic macrocosm a principle of geometrical equality that brings order within it as well as within society and the human microcosm of the soul. An individual or ruler of the kind extolled by Callicles 'would be incapable of sharing, and where there is no sharing there can be no friendship' (507e). Plato combined two different but related principles, 'sharing' and geometrical equality, or what later in the *Laws* Plato called proportional equality, giving each individual what he deserved (*Laws*, 757b–d). The observance of the principle of geometrical equality results in 'sharing' and is necessarily accompanied by friendship, self-control and justice. Plato was surely implying here that the Calliclean ideal of the 'strong man' who is constantly striving for excessive self-gratification against convention would make impossible the notion of friendship and community which were so integral to the unity of the polis. Socrates chided Callicles for neglecting geometry, and so believing that 'one should strive for a share larger than that which other men possess' (508a). Against Callicles' contention that the natural world is subject to no order, Socrates noted that the world itself is literally a kosmos or order. And he implied that just as the order in the soul that constituted its virtue or arete did not arrive by 'accident' or chance, so the order in the universe did not come about by chance or necessity (in the Platonic sense) as some of the physiologoi may have influenced Callicles to believe (Cornford, trans. *Timaeus*, 1957, pp. 165–9).

> The excellence of each thing, whether of utensil or of body or (to extend the definition) of soul or of any living thing—this excellence surely cannot be best acquired by mere chance, but by correct arrangement and by an art which is peculiar to each class individually. (506d–e)

Applied to man's soul the order that is natural to it is brought about by nomos or law.

> The word for harmony and order in the soul is 'lawful' and 'law', by which men become law-abiding and orderly. These qualities, then, are justice and self-control. (504d)

The virtue or arete a thing has is, according to the *Republic* (353d), the well performance of the function uniquely or most appropriately attributed to members of a class of any objects according to principles of nature (428e). Virtue, the realization of the function of the soul, is conceived of as justice and self-control. It is achieved through its constitution as regular and orderly, a condition which is called 'lawful', and 'law' and makes the individual himself law-abiding and orderly. Thus nature or physis conceived as what things really are is identified with law and order. Further, virtue within the individual is brought about by the true art of rhetoric which studies how justice may be brought about within the soul by applying the principle of geometrical equality in the soul to make it ordered or kosmos just as it brings about order or kosmos in the universe (*Gorg.*, 503a–b, 504d–e).

The universe, then, displays an order due to the observance of a geometrical equality which is by no means always matched in observance in the human sphere. The visible universe by its apparent order does follow the principle of sharing in a way in which men, beset as they are by jealousy, strife and factions, do not. The principle of geometrical equality underlies the physical universe, and should, although it does not always, underlie the human world. Through the application of that principle, physis and nomos are virtually identical especially in man's soul, although the principle of geometric equality does not appear to give an adequate basis in society to law and morality. It is a principle whose abstractness does not allow us to see just how its application by the good orator makes the soul just. Like the similar unifying principles of some of the early presocratics, the principle of geometrical equality is immanent within the world and descriptive of it. It does not stand outside of the world and give to it and all that is within it purpose and intelligent direction (Maguire, 1947, pp. 159–63).

To effect the union of being and value lacking in the *Gorgias* Plato literally took the concept of physis out of the world around us. For the presocratics, physis and its different manifestations *were* the world. Plato, however, took these various aspects and made of them intelligible entities, the forms, which exist in an intelligible realm completely apart from this world. In the *Phaedo* and in the *Republic* Plato formulates not an immanent dualism, but a dualism of two separate worlds: the world of forms, static, perfect, unchanging, a model for emulation; and the world around us, the imperfect, transitory, changing world in which things pass in and out of existence (*Phaedo*, 65, 74–5; *Rep.*, 476a–80a). For every class of objects in this world around us, animate, inanimate, for qualities, virtues, beautiful things, there is one archetype or form which, in addition to its above-named characteristics, is also a standard or model to be imitated or approximated in its copies in the physical world. Not only are the forms what is most real, but they are also what is most valuable. Physis, then, for Plato has become supersensible and transcends the empirical world. Physis as the world of forms provides a model or standard of justice not only for laws, but also for the individual soul, which is more akin to the forms than it is to the surrounding physical world (*Phaedo*, 79a-80b).

Plato's affirmation of an intelligible and purposeful universe is further developed in the *Timaeus*. The intelligibility and purpose of the universe is due to the direction of an all-good, but not all-powerful god or architect of the order in the universe, the demiurge, who stands apart and transcends the universe which he has ordered to be as good as possible (29e-30b). In this discussion of the mythical creation of the world in the *Timaeus*, Plato emphasized that the physical or mechanical causes of the universe cited by the presocratics were insufficient for explanation of the nature and purpose of the universe and its elements and forces. The mechanical causes were to be supplemented by intelligent causes 'that work with intelligence to produce what is good and desirable', for they 'being destitute of reason, produce their sundry effects at random and without order' (46e). Thus the metaphysical basis for dealing with nomos as mere convention was supplied by the identity of being and value. The forms, especially the moral forms, served as a standard or criterion of positive law and morality. They prescribed through those who have knowledge of them the habits, custom and laws men should follow. Here, then, was perhaps the first statement of the natural law doctrine, that laws of the polis should be grounded on the nature of reality as embodying unchanging standards (Solmsen, 1942, pp. 161-72; Maguire, 1947; Morrow, 1948).

As if testifying to the continuing influence of the materialistic world outlook of the physiologoi and its influence on theories of nomos, Plato in his last work returned again to the unity of physis and nomos (Guthrie, 1957, p. 107), though now nomos is replaced by art or techne. The Athenian Stranger, Plato's spokesman in the *Laws*, developed first the materialistic position (Pangle, 1976, pp. 1065-70), which claimed

> that the greatest and finest things in the world are the products of nature and chance, the creations of art being comparatively trivial. The works of nature, they say, are grand and primary, and constitute a ready-made source for all the minor works constructed and fashioned by art—*art*efacts, as they're generally called. (889a)

Nature and chance first brought about the material elements. These in turn 'by their own inherent properties' were the cause of the 'secondary physical bodies'—the earth, sun, moon and stars. Next, again by nature and chance, plants and animals began to exist. Art or techne the materialists disparaged as 'the mortal child of mortal beings' that has produced such 'amusing, hardly real trifles' as music and painting and their kindred arts. The only arts worthwhile are those which in cooperation with nature produce useful results: arts like medicine, farming and gymnastics which have a basis in nature (889d). But government had, the materialists contended, little or nothing to do with nature. Legislation was not a 'natural process', but was grounded on a technique and was 'quite artificial' (889e).

The gods had no basis in nature according to the materialists, but were legal fictions adopted by people, and the beliefs people had of them differed as widely as did the different conventions on which people based their legal codes (889e). Reflecting the presocratic emptying of physis of any moral or legal significance, the materialists, according to the Stranger, contended that

> goodness according to nature and goodness according to the law are two different things, and there is no natural standard of justice at all. On the contrary, men are always wrangling about their moral standards and altering them, and every change introduced becomes binding from the moment it's made, regardless of the fact that it is entirely artificial, and based on convention, not nature in the slightest degree. (889e–90a)

As a result of the relativity of moral standards and belief in the gods, the youth were influenced by the poets and the Sophists to adopt something like the Calliclean view of life, 'the true natural life' which was 'nothing but a life of conquest over others, not one of service to your neighbor as the law enjoins' (890a). These forays into individual self-gratification were strengthened by the spread of impiety among the youth which arose from the variability in the nature of the gods prescribed by the different codes of laws and led to the conclusion that there are no gods.

The Stranger was not attempting to deal with all theories that result from the separation of law from nature, but those which either lead to or represent the excessive individualism that emphasized that might was right since 'life is a conquest over others' (890a). For such an aggressive egoism leads to the disunity of the polis and not to the sense of fellow feeling and cooperation 'of service to your neighbor' which is enjoined by law. The Stranger found the Calliclean position dangerous not only in questioning the legitimacy of the conventions of society, and encouraging factionalism at the expense of cooperation in the state, but also in offering the youth a carte blanche for such a life of nature by affirming 'that anything you can get away with by force is absolutely justified' (890a).

Yet, in opposing the Calliclean position on nature as the standard for action, the Stranger is also opposing the conventionalism of Protagoras himself and its more realistic version presented by Thrasymachus and Glaucon. Although Protagoras took a more 'civilised' view of society in giving a more positive role to law and convention than the others we are discussing, he still based his account of the physis or nature of man as it appeared to the senses, employing a different selection of the empirical data available to him. Along with the analyses provided by Thrasymachus, Glaucon and Callicles, he, too, offered what was a purely naturalistic or mechanistic interpretation of man's nature. But Protagoras would contend that though law was not a part of man's physis, he was naturally disposed to follow law and convention once they had been established.

The Stranger would agree with the materialists' criticism of the Protagorean contentionalism when it showed the relative and arbitrary character of moral principles that 'men are always wrangling about their moral standards and altering them, and every change becomes binding from the moment it's made, regardless of the fact that it is entirely artificial and based on convention not nature in the slightest degree' (889e–90a).

But as the Stranger observed, it was the Protagorean doctrine of relativity that really bred the notion of the 'true natural life', 'the life of conquest over others'. The materialists in the Stranger's account implied that any intelligent youth who reflected on the implications of Protagorean relativism, that 'whatever practices seem right and laudable to any particular state are so, for that state', and on the conflicts in moral standards, would conclude that only the individual himself in his own nature was the valid arbiter of how he should act. All attempts to maintain standards outside of the individual judgment were merely sham and a cover-up by the upholders of convention who wished to maintain their power over the exceptional individual.

In his restatement of Socrates' position Guthrie brings out the moral confusion and relativism in Protagoras' conventionalism that led to the natural justice of a Callicles:

> Here are our orators, and other people talking about loyalty, freedom, equality, and other fine things as if they meant the same for everybody everywhere, yet men like Protagoras deny that such conceptions have any universal validity. We are each entitled to our own private notion of them, which remains true for us so long as we hold it. If that is so, people ought to be stopped from using these as if they were absolutes. The situation is intolerable both intellectually—for it obviously leads to a confusion of thought–and morally, since in such a situation there is no means of knowing what constitutes right action. (1968, p. 13) trans. *Protagoras and Meno*

The Calliclean position, then, naturally flowed from Protagorean relativism and really meant the abandonment of universal principles apart from man's social sense which by itself only prevents anarchy, but does not foster 'service to your neighbor'. Although Protagoras' 'man is the measure' doctrine may be applied to the moral standards and values of societies, nothing in principle precluded its extension to each individual making his own standards and values in accordance with his conception of nature. Dodds (1959, p. 14) suggests that many individuals in the late fifth and the fourth centuries did, in fact, follow a life according to natural justice. Any notion of convention as the basis of right and wrong, Plato thought, inexorably leads to each individual's claiming his own sense of values to decide what is right and wrong in politics, morality and art. The Athenian democracy in its heyday, Plato believed, allowed such relativism. Plato in the *Laws* traced the growth of lawlessness to the spreading of the belief that any individual could be an adequate judge of the value of the music he heard. This sanction of the validity of one's private judgment in music matters led to 'everyone's conviction that he was an authority on everything, and of a general disregard for the law. Complete license was not far behind' (701a).

The nomos–physis distinction, whether in the apparently milder and more humane version of Protagoras, or the more hard-boiled and realistic view presented by Glaucon and championed by Thrasymachus, or the romantic will to power glorification of life according to nature thrust forward by Callicles, underlay, Plato believed, the destruction of the moral values and political stability of the Athenian democracy. In the *Laws* Plato attempted a final reconciliation or synthesis between law or art and nature.

This is not the place to consider in detail the Stranger's refutation of the materialist claim that nature was prior to art or to law. He argued that motion or change must be caused by a principle or force that is not itself moved. This is soul, a principle of dynamism in the universe that is original, uncaused and the source of all movement. Since the soul is spiritual and the cause of all movement, its properties will be prior to material qualities: 'habits, customs, will, calculation, right opinion, diligence, and memory will be prior creations to material length, breadth, depth and strength, if (as it is true) soul is prior to matter' (896c).

As in the account of the universe in the *Timaeus*, in the *Laws* intelligence and purpose as the activity of soul were prior to mechanical explanation. Just as this soul was the source of good, so there was another soul in the *Laws* that was the cause of evil (898c). But the good soul underlay the achievements of art and legislation and its activity was what makes them truly natural in Plato's sense of the term. Plato, then, in his new synthesis of being and value provided an unchanging right or justice for law and morality, a basis which provided the content of the art of rule by the philosophers of the ideal state discussed in the *Republic*.

Chapter 3

The Inadequacy of Convention as a Basis for Society

The distinction between nature and convention removed any divine basis from society and its laws. The grounding of society's values, moral principles and written laws on custom and tradition became widely accepted. Tradition and custom were, however, subject to change. Their validity depended on how useful they were to the aims of the society and its citizens. Those traditions and customs that advanced the economic, political and military power of the polis and gave it an influential role in foreign affairs were worthwhile and 'true' for the society. The same valuation applied to the individual. Whatever gained him political and material success was useful and valuable. Any individual who realized material and political success was thought to have attained his arete or excellence.

In his examination of a society based on conventional values Plato in the *Protagoras* elected to question not the meaning of arete, but the way in which it was transmitted. Socrates observed that in the assembly the opinions of all individuals were allowed on political questions affecting the polis as a whole, whether to declare war or peace, whether to build a navy or to emphasize land forces. But a cobbler whose views on such matters would be listened to by the assembly would be howled down if he attempted to discuss technical aspects of which he had no knowledge, such as, for example, the details of building a swifter ship than existing vessels. The problem perplexing Socrates was that since everybody could give an opinion about political matters, political arete (and arete itself) is not an art that can be taught. How was it transmitted from parent to child? Socrates was particularly concerned with the problem that since a parent naturally wanted the best for his children, why were those the most renowned for arete in private and public affairs not able to transmit that arete and knowledge how to attain it to their sons (319e–20b)? Protagoras dealt with this problem in his great speech (320c–8c) by maintaining that political arete, the sense of aidos and dike, is within all individuals in varying degrees as brought about by the traditions and values of society itself. He himself claimed to be able to teach political arete to those who could pay for such teaching so as to make some more outstanding in such arete.

Protagoras' account of the educational process stressed what has been called the semi-automatic transmission of such virtue or the culture of the existing society. Such morality has 'never been a fixed and permanent quantity, but an evolving pattern of habit and response and value' (Havelock, 1957, p. 170). The educational process did not impart knowledge to the young or enable them to make informed choices. It molded them so that they were naturally disposed, without reflection, to the kind of behavior and value system that prevailed in the existing society and was considered as right and good. To bring about the conformity of the youth with the traditions into which they were born was the goal of the efforts of parents, teachers, tutors and statesmen.

It seems to be Plato's contention in the *Protagoras* that the unreflecting opinion and acceptance of values the youth absorbed in their education underlay the acceptance of the good of society as pleasure and its surplus over pain (354e–5a). Virtue as the ability to manage one's public and private affairs so as to get a maximum of pleasure over pain was acquired through the habits, routines and customs that had become ingrained in people. Virtue transmitted in this sense Socrates thought was not teachable (361b). But Socrates contended that within the hedonistic position adopted by the society the virtuous action which would be able to secure pleasure required a knowledge of the measuring art of pleasures and pains so as to acquire a maximum of pleasure with a minimum of pain (356a–c). Convention as the semi-automatic transmission of culture and values related in Protagoras' account of the educational process was unable to achieve such a goal. Without committing himself to a hedonistic position, Plato showed that pleasure for the individual could not be acquired in this fashion, but required the measuring art of pleasures and pains.

Yet Plato, as the *Gorgias* revealed, was opposed to the ethical hedonism propounded by Callicles (495a–9b) that was no different in quality than that of the *Protagoras*. Although Protagoras himself did not uphold a hedonistic theory of individual action, his grounding of society and its values on convention allowed for that kind of hedonism and its excessive gratification. For there was no way in which such a theory could be labeled false according to his principles, or any other theory of human action or behavior as long as all or most members of society agreed on it.

The *Meno* continues the problem begun in the *Protagoras*: how adequate is convention as a basis for teaching and acquiring virtue as it is commonly understood in society? Socrates asked Anytus to whom the young Meno should be sent to learn about virtue in the conventional sense in order to 'manage an estate or govern a city, to look after their parents, and to entertain and send off guests in proper style, both their own countrymen and foreigners' (91a). Anytus scorned Socrates' suggestion that perhaps the Sophists would prove to be good teachers of virtue. For, complained Anytus, they were 'the manifest ruin and corruption of anyone who came into contact with them' (91c). Socrates, curiously enough, appeared to defend the Sophists (91c–2a). Protagoras, he said, enjoyed a great following, wealth and fame throughout the long years of his profession as a Sophist. People would not have regarded Protagoras so highly and employed his services so frequently and enthusiastically if he had corrupted his students and sent them away worse off than before they came to him. And, claimed Socrates, there were many other Sophists like Protagoras, contemporary with him and even practicing during their own times, who were well thought of.

This surprising defense of the Sophists does have a subtle cutting edge which reflected Plato's distrust of the Sophists and of their abilities. Socrates compared the work of Protagoras with a restorer of shoes or clothes instead of the work he usually employed in his analogies: painting, medicine, carpentry, navigation and other such arts. It's possible to take this kind of analogy as indicating that the restorer did the best he could with the shoes or garments he was given, that he patched them up to give them a good appearance and added serviceability, but he could not restore them to their true nature. So it was with the Sophists. They could take an individual and try to cover up what for Socrates was the effect of the corruption of the existing society and its citizens by giving him the ability, chiefly through rhetoric and the political art, to win power, fame and the other trappings of success, as the Sophists and society viewed it. But the Sophists were able to give him only the conventional appearance of the fulfillment of human excellence. For Socrates these achievements won under the tutelage of the Sophists were illusory. He wondered whether the Sophists were deceiving others as to the true product of their 'art', the further ruin and corruption of the individual, or were themselves unaware of their harmful effect. Although he gave no direct indication here, we know from other dialogues, notably the *Gorgias;* that Socrates considered that the ideals inspired by the Sophists had, in effect, corrupted those Athenian leaders influenced by them, despite their outward appearance of success in politics and their making Athens during the Periclean age a greater power politically and economically than it ever was before. But Socrates probably would admit that the Sophists, on the whole, were unaware of the true harm they did because they, too, were ignorant of what was the proper excellence of man and the true art of government.

Instead of relying on the abilities of the Sophist, Anytus would send a youth eager to learn virtue to any Athenian gentleman who, in turn, was taught virtue by his 'forebears who were gentlemen themselves' (93a). In this notion of the youth assimilating virtue from his virtuous relations, Anytus displayed the Protagorean concept of education in arete as a semi-automatic transmission of the values, customs and traditions of society. Socrates conceded that there were many virtuous gentlemen in Athens, especially its leaders (virtuous, of course, in the sense described above).

But Socrates makes the same objection as in the *Protagoras* (319e–20b). If these virtuous gentlemen were able to, they would transmit their virtue by means of education to their sons, but this had not happened. It looked as if, said Socrates, virtue could not be taught, even by the great leaders of Athens (93c–4e).

But if virtue can not be taught, how did the statesmen of Athens attain their virtue and skill in political affairs? Here Plato did not mount a frontal attack on Themistocles, Pericles and the other prominent politicians of Athens, but by implication allowed us to see that he did, in fact, disdain whatever excellence they displayed as not being real arete. Having earlier in the *Meno* established that virtue was not teachable because it was not knowledge (since it apparently had neither teachers nor students), Socrates suggested that the statesmen were virtuous through eudoxia, ordinarily, though mistakenly, translated as right opinion (99c). Whatever favorable connotation in the *Meno* has been attached to right or true opinion is then applied to the eudoxia of the statesmen and the arete which it brings about. But eudoxia connotes something quite different from the true or right opinion (orthe or alethes doxa) previously discussed in the *Meno*.

The notion of right opinion developed in the *Meno* was Socrates' response to the objection, how can we inquire into something of which we are ignorant? Either we know something, and there is no need for any inquiry, or we don't know, so how can we inquire about what we don't know? (80d–e) Socrates maintained that, as 'certain priests and priestesses claim', there were within us certain right opinions, traces of a former knowledge gained in a previous existence (81a–b). Through proper questioning these opinions, Socrates asserted, could be stirred up in the individual. Under repeated questionings of the right sort, they became knowledge when 'fastened down' by knowledge of their causes. Learning was a process of recollection. Socrates believed himself to be a 'midwife' to the birth of such right opinions. The theory of recollection was developed in the famous 'slave boy' passage where Socrates interrogated a Greek slave with no previous knowledge of mathematics. By the proper sort of questioning Socrates brought to birth within him right opinions of mathematical principles (82a–6d). As Socrates' discussion with the slave boy revealed, right opinion had the same object as knowledge that came about through recollection. Unlike knowledge, right opinion was unstable, liable 'to fly away' until tethered down in the mind by knowledge of the causes.

In contrast to the frequent use of orthe or alethes doxa translated as 'right' or 'true opinion', eudoxia was used only at one place in the *Meno* in a manner which might make it appear to have the connotation of right opinion as the means whereby the statesmen of Athens acquired their virtue. Wherever the term eudoxia is used elsewhere in the dialogues it bears its usual connotation of a good reputation, name or notoriety or fame (des Places, 1970, p. 217). It is something like this kind of connotation that best suits eudoxia in the *Meno* rather than that of true opinion. Tempting as it may be to render eudoxia as right opinion because of the prominence of the use of 'right opinion' and the association of both orthe doxa (or alethes) and eudoxia with beneficial consequences, the two terms in the *Meno* should be kept quite distinct in their meanings (Hall, 1964).

Those statesmen like Themistocles 'and the rest of them' who were virtuous and controlled their states through eudoxia were likened to the soothsayers and diviners, and all those with a poetic bent in having as little to do with wisdom (99c–d). The statesmen shared the same bond of irrationality as those with whom they were linked. Like them, the statesmen 'under divine inspiration utter many truths, but have no knowledge of what they are saying' (99c). Although having no understanding, they were 'repeatedly and outstandingly successful in what they do or say' (99c). Socrates' depiction of the great statesmen of Athens as gaining their arete through eudoxia as a gift of the gods was ironic. He in no way complimented these statesmen in associating them with the poets, diviners and prophets for whom Plato had scant respect (Dodds, 1959, p. 23).

'Eudoxia' suggests that those individuals had an intuitive ability or a knack to feel the pulse of the people and then, through the persuasion of rhetoric, they did whatever was necessary to preserve and increase their power. Here the primary and conventional meaning of eudoxia is apparent. It catches the flavour of expediency, of external rightness or propriety, of bringing about the material well-being of the people and the expansion of the power and greatness of the polis, the achievement of which underlies the 'good fame' and 'charisma' of the great statesmen.

The association of the prominent statesmen of Athens with poets, seers and prophets who like them were god-gifted with eudoxia strongly indicated Plato's disapproval of the statesmen and their accomplishments. The conventional interpretation of virtue that was the basis for the praise of the statesmen was questioned when Socrates hinted that through recollection the true meaning of arete could be brought to light (86d), a suggestion not carried out in the *Meno*. Thus against the prevailing convention of arete Plato implied that there may be a true kind of arete which can be acquired and transmitted through a new kind of knowledge. This knowledge will make possible 'a kind of statesman who can create another like himself' (100a). This was, of course, an anticipation of the ideal polis of the *Republic* with its educational scheme for the development of philosopher rulers.

Although probably later than the work to be considered next, the *Gorgias* (Dodds, 1959, pp. 22–3), the *Meno* was considered in conjunction with the *Protagoras* because both, unlike the *Gorgias*, seemed to have a more tolerant view of the Sophists and the accomplishments of the great statesmen. But Plato's apparent approval in the *Meno* of the statesmen and their works is based on the conventional description of virtue offered earlier by Meno. Sovereignty or keeping a city in good order seemed to be giving the people what they wanted in terms of more magnificent buildings, more ships, increased trade and commerce, more tribute money and an ever-expanding imperialism, a view of the statesman's function which Plato thought brought the moral ruin of the Athenian democracy and its institutions.

In the *Gorgias* rhetoric appeared as the principal means whereby the great statesmen displayed their political arete and acted for what they considered the good of the polis as a whole. According to Callicles, however, rhetoric was to be used by the aspiring, unscrupulous politician as a means for winning absolute and tyrannical power in accordance with Callicles' concept of the law of nature. As we see from the history of the Athenian democracy and in the *Gorgias,* rhetoric was also a principal means whereby the statesmen and others acted according to convention in the advancement of their political and individual arete.

Rhetoric was a sign of excellence in its possessor according to Gorgias for it enabled him to persuade those ignorant of any art that the rhetorician was an expert in that art, 'for not a single craftsman is able to speak in a crowd, on any subject in the world, more persuasively than the rhetorician. This is to show you how great and how splendid is the power of his art' (456c). Specifically, rhetoric was an ability to effect 'a persuasion which can produce belief about justice and injustice, but can not give instruction about them' (455a).

Although Socrates at times used rhetoric in a somewhat specialized sense as the sham counterpart of justice whose effective use by a defendant won acquittal from the courts, he also saw its more general use as sophistry employed by the politician in gaining and using political power. The most satisfactory place in the *Gorgias* to see both uses of rhetoric, as well as the starting-point for the Platonic criticism of the great statesmen of Athens, is the well-known analogy between the arts governing the well-being of the soul and the body, and the sham 'arts' which profess concern for the well-being of the same objects (464b–e).

Attending to the care and well-being of the body were the twin arts of gymnastics and medicine. Gymnastics built up the body through exercise to strengthen it and make it fit for all sorts of strenuous physical activity. When through illness the body lost the balance or order that constituted health, the art of medicine restored its physical well-being. While Plato can find no name common to the activity of the arts of gymnastics and medicine, he compared the two sub-branches of the art of politics, legislation and justice, to gymnastics and medicine. Legislation developed the moral health and order of the soul, and justice cured the evil soul. These four arts have, according to Socrates, 'the greatest good of the soul or body in view'. As a counterpart to these arts that deal with the genuine well-being of the body is the knack of flattery which tries to please rather than to do what is good; 'it aims at pleasure without consideration of what is best' (465a). Flattery is a knack because unlike a genuine art it is irrational; it is unable to explain its methods and, therefore, how it brings about its results. The sham counterpart of gymnastics is the flattery of make-up which gives the deceitful appearance of health 'by means of forms and colors, polish and fine garments, assuming a borrowed beauty to the neglect of natural loveliness which comes only through gymnastics' (465a–b). The deceit of the knack of cookery is to replace medicine by claiming to know better than a physician what foods are best for restoring health in a body and convincing any ignorant hearers of its wisdom.

Sophistry, the 'knack' whereby the statesmen gain their power, is the sham counterpart of legislation. Statesmen made extensive and effective use of rhetoric in winning power in Athens as the history of the radical Athenian democracy vividly showed. Rhetoric, as the knack of flattery that is the sham counterpart of justice, aimed by persuasion, special pleading and advocacy of all sorts to win the day in court and enable the defendant to avoid punishment. Flattery as a whole, then, through the sham arts of cookery, make-up, sophistry and rhetoric used guesswork to displace the four genuine arts and sought to 'entrap ignorance with the bait of the pleasure of the moment' (464d).

Sophistry, as a knack of flattery, was clearly the so-called virtue which the eudoxia of the *Meno* brought about in the statesmen as a dispensation of the gods. Sophistry was irrational like eudoxia; it had no knowledge of rational procedure or of its underlying causes. It won the allegiance of the people by pleasing them, by giving them what they wanted instead of what was best. Whether through the sophistry of the *Gorgias* or the eudoxia of the *Meno*, the so-called virtuous statesmen of Athens (like the poets with whom the statesmen were linked as also being gifted by the gods with eudoxia in the *Meno*)

> strive to gratify their fellows and, in seeking their own private interest . . . neglect the common good, dealing with public assemblies as though the constituents were children, trying only to gratify them, and caring not at all whether this procedure makes them better or makes them worse. (502e)

While there may be a 'good' kind of rhetoric which always strives to make the souls of the citizens as excellent as they may be, no leader of Athens past or present has displayed it (503b). The past greats of Athens, those who might be claimed to have such a rhetoric – Themistocles, Cimon, Miltiades and Pericles – only fulfilled their own desires and those of the people. In Socrates' opinion, those desires made the people worse instead of better.

The criterion Socrates employed to judge if these past statesmen really did practice the true art of rhetoric was how they were treated by the people. If these great statesmen of the past had really performed their function of making the people better after their rule, why did the people exile Themistocles, ostracize Cimon, vote condemnation of Miltiades, the victor of Marathon, and even find Pericles guilty of embezzlement? Socrates' arguments may not appear altogether cogent or convincing to some (Dodds, 1959, p. 355), and may be exaggerated.

Nonetheless, if the education of the citizens in morality was the primary object of the statesman's rule, and if the statesmen were genuine statesmen throughout their rule, then the main point of Socrates' criticism is valid: that these four great statesmen and others like them did not do what was truly good for the people, but rather concentrated on building up the economic, military and imperial power of Athens which culminated in her physical and moral destruction. Of these four statesmen Socrates noted that, in a sense, they were better than present statesmen in giving the city what it wanted.

> But as for transforming its desires instead of toadying to them, as for persuading and coercing fellow citizens to the point of self-improvement, there is not, in a word, a whit of difference between generations. Yet this and this alone is the task of a truly good citizen. I freely acknowledge that the former age was cleverer at providing ships and walls and docks and the rest of it than are our contemporaries. (517b–c).

By giving the people what they wanted, these four statesmen allowed Athens to be a great imperial power. Her imperialistic attitude resulted in Athen's military defeat and moral decline.

> Men say that they made our city great, not perceiving that it is swollen and ulcerous because of its ancient counselors. With no regard for self-control or justice they stuffed our state with harbors and docks and walls and tribute-money and all such nonsense; so when this presumed attack of illness finally comes, they will blame the advisors who happen to be about at the time while praising to the skies Themistocles, and Cimon, and Pericles, though they were the true authors of the trouble. (518e–19a)

Dodds rightly sees Plato as not merely holding that the four great statesmen, especially Pericles himself, and their predecessors in the early fifth century were responsible for Athens' moral and political decline, but that the very way of life of the Athenian society itself, its conventions, values and laws (which according to Protagoras were right because that was what the society considered right), brought Athens to ruin. What

Plato attacks in the *Gorgias*, according to Dodds,

> is the whole way of life of a society which measures its 'power' by the number of ships in its harbours and of dollars in its treasury, its 'well-being' by the standard of living of its citizens. Such a society, he holds, was Periclean Athens, a society whose basically corrupt principles led to the corruption of all its institutions, musical and dramatic, as well as political and social. (1959, p. 33)

When Socrates at the end of the *Meno* attributed the virtue of the statesmen to eudoxia he was perhaps more subtly, but no less effectively than here in the *Gorgias*, pointing up their ignorance and the sham of any notion of their ruling as an art or science. He likened their ability to say and do the right thing to similar abilities in 'soothsayers and divines'. For nowhere do the statesmen do what a statesman should – convince the people to look after the true well-being of their souls – although they succeeded in making the 'city great'.

Plato does introduce in the *Gorgias* the idea that government, in fact, can be a science dedicated to the well-being of its object, the citizens. Socrates emphasized the importance of the individual's tendance of soul in the *Apology* (30a–e), but apparently gave up the possibility that the activity he was engaged in, his mission in life of bringing people to see the true importance of their souls and to care for their souls, properly could be conducted on a public basis (*Apol.*, 31a–e). As a private individual he claimed in the *Gorgias* to be the only true statesman of Athens (521d) because he went about, as he said in the *Apology*, exhorting people to look after the highest good in their souls, and not merely in what was pleasant, an impossible task for a statesman of the times. Yet in the *Gorgias*, indications are strong that there was a movement by Plato towards putting the Socratic tendance of the soul as the primary aim of the statesman armed with 'a good rhetoric' which would be devoted to the maximum improvement of the citizens (502e–3a). With such a good rhetoric, all that the statesman said and did would be towards 'the engendering of justice in the souls of his fellow citizens and the eradication of injustice, the planting of self control, and the uprooting of uncontrol' (504e). The introduction of a 'good rhetoric' devoted to the well-being of the soul was amplified in the *Meno*'s intimation that it may be possible that through education virtuous statesmen may be able to create others like themselves (100a). But such virtue would be quite different from that produced by eudoxia. Both the *Gorgias* and *Meno* look forward to the *Republic* with its theory of justice of the individual brought about in the polis through a 'good rhetoric'. Such a rhetoric is used by the philosopher rulers who have been educated in a science or art of government based on knowledge of the forms. In the *Republic* Plato implemented the Socratic ideal of tendance or moral care of the soul. The rulers of the ideal state would be genuine practitioners of the art of governing so that through their guidance and instruction the citizens can realize their arete.

Throughout these dialogues we have been considering there is a curious ambiguity. On the one hand, they either explicitly or implicitly praise law and obedience to law. On the other hand, in the *Gorgias* there is an explicit condemnation of the existing state and its leaders, and an implicit one in the *Protagoras* and *Meno*. But this condemnation depended on the kind of laws that the state had developed. When Socrates was attacking the ability of the statesman to provide greater harbors and ships and to make Athens an imperial power, he was also attacking the laws or decrees that the assembly passed which made Athens an imperial power and sustained her ambitions of pleonexia. Yet there can be no doubt of the sincerity of the praise that he lavished on the law in the *Gorgias*. In the *Gorgias* Socrates praised law as being beautiful (474e). Beauty was defined as what was either pleasant or useful. Obviously laws applied by the courts in punishment of those who had run afoul of the laws were useful, not pleasant for them. Laws and the obedience they required, and the punishment that they inflicted on those who transgressed against them, were necessary to prevent that lawless society which was typified by the tyrannical rule of Archelaus (470d). The sort of unjust actions Socrates had in mind were the obvious ones of theft, murder, fraud and all the other illegal means that an aspiring tyrant would employ in his quest for power. Justice was useful not only in ridding the soul of evil, but also in bringing about the stability and order in society. The quality of the just punishment 'rubs off' on the object of the punishment and obviously, not being pleasant, it was useful in purging him of the evil. Of the tendance of the soul these laws of justice said nothing. There is something odd about the unjust individual being 'restored' to justice by simply bringing himself to the court to be purged of his evil. It suggests a passivity which is incompatible with morality in any real sense of the individual's being responsible for attaining his own morality. Although it may be implied that such punishment took the form of instruction to rid the soul of the ignorance which brought about that evil, this is only conjecture and can not be based on the text. Similarly, the function of the statesman was the making of legislation that would bring about morality within the individual. According to the *Gorgias*, morality was achieved by the statesman and his appropriate laws. The craftsman of the political art looked after the well-being of the soul as the physical trainer did after the well-being of the body, and could give an account of 'the real nature of the methods it applies', and could tell the cause of such methods (465a). The analogy Socrates drew between legislation and justice and the art of gymnastics and medicine did not allow a role for the individual in acquiring or regaining morality within the soul (Hall, 1971, pp. 202–4). Like the other arts, especially those of gymnastics and medicine, all was done at the behest of the craftsman; the individual himself did nothing but make himself available to the legislator or judge for appropriate treatment.

Thus in the *Gorgias* the craftsman, the statesman, rather than the individual concerned, the citizen himself, was charged with making the individual moral; and the judge, instead of the individual, was concerned with removing the injustice from the wicked individual. But any consideration of morality stresses the moral responsibility of the individual. Regardless of how the morality of his action was characterized, whether by the motive underlying the action or by the consequences of the action, the moral character of the individual was his own responsibility and achievement. The conditions making possible the winning of morality and moral regeneration may be due to others, but the actual acquisition or moral restoration must be the individual's own doing. Plato in the *Republic* and in the *Laws* explicitly affirmed the moral responsibility of the individual within the surrounding social, political and educational context (*Rep.*, 617e; *Laws*, 770d–e, 959a–c).

Socrates' apparent preoccupation with an account of justice in the existing society rather than with legislation concerned with tendance of the soul suggests how he may both be praising law and damning law at the same time. For although there may be a normative role of the statesman in instructing the citizens on how to acquire morality, little is said concerning this science or art of legislation other than that it could exist. Not so with justice. Whatever shortcomings the law courts may have, Socrates advised the individual who had committed injustice, theft, murder, fraud, and so on, to take himself post haste to the law courts for just punishment and the removal of whatever evil was in his soul (480a–c). What this suggests was adequacy of the existing law in Athens so far as it dealt with breaches to the social order. In this sense law was praised by Socrates and was a bulwark of the preservation of social tranquility as in the *Protagoras*, even though the administration of such law might be defective. But in the *Gorgias* there appears to be no art of statesmanship in Athens, past or present, that was as adequate in leading individuals to morality within the souls, as there was an art of justice in removing evil from unjust individuals and ensuring a stable and orderly society of sorts.

Plato recognized that a kind of order and stability might be present in the state without necessarily implying that the individuals of the society were moral. This appeared evident when he noted in the *Republic* that the oligarchic man practiced a kind of 'enforced moderation' and obedience to law not because he was inwardly moral, but because he feared that in acting illegally or at the behest of his desires he would lose his fortune (554d–e). And again in the Myth of Er which concludes the *Republic*, Plato mentioned a soul in the afterlife who made a poor choice of a future life because he was from a well-ordered state with laws that were observed by its citizens, and so he was just by habit rather than by pursuing wisdom (619c–d). It was possible, then, for the laws of the state to be reasonably effective in maintaining social order and unity without making the individual citizens moral. To the extent that the art of politics through its sub-art of justice brought about political order and stability Socrates praised the applicable law; to the extent that the sham 'art' of politics through its legislative branch, in this case sophistry, made the people worse and gave them what they wanted instead of making them better, Socrates condemned the law, the state and the so-called statesmen for failure in performing the art or craft of legislation and in convincing the people that their most important concern should be the well-being of their souls. This Socratic distinction between the function of law as educating the citizens to morality and as maintaining order and stability in society leads to the development by Plato of constitutions and laws that would make possible both the maintenance of order and stability of the state and the bringing about of morality within the individual. The concept which is essential in this development is education.

Chapter 4

The Education of the Rulers in the *Republic*

While Socrates thought that government should be a science which had the tendance of the soul of its citizens as its chief concern, he could never provide a content to that science (*Euthyd.*, 292c–e). Plato succeeded in that effort in the *Republic*. Ostensibly beginning with a quest for the definition of justice of the individual in its first book, the *Republic* soon broadened its inquiry into the nature of the good society and of the good man. Justice for Plato meant much more that it does for us today. We usually give it a legal significance and think of it as related to the process of courts and the judicial arm of government. For Plato it connoted more a sense of righteousness, of what constituted man's unique or peculiar excellence or arete.

After some preliminary jousting between Socrates and his companions on the nature of justice, Thrasymachus launched his bombshell that justice was described or defined as the rule of the stronger for the stronger's interest and to the detriment of the weaker, the subjects (338c–e). Thrasymachus' argument might not be as polished and cogent as some would desire, but it does reveal his impatient and impulsive nature which blunts the fine edge of any logic he may have. It also provides ample opportunity for scholars and philosophers to write about what Thrasymachus actually did say or what he should have said. But Thrasymachus' main point is clear. Any form of government, democracy, monarchy or aristocracy, always made laws that the citizens had to obey that benefited the ruler and were harmful to the well-being of the citizens (338e–9a, 343b–c). Justice was obedience by the citizens to the laws, and injustice appeared to be the actions, such as passing the laws, of the ruling power. In a way Thrasymachus sounded two of the central thematic questions of the *Republic:* whether a man should live justly or injustly, and whether government was an art or science.

Actually the two themes are interlocked in the discussion of the *Republic*. To show that the just way of life is better than the unjust both intrinsically and in its consequences, Socrates first defined justice of the individual by showing how it was related to the justice of the state. But justice of the state and justice of the individual which can develop only in a just state (as Socrates concluded ruefully in the *Gorgias,* always, of course, excepting himself [521d]) depend on the implementation of the Socratic-Platonic principle that government was a science.

The second theme was unwillingly sounded by Thrasymachus in dealing with Socrates' initial rejoinder to his description of justice as the obedience by the weaker to laws passed by the rulers in their own interest. What, asked Socrates innocently, if the stronger made a mistake in passing their laws (339b–40c)? They passed a law which would not be to their interest if the people obeyed it. Would not this be inconsistent with Thrasymachus' initial description of justice? Failing to take the suggestion made by one of the participants that the rulers made laws which they thought were in their favor, Thrasymachus adopted the headstrong course of asserting that his rulers were to be experts and, as such, never made mistakes in their art of rule (340d–e). Pricking up his ears at this tactic by Thrasymachus, Socrates rapidly gained Thrasymachus' acquiescence in the proposition that no craftsman worthy of the name would be interested in any material benefit from the exercise of his craft but only in the well-being of the objects of his art. Therefore the ruler as a craftsman was not interested in his personal aggrandizement at the expense of the subjects, but in their true well-being (341c–2e).

If government is an art or science for the benefit of the people, then of course it must, like all arts, be in some sense taught, even if only in terms of the Platonic view that all learning is a process of recollection, a view hinted at later in the *Republic* (518d).

The content of the art of government was found in the world of forms which provided the moral and political standards and models of individual and civic life which were to be implemented in the existing society to make it and its citizens just. Only philosophers with knowledge of the forms and of the highest instance of the forms – the idea of the good, the ground of the forms, and of certainty and knowledge – would be able to practice the art of government as envisaged by Plato.

> Unless . . . either philosophers become kings in our states or those whom we now call our kings and rulers take to the pursuit of philosophy seriously and adequately, and there is a conjunction of these two things, political power and philosophical intelligence . . . there can be no cessation of troubles . . . for our states, nor I fancy, for the human race either. Nor, until this happens, will this constitution which we have been expounding in theory ever be put into practice within the limits of possibility and see the light of the sun. (473c–e)

The entire process of education from its beginning seeks to actualize in the souls of those being educated the capacity for knowing the forms and the idea of the good. The point of the famous allegory of the cave (514a–17d) was to reveal that at the successful conclusion of his education the philosopher had emerged from the cave and its shadows into the sunlight and had grasped the forms and the idea of the good, the entire soul must be turned away from this changing world, until its eye can bear to contemplate reality and that supreme splendour which we have called the Good. (518c–d, Cornford trans.)

It was this process of education which we are about to describe that was

an art of the speediest and most effective shifting or conversion of the soul, not an art of producing vision in it, but on the assumption that it possesses vision but does not rightly direct it and does not look where it should, an art of bringing this about. (518d)

Putting aside the practical difficulty as to how the ideal state of the *Republic* came into existence, let us consider the principal aspects of the educational programme from which selections would be made at each stage of those who were to continue their education and training and finally to emerge as philosopher rulers and take their turn at the helm of state.

Plato's ideal society was divided into three orders: rulers, auxiliaries and the artisans. They were placed into these orders in terms of their natural social abilities, and usually, but not always, these abilities were handed down genetically from parents to children. But in some cases those born in the ruling order might display abilities which would qualify them for membership in the artisan order, while members born in that order might show leadership qualifications and be moved up accordingly (414d–15c). Such mobility from one order to another, if taken seriously, suggests that there must be a common education of all children of the ideal state so that these unexpected talents or abilities could be discovered (Cornford, trans. *Republic*, 1978, pp. 63–4).

Initially, then, education was given to young people from whom later on a selection would be made at age 20 of those who should receive further training that would result in their becoming philosophers (537c). Those not selected would be members of the auxiliaries, the soldiers of the state. The youth who were to undergo training must display those qualities which will make them able defenders of the state, and yet cherish a sense of fellow feeling and comradeship with their fellow citizens. They should have the necessary temperament and qualities of a watch dog. They were to display the exemplary military qualities of defense–detection, speed and strength. A high-spirited nature of fearlessness was combined with the disposition to be gentle and considerate to their own people. And Socrates believed that those qualities that enabled one to detect a friend and foe were the beginning of the philosophic temperament, the passion for knowledge and understanding. Thus the guardians displayed those natural qualities which would make them 'swift, strong, spirited and philosophical' (374e–6d). Then, Socrates asked, what kind of education should these youth receive that would develop these abilities in the best way?

Clearly the beginning of this education was drawn from the traditional
Athenian mold.

What, then, is our education? Or is it hard to find a better than that
which long time has discovered? Which is, I suppose, gymnastics for
the body, and for the soul, music . . . and shall we not begin education
in music earlier than in gymnastics? (376e)

Plato believed that the environment and surroundings within which
the young are developed and nurtured were vital to what finally they
made of themselves. Given that human nature is imitative, it is all the
more important that the right sort of stimuli were presented for imitation
and the wrong excluded. The goal of the program of education was
ultimately that the guardians who were to be philosophers would 'see' the
forms and the idea of the good. These constituted the content of the art of
rule that was to be applied in the right fashion to the society. It was for
this final insight that the soul must be prepared at various stages of
education to see what was good in different manifestations leading up to
the vision of the idea of the good itself.

The first aspect of education is music. By music was meant much more
than what we today understand music to be. Music for the Greeks of
Plato's day meant the liberal arts as well: literature, art, culture and
philosophic insights. But before considering his plans for the training of
the young in music, it would be well to clarify what Plato meant by
mimesis since his views on the right kind of education depend on its
bringing about the right sort of mimesis.

Plato's use of mimesis in the *Republic* suggested a twofold meaning of
the term (395b–d). Mimesis as reflected by its context in the *Republic*
means (1) an approximation or likeness of a model, and (2) an exact,
'mirror' copy, a precise and faithful impersonation attaining a kind of
mimicry (Grube, 1958, pp. 185–90; Else, 1972, p. 35; Hall, 1974, p. 76).
Plato was concerned with the extent to which the desire for imitation as
mimicry or impersonation had permeated every aspect of Greek art and
culture. Plato thought that the individual was prone to lose what has been
called in aesthetic theory psychical distance, and to a greater or less
extent, identify himself with the character he was observing, or to place
himself in the situation he was watching. Much depended on the nature
of the object which was viewed, whether it was the 'imitation or
representation of reality as it is' or of 'appearance as it appears' (598b). It
was the latter kind of mimesis which drew the spectator into
impersonation or mimicry, while the former represented the way things
are and attempted to represent the universal rather than the particular.

For the Greek world poetry and art had a much greater force on the
development of character than we think possible today. What may seem
odd to us is not so much the fact that the young as well as the not so young

tended to impersonate those deemed worthy of impersonation by their peers, but that their models were drawn especially from tragedy or comedy. But, of course, along with music these were a principal source of participation in a common experience of culture among the Athenians. To Plato it seemed obvious that for the impressionable young, impersonation was natural.

Plato laid down norms or laws covering the content and form of poetry and literature. He had in mind a standard set down by the nature of reality which music in its extended sense should not transgress. Children were first exposed to fictitious stories about the gods which still contained a measure of truth. Such stories had to meet certain standards of content. The standards were initially termed typoi, patterns for the content and form of poetry, and were explicitly termed laws, nomoi, as well (380c). The first law or pattern stipulated that the gods were not to be pictured as acting contrary to their true nature, that they were to be represented as the cause of good only, not of evil. The fact that a god had been pictured as the source of evil was harmful because it produced a model for emulation by children. It meant that one copied badly in his speech the true nature of gods and learned a bad representation of the character of the gods, 'like a painter whose portraits bear no resemblance to his models' (377e).

The second law concerning the content of poetry required that the gods be again portrayed as they were, that they did not take on a different appearance and that they did not deceive men either in word or in deed because such deception would be inconsistent with the nature of the gods and conflict with what really is: is it not true that the gods 'are neither wizards in shape-shifting nor do they mislead us by falsehoods in words or deed' (383a)? These laws or standards, then, were based on Plato's demand that reality be imitated or represented as it really is, and not impersonated as it appeared to the ignorant artists.

In addition to the right stories about the gods, children were also to be taught in their stories to revere parents as well as gods, and to recognize the importance of getting along with one another (378a–d). Tales about how heroes and men faced death must not make their listeners afraid of death (386a–7c). The underworld, or life after death, should not be described in gloomy or terrifying terms. Heroes should not be presented as indulging in excessive grief or lamentation over the death of their comrades (387d–8c). But just as stories should avoid too much grief, so they should shun excessive laughter (388e). Truthfulness was stressed. The stories, though in a sense false in their details, nonetheless conveyed certain truths about the gods. The young should not learn deception from their stories, but only concern for the truth (389b). Fictions could be used by the ruler either against external enemies or presented to the people for the good of the state. In this way they had a medicinal or useful value (382c–d), and were not really equivalent to what some have called the big lie (Richardson, 1951). They did not say what was false in the sense of

deliberately claiming something to be what it was not. Rather they used
the fictitious to bring out certain important concepts for the well-being of
society.

Plato's falsehood or medicinal fiction of the earthborn, for example,
was not an attempt at a 'big lie'. The myth that the original inhabitants of
the ideal state slumbered and developed underground along with their
weapons had no claim to a factual basis. Obviously the myth was fabulous
and intended to be so. Plato resorted to myths in his dialogues to express
ideas or truths which in principle could not be literally substantiated,
such as the charioteer myth of the *Phaedrus* (246a–56e), and the moral
responsibility of the individual soul (*Rep.*, 614b–21d). In the myth of the
earthborn Plato was simply following a traditional practice used by the
Greeks to forge an emotional bonding and fellow feeling among the
citizens of a state. The myth that they all came from the earth was used by
the leaders of the city to imbue the Athenian citizens with a sense of
loyalty and kinship. Whether the citizens literally believed in the myth
seemed irrelevant. In remaking the political map of Attica, Cleisthenes,
for example, gave to each of the ten new tribes of citizens he created a hero
after which the tribe was named. The people of the tribe could identify
and relate to each hero as a source of kinship.

The political significance of the myth of the earthborn, then, was to
provide the inhabitants of the city with a sense of a common origin and of
being of one kind, even though as the allegory of the metals revealed they
have different social capabilities. With this penumbral association of a
common origin provided by the myth of the earthborn the citizens 'may
care more for their city'. Plato resorted to myth here because no factual
statement would bring about the close sense of kinship implied in the
myth. He, of course, intended that the myth, if possible, be accepted by
all members of the society. Socrates' hesitation about introducing the
myth indicated his reservations as to its literal credibility. Plato did not
regard the acceptance of the myth of the earthborn as vital but would
leave its fate to the tradition that may be built up about it. The myth of the
earthborn had no sinister connotation, but was a way of conveying a
unifying sentiment he thought necessary for the city that would hold the
citizens together despite their division into different orders. This
differentiation of course was not part of the myth.

Finally, Plato thought that the stories used in the portrayal of heroes
should develop a sense of temperance and self-control by restraining the
appetite for drink, food and sex, and at the same time by cultivating
courage and fortitude (389d–91e). The youth learned that they should not
be bought by money or try to bribe others. These were the norms which
Plato would want to see hold sway in all tales concerning the gods,
demons, heroes and the underworld.

Plato's discussion of style or form (lexis) was also an important aspect
of education (392c–8b). What is emphasized was the proscription of a style

of excessive impersonation. The most appropriate style was simple narrative where the author simply recounted the details of an incident. In diction as impersonation the author impersonated characters and happenings in tragedy or comedy. Plato's approval of the simple narrative style was as obvious as his disapproval of the mimicry of complete impersonation, the second kind of style or diction. Of the third kind of style or diction Plato distinguished between a good and bad kind depending on the nature and extent of the mimesis involved. This third kind was a mixture of mimesis and narration. If the mimesis was not excessively representative and the diction was primarily narrative, this mixed imitative or representative style was good. If the mixed style involved much impersonation and little narration it was bad. What this mixed style revealed of mimesis was complex, intricate, varied, and many times was violently realistic. Its practitioner attempted seriously and in the presence of many

> to imitate all things . . . claps of thunder, and the noise of wind and hail and axles and pulleys, and the notes of trumpets and flutes and pan-pipes, and the sounds of all instruments, and the cries of dogs, sheep and birds . . . so his style will depend wholly on imitation [impersonation] in voice and gesture, or will contain but a little of pure narration (397a–b).

In contrast, the mixed representative style represented or imitated the good man and had few variations in what it depicted. It allowed for few changes in the musical mode. The speaker maintained the same or similar rhythm throughout the composition, a rhythm suited to the mixture. While the youth should know what is evil they should not know it first hand. Plato's thesis seems to be that by being exposed through poetry, that is, tragedy and comedy, to undesirable, weak and emotional characters the youth would tend to imitate personally what they experienced.

> But if they imitate they should from childhood up imitate what is appropriate to them—men, that is, who are brave, sober, pious, free and all things of that kind; but things unbecoming the free man they should neither do nor be clever at imitating, nor yet any other shameful thing, lest from the imitation they imbide the reality. Or have you not observed that imitations, if continued from youth far into life, settle down into habits and (second) nature in the body, the speech, and the thought? (395c–d)

In addition to having the kind of literature appropriate in content and form for the development of the guardians, Plato stressed the importance of the right kind of song or music in a narrow sense (398c–400d). Plato thought of musical modes or harmonies (harmonia), words and rhythm as inseparable elements in song. The words of every song should conform to the standards already set down. Those musical modes which were dirge-like and funereal, the Hyperlydian and the Mixed Lydian, were rejected. Plato also found harmonies unsuitable for the development of the guardians, such as the 'slack' Ionian and Lydian modes which underwent frequent modulations, expressed many changing moods and were drenched with languor and effeminancy.

He found only two kinds of musical modes acceptable. One provided a representation of 'the utterances and accents of a brave man who is engaged in warfare or in any enforced business . . . who . . . in all these conditions confronts fortune with steadfast assurance' (399a–b). The other allowable kind of harmony or musical mode expressed the mood of temperance or mental equilibrium gained by a prosperity 'won by peaceful pursuits'. These acceptable modes were the Dorian and Phrygian. They best 'impersonate the utterances of men failing or succeeding' (399c). Rhythms were selected on the basis of conforming to the requirements of the musical mode. Plato would also allow only simple instruments for accompaniment excluding triangles, harps, flutes and all other 'many-stringed and poly-harmonic instruments' (399c–d). Here Plato seemed to be observing the ethical approach to music developed by Damon, a well-known musician and friend of Pericles (Anderson, 1966, pp. 38–42, 102–4).

When Plato warned that any change in music should be watched closely as endangering the basic laws and conventions of the state (424b), it is unlikely that he thought that a direct causal relation existed between a change in music and the endangering of the social fabric. Rather, as Plato suggested in the Laws, change in music was initially infectious and its example was followed in other areas, especially in the laws and constitution of the state (700a–1b).

Given the fact that the young were naturally drawn to a mimesis of what they were exposed to, Plato wanted the youth of his ideal state to be exposed in poetry, painting and music only to the representation of what was true, and hence what was beautiful. It is not that true art was didactic, but it provided a medium whereby the young were drawn to a love of the beautiful by being constantly exposed to it rather than to what was bad and meretricious. The ability to speak well in both style and content and to display a sense of good rhythm depended on the nature of the individual himself and the kind of mind and moral character he had.

Good speech, then, good accord, and good grace, and good rhythm wait upon a good disposition, not that weakness of head which we euphemistically style goodness of heart, but the truly good and fair disposition of character and the mind. (400d–e)

To realize the good and noble characters and dispositions that they potentially had the youth must constantly be exposed only to what was beautiful, harmonious and graceful both in objects of the natural world. and in the objects of the craftsmen. Speaking of the good and fair disposition of character and mind Socrates observed:

> there is surely much of these qualities in painting and in all similar craftsmanship—weaving is full of them and embroidery and architecture and likewise the manufacture of household furnishings and thereto the natural bodies of animals and plants as well. For in all these there is grace or gracelessness. And gracelessness and evil rhythm and disharmony are akin to evil speaking and the evil temper, but the opposites are the symbols and kin of the opposites, the sober and good disposition. (401a)

The youth, then, should from the beginning be exposed to those works of art produced by 'those craftsmen who by a happy gift of nature are capable of following the trail of true beauty and grace' (401c). Through the works of beauty that come to them through the eye and ear, the youth insensibly would be led to 'likeness, to friendship, to harmony with beautiful reasons' (401d). In the products of his craft, the able craftsman presented the order, rhythm, harmony and underlying rationality which belonged to the universe as a whole. Through exposure to such works of art, the youth realized similar qualities within themselves and developed a moral and rational character (401d, 402a). They became acquainted through sight and hearing with a sensible beauty that they would later come to know in its rational form through science and philosophy (Nettleship, 1961, pp. 112–18).

The early stage of education in poetry and music ended when not only could the youth see and love instances of beauty, harmony and rhythm in works of art, but also approximations of the virtues of temperance, courage, liberality, high-mindedness and similar qualities joined with bodily harmony and beauty (402c–d). This perception of the manifestation of the forms of virtue in beautiful sensible things was a preliminary stage in the eventual intellectual comprehension of the world of forms themselves and their approximation in things, a comprehension which characterized the true guardian (402c).

The concluding aspect of the education and training of the young guardians was physical education (403c–4e). Plato stressed that this was not simply developing the body as ordinary athletes did. Such athletes were frequently sleepy and sluggish from their one-sided training and exertions. They would be unable to withstand the onslaught of disease if they had to vary even slightly their diet and regimen. In contrast the guardians were not to develop the body at the expense of the development of the soul. Their life was to be simple and moderate so as to produce bodily health. They were to be trained to withstand changes in food, drinking water and weather. Being used to such changes of condition, they would be able to maintain their soldierly qualities at all times, and stay alert and watchful. Indeed Plato likened the appropriate training in physical education to that in poetry and music, as being 'simple and flexible' (404b-e). Both the liberal arts as embodied in the Greek conception of music and physical training were necessary, then, to bring about the right blend of the two elements of the soul, the spirited and philosophic (411e-12a).

The early stages of education including geometry, literature, music and gymnastics constituted a preliminary training which prepared the youth for the later study of dialectic (536d). Such education, Plato believed, should not be conducted as compulsory learning, but as play. For enforced learning does not stay in the mind and the natural abilities of the young can be seen better in play.

After the completion of their early education at age 17 or 18, the future guardians had to undergo an intensive military and physical training (537b). Such training, Plato believed, presented an important test of character. During this period of arduous training there would be no attempt at study since being constantly tired and in need of sleep from their physical exertions the young people would not be able to concentrate on study. Some of these young men, and presumably women, when they are 20 would be selected to study advanced mathematics in a new way by providing a comprehensive and unified view of the connection of the various branches of mathematics, including arithmetic (524d-6c), geometry (526c-7c), solid geometry (527d-8e), astronomy (528e-30c) and harmonics (530c-1c), and their relation to reality. This, averred Socrates, was the only kind of instruction which attains permanence in the mind (537c). It was mathematics which was a propadeutic or preliminary to the study of dialectic (531c-5a). Its ability to see the interconnection of mathematical objects was a valuable and necessary preliminary to the study of dialectic which grasped the interrelationship of the forms in the ways in which they do and do not combine with one another. Based on their display of character and their ability in mathematical studies, a still further selection of those who have reached age 30 would be made to study dialectic for five years. With dialectic the students no longer needed the senses and could 'follow truth into the region of pure reality' (537d, Cornford trans.). Of particular concern would be the study of moral forms or principles, especially justice.

From age 35 to 50 those who had completed the study of dialectic would be sent away from their studies to gain practical experience in political and military positions suitable for those who were taking 'on the job training' to become future philosopher rulers (539e-40a). This training period would also be a further testing period to see if the candidates could withstand temptations of various kinds. Then at age 50 those who had withstood the winnowing process and had come through all trials and 'have proved to be the best at all points of action' at last were brought to the final goal when they view that 'which sheds light on all things', the supreme form, the idea of the good. This is the capstone of the education of the philosopher king. After having seen the good itself, they take it 'as a pattern for the right ordering of the state and the citizens and themselves' (540a).

Having completed the training which began in their childhood, the philosophers would be able to alternate between study and assume the 'toils of public life' (540b). Should the philosopher

> find himself compelled to mould other characters beside his own and to shape the pattern of public and private life into conformity with his vision of the ideal, he will not lack the skill to produce such counterparts of temperance, justice, and all the virtues that can exist in the ordinary man. (500d, Cornford trans.)

After making a new start by taking 'citizens and human character as his canvas' and scraping it clean, the philosopher would 'sketch in the figure of the constitution' (501a). Then Plato went on to compare the process of rule in terms of the painter referring to his model and to the object he was painting in language he used to refer to the theory of forms.

> In the course of the work they would glance frequently in either direction at justice, beauty, sobriety [temperance], and the like as they are in the nature of things, and alternately at that which they were trying to reproduce in mankind, mingling and blending from various pursuits that hue of the flesh, so to speak, deriving their judgement from the likeness of humanity which Homer too called, when it appeared to men, the image and likeness of God. (501b)

Plato's use of language vividly brings home the way in which knowledge of the forms was intertwined with knowing the right way to govern—a rule which showed finally how Socrates' aim of tendance of the soul could be achieved in society.

The final aim of such rule made possible by this outline of the education of the philosopher king was to provide the necessary social and political conditions wherein the individual could attain justice within a just state.

Chapter 5

The Justice of the State and the Justice of the Individual

While students of Plato's political philosophy may well focus on the political implications of the well-known analogy between the soul and the state in Book II of the *Republic* (368c–9a), its underlying ethical implications should not be lost sight of. The purpose of the political analogy is to help solve an ethical problem—the definition of justice as a necessary preliminary to the answer to Thrasymachus' claim that injustice is superior to justice as a mark of the individual's arete or excellence (348e–9a). As it unfolds the political analogy does, in fact, develop a theory of the underlying basis of the state, but our keeping in mind the ethical perspective of the analogy will keep us from making the common mistake of making the analogy into an identity. Too often studies of Plato's political philosophy assume that the definition of the justice of the state ends the inquiry, that without further ado the justice of the state is applied to that of the individual (Sabine, 1959, p. 58; Wolin, 1960, p. 33; Popper, 1962, pp. 107–8). But not only does this identification alter the intent of the analogy, but it also seriously disrupts the relation of the individual to the state, and, consequently, the underlying purpose of Plato's political philosophy as it appears in the *Republic*. The *Republic*, of course, is a many-sided work and is almost a seamless web of moral, political, metaphysical and epistemological issues. To concentrate on one kind of issue to the exclusion of its relationship with the others is bound to give a false picture of that issue, as well as of the *Republic* itself.

Before undertaking an analysis of the analogy, then, let us recall in more detail what brought about the analogy. The attempted definitions of justice early in the *Republic* are ways to find out how the individual gains the arete or excellence of man so prized by the Greeks and in Plato's day considered as justice. After two unsuccessful attempts to define justice by Cephalus (331a–d) and Polemarchus (331e–5e), Thrasymachus proffered his definition or description of justice as the interest of the stronger or the unjust and launched the inquiry that finally probed into the underlying issues of statesmanship, the soul, knowledge and morality (338c). Totally rejecting Thrasymachus' claim that injustice was really a sign of greatness, Glaucon and Adeimantus pleaded with Socrates to show that justice is intrinsically valuable apart from its consequences. This was an

54

ethical innovation in the moral thought of Greece which had always emphasized the value of morality for its consequences (366d–7e; Hall, 1963, pp. 34–54). To begin to answer Thrasymachus, Socrates and his companions must provide a definition of justice, not only of the individual, but of the polis or state. For although Thrasymachus began with an account of the justice of the state, he applied his argument to a way of life in which the individual acted on the principle of pleonexia, of getting more than his share. To discover the justice of the individual Socrates proposed to his friends that they inquire into the nature of the justice of the state first, since he divined a resemblance between the state and the individual. Because the state is the larger of the two, it may be easier to find the justice of the state, and then to apply its results to the justice of the individual.

Socrates succinctly stated the essential aspects of the analogy:

The inquiry we are undertaking is no easy one but calls for keen vision, as it seems to me. So, since we are not clever persons, I think we should employ the method of search that we should use if we, with not very keen vision, were bidden to read small letters from a distance, and then someone had observed that these same letters exist elsewhere larger and on a larger surface. We should have accounted it a godsend, I fancy, to be allowed to read those letters first, and then examine the smaller, if they are the same. 'Quite so', said Adeimantus; 'but what analogy to this do you detect in the inquiry about justice?' ... 'there is a justice of one man, we say, and I suppose also of an entire city?' ... 'Is not the city larger than the man?' 'It is larger', he said. 'Then, perhaps, there would be more justice in the larger object and more easy to apprehend. If it please you, then, let us first look for its quality in states, and then only examine it also in the individual, looking for the likeness of the greater in the form of the less'. (368c–9a)

Here, at the commencement of the analogy, every effort should be made to understand its intent. Does the statement of the analogy tell us that the search for the justice of the individual will be over once the definition of the justice of the state is found, or does the definition of the justice of the state serve as an aid in discovering the justice of the individual, which is quite distinct from, though related to, justice of the state? This is an important question because it is a point on which many interpretations of Plato's political philosophy founder by assuming that they are the same. Socrates remarked that only after finding the quality of justice in the state should they go on to find its likeness in the individual; 'let us first look for its quality in states, and then only examine it also in the individual looking for the likeness of the greater in the form of the less'. Here he clearly thought of justice of the individual as distinct from that of the state, but like it.

To find the nature of the justice of the state Socrates proposed to bring a state into existence in discourse not to serve as an historical account of the origin of the state, but to show analytically the underlying principles of existing society (Cornford, trans. *Republic,* 1978, p. 53). Beginning with the economic sphere of society, Socrates discerned an underlying principle of the division of labor that based the individual's economic job on what he was naturally suited for. Instead of a man trying at the same time to forage for his own food, to weave his own clothes and to build his own shelter, he does that one task for which he is naturally suited. As a result, there is greater efficiency in the utilization of the society's resources. The underlying ground for Socrates' view was his observation that men are naturally unequal in the sorts of jobs they can do in society, 'it occurs to me myself that . . . our several natures are not all alike but different. One man is naturally fitted for one task, and another for another' (370a–b). This declaration of a fundamental difference in natural aptitude has been taken to signify a difference in human nature and value. Men intrinsically were superior or inferior as men because of their social abilities. But, in fact, the inequality of natural social abilities was balanced by an earlier, preliminary definition of the justice of the individual which showed that in a real sense men were naturally equal.

Before the statement of the political analogy, Socrates advanced a preliminary definition or description of justice of the individual. Noting that the distinctive function of the soul, the 'work which you couldn't accomplish with anything else in the world', was 'management, rule deliberation, and the like', Socrates asked, 'is there anything else than soul to which you could rightly assign these and say that they were its peculiar work?' (353d) Excellence in the performance of such activity constitutes justice. Although Socrates ironically confessed that he had not yet hit upon a definition of justice, he anticipated the definition of justice of the individual in Book IV. He emphasized the primarily inward character of justice with its emphasis on rational self-control of the soul. The 'peculiar work' of the soul applied to every soul with the implication that any man could acquire the excellence of justice through performing well his peculiar or unique function as a man. The concept of function clearly implies that it is the defining property of a class as Socrates' previous examples of the defining function of such diverse classes as eyes, ears and knives show. The distinctive function of a class is described as 'the work of a thing which it only or it better than anything else can perform'. The defining function of the individual, any individual, is the capacity to act in a manner in which he may achieve the distinctive human excellence or justice. It is this concept of a distinctive function of man which underlies the justice of the individual in Book IV.

The individual, then, can be viewed from two aspects. As a man he is equal to all other men in his capacity to acquire justice, since justice is the excellence of the function which uniquely determines the class of men. As a citizen the individual is unequal with regard to his natural, social abilities. These two aspects are complementary, rather than contradictory. They refer to different sides of the same individual, as a man, and as a citizen.

This principle of the division of labor stemming from differences in the natural capabilities of the citizens is the basis of the justice of the state. For the observance of the division of labor principle not only produces the most effective use of the economic abilities of the citizens, but also brings about the justice of the state: 'The proper functioning of the money-making class, the helpers, and the guardians, each doing its own work in the state . . . would be justice and would render the city just (434c–d).

Basic to Socrates' quest for the justice of the state is his division of society, any society, into three broad areas of social activity grounded on a similar principle of the division of the natural abilities of the citizen. Every state, argues Socrates, has a small number of individuals who by nature have an ability to rule the society. Still more individuals display a natural capacity to participate in the military or defense activities of the state. By far the greatest number of citizens is capable of attending to the legitimate and varied needs of the appetitive side of the state. The difficulty with all existing states is that citizens were not actually performing those social tasks for which they were naturally suited. In bridging this gap lies the problem of achieving, as we shall see, the just state. The problem of realizing the just state turns on the citizens doing those social activities for which they are fit by nature.

Before coming to the definition of justice of the state, Socrates first defined the other virtues and showed their relation to the different classes or aspects of society. What made a state wise was that it was ruled by those who had a distinctive flair for rational activity of a particular sort, a rational facility for the rulers to take advice 'about the city as a whole and the betterment of its relations with itself and with other states' (428d). Such a state would be 'wise and well counseled'. But contrary to many interpretations of Plato's political thought, it is not the case that all wisdom in the state was arrogated to the rulers, but only that which made a state wise. Other kinds of wisdom existed in the appetitive order. Plato's conception that a state was wise because of its rulers is a reasonable one. Today, we think of a state as wise or foolish according to the actions, statements and policies of its leaders, not of the populace as a whole. To indict the American policy towards Vietnam as 'foolish or wise' is not to say that all Americans were foolish or wise but only those who set national policy.

Like wisdom, courage of the state stems from the correct activity of those individuals naturally suited for the task of holding fast to what ought to be feared and what ought not to be feared in regard to 'pains and pleasures and in desires and fears' having to do with the welfare of the

state. Most significant for understanding the epistemological basis for
justice of the individual is Socrates' rejection of mere right opinion as a
source of genuine courage (430c). Genuine courage must not be
accidental or lucky, but the product of education in those displaying the
appropriate talent. This account of courage based on right opinion
produced by education results in the notion of an 'educated right opinion'
allied with knowledge in contrast to an inferior and empirical right
opinion.

While wisdom and courage are the well functioning of what might be
called the rational and spirited aspects of the state, temperance depends
upon the proper functioning of all three aspects of the state. It is not, as
some think, the virtue, or well functioning of the members of the
appetitive order. Temperance entails the willingness of the ruled, that is,
the appetitive order to be ruled, and the rulers, including the auxiliaries,
to rule. Temperance, then, is a kind of harmony or consensus stretching
across the whole state and creating a unified whole of the disparate orders
(432a-b). Deprived of actual political activity, members of the appetitive
order nonetheless play a significant, if hitherto largely unnoticed, role in
achieving and maintaining the justice of the state. For Socrates
emphasized that the only way in which the ideal state could be realized
was through the agreement of the citizens to be ruled by the philosopher
rulers. And it is clear that temperance must be a persistent feature of the
just state so that the agreement or consent of the citizens must be
continually presupposed. While hardly a representative democracy, the
ideal state is still by no means a benevolent dictatorship. The state would
cease if the members of the appetitive class, by far the most numerous,
were unwilling to continue to accede to the rule of the philosophers.

There has been a persistent tendency to underplay or demean the
members of the appetitive order, perhaps almost necessarily so from their
being labeled, however the Greek be translated, as workers, or artisans or
members of the appetitive order. We are accustomed to think of the
artisans, as perhaps of the proles of Huxley's *Brave New World*, as well
nigh mentally defective or people with frontal lobotomies equipped for
the menial tasks and to be considered as 'drawers of water and hewers of
wood'. But, in fact, the tasks performed by members of the appetitive
order are varied and call for different types of skill and knowledge.
Socrates himself observed that apart from the ruler's wisdom, 'there are
many different kinds of wisdom in the state' (428b). Farmers and
carpenters, for example, require knowledge to carry on their crafts.
Doctors and navigators also need knowledge of a more sophisticated sort
to practice their arts.

Knowledge is required to carry on the commercial and business
activities of the state which would be conducted by members of the
appetitive order. If, for example, we consider the many, diverse and
sophisticated kinds of knowledge that minister to the appetitive needs of

present-day society we may have a better idea of what kinds of experts are necessary to take care of the appetitive needs. In addition to what we have already named, we may include bankers, lawyers, architects and other professionals who are presupposed to have a high degree of technical competence. Surely the level of performance of the various technai to achieve the aim of the division of labor assumes considerable knowledge.

Underlying this devaluing of the appetitive order is the near identification of the two terms of the analogy, individual and state, with the term 'appetitive or artisan' being emotively charged to signify individuals intrinsically inferior to the members of the other orders. Some commentators tend to equate the task one is doing with his total personality (Foster, 1935, pp. 59, 61, 76, 99–101, 128). The artisan is pictured as appetitive from head to toe, the soldier as a warlike mesomorph and the ruler as a brilliant intellectual deprived of the spirited and appetitive aspects of the soul. Of course, nothing can be further from the truth. Plato considered that all individuals had all three aspects of soul: reason, spirit and appetites. A member of the appetitive class may be best suited to perform some task related to the appetitive needs of the society, but that does not mean that he appears as all appetite and does not use reason (Williams, 1973, pp. 198–9). The doctor takes care of the appetitive needs of society so far as the health of the individual is concerned, but surely his personality as an individual is more than appetitive, and in his activity as a doctor he uses reason rather than appetite. Simply because an individual is capable of performing an appetitive (in the larger sense) task, it does not follow that he himself is all appetite.

The fact, then, that because of a characteristic predominating in him, the individual is placed into one order rather than another simply indicates his particular social skill. It hardly means that he lacks the other aspects of psyche or soul. They are not mentioned here because there is no need. Plato was discussing the fundamental characteristics of the state, not of the individual. The virtues resulting are not those of the individual, but of the state. Consequently, Plato need only discuss those aspects of the individual which are relevant to laying out the basic structures of the state. The absurdity of depersonalizing the individual is only too clear when we consider that for Plato the three aspects of the soul belong to all human beings (Joseph, 1935, pp. 119–21).

Two problems are apparent in the definition of justice of the state, 'the proper functioning of the money-making [i.e. appetitive] order, the auxiliaries and the guardians, each doing its own work in the state . . . would be justice and would render the city just'. The first difficulty turns on the questionable manner in which Socrates alighted upon justice. The second stems from the apparent synonymy of justice and temperance. Can justice and temperance be meaningfully separated? Socrates' derivation of justice as being entailed by the discussion of the other virtues of wisdom, temperance and justice seems 'surprising' and hardly deserving of serious attention to some scholars (Popper, 1962, pp. 96–9). But, as a matter of fact, Plato has argued well. Justice comes 'tumbling out' after the discovery of the other three virtues, because they are dependent on 'the doing of one's own', which is the principle of justice (432a). The fact that the basis for the other virtues is justice (of the state) so that each man does the task for which he is best suited naturally is the way in which we come to know what justice of the state is. The virtues of the state are applications of the principle of doing that social task for which one is naturally suited. When those naturally suited for ruling are in fact ruling, or 'doing one's own', guarding the state against its internal and external enemies, the state is courageous. Temperance occurs from the willingness of both rulers and ruled 'to do their own'; by the rulers, including the soldiers or auxiliaries, to exercise rule, and by the artisans to be ruled. Yet, although special applications of justice, these virtues are not the same as justice. The fact that these virtues owe their existence to the 'doing of one's own' is the way in which the principle of justice of the state is discovered as the underlying principle of the specific virtues.

The second difficulty in considering justice as a virtue of the state is its apparent synonymy with temperance (Larson, 1951). Both temperance and justice appear to be a sort of harmony extending among the three orders of the state. Temperance implies the doing of one's social function and justice implies an agreement or harmony among the citizens. But the primary connotation of justice is active, entailing the doing of one's social function in contrast to the explicit significance of temperance as a harmony or concord among the three orders of the society as to who should rule and who should be ruled. Temperance and justice, then, are distinct virtues of the state.

The definition of the justice of the state completes the first stage in the search for the definition of the justice of the individual. But what has been defined are the justice and other virtues of the state, *not* the virtues of the individual. To overlook this fact is to pave the way to an interpretation of Plato as a totalitarian who believed the individual's primary function was to serve the state in 'his station and its duties'.

As if to make clear that the discovery of justice of the state is an aid to discovering the justice of the individual but not the same as it, Socrates urged his companions to go forward to discover the original object of their search, the justice of the individual.

> But now let us work out the inquiry in which we supposed that, if we found some larger thing that contained justice and viewed it there, we should more easily discover its nature in the individual man . . . But if something different manifests itself in the individual, we will return again to the state and test it there. (434d–e)

Here Socrates obviously distinguished between the two, justice of the state, and justice of the individual. The justice of the state may aid them in uncovering the justice of the individual, but it is clear that although there is some sort of similarity between them, the two kinds of justice are distinct.

A similarity of form as well as content exists between the justice of state and that of the individual. The similarity in content stems from the characteristics of the soul that can become the virtues of both state and individual. For Plato suggested that the characteristics which made up the three orders of the state were derived from those of the individual. 'Is it not, then . . . impossible for us to avoid admitting this much, that the same forms and qualities are to be found in each one of us that are in the state' (435e).

The virtues of the state come about because of the right functioning of its generic parts, the three orders of the state, just as the virtues of the individual, Socrates later showed, came from the right functioning of the three generic parts of his soul. Presumably the same, by analogy, would be true of the individual soul if it could be shown to have similar generic parts or characteristics.

These characteristics, forms or generic parts, contrary to customary interpretations, are not the virtues although they are the basis for virtues (Vlastos, 1969, p. 512). It makes sense to take characteristics or dispositions as non-moral, rather than moral, derived from all or most of its citizens. Socrates, for example, noted how absurd it would be to assume that 'the element of high spirit was not derived in states from the private citizens who are reputed to have this quality' (435e). Similarly, he considered it foolish that the love of knowledge was not to be predicated of the region where Socrates and his friends live, or that the love of money found in Egypt or Phoenicia was not to be derived from its citizens. It could be argued that the example of the Egyptians' love of money had a morally deprecatory meaning, rather than a morally neutral sense. But at the same time, Socrates attributed to Athens the love of knowledge. Yet, surely he would not admit that the Athens of his time exhibited the wisdom that he later would find in the ideal state. These examples merely indicate that the state manifests the non-moral characteristics of its citizens. The rational, spirited and appetitive characteristics, or generic parts of the state, come from individuals whose natural capacities for social tasks are unequal and are the reason for their belonging to one of the three orders of the state.

Basic to understanding Plato's analysis of the relation of the justice of the state to that of the individual is his account of the three aspects or 'parts' of the individual soul (435a–41c). For not only does the threefold grouping of generic parts or characteristics which are the bases of the virtues of the state come from the three aspects of the soul, but the virtues of the individual, too, come from them as well. Plato obviously here was not so much discovering the fact that there are three aspects of the soul as he was justifying his belief that there were these three aspects. For the orders of the state were predicated on a similar distinction in the individual soul. So that in 'proving' that the individual soul had three aspects, Socrates was merely establishing for the record what he already assumed. In his account of the state and its virtues, Plato's placement of the discussion justifying and explaining the three aspects of soul was not so much logical as transitional. Logically the discussion of the three aspects of the soul should have preceded the analysis of the state and its three orders. But it serves as a bridge between the justice of the state and that of the individual. The analysis of the three aspects of the soul further refines and clarifies Socrates' earlier statement of the distinctive function of the soul as (353d) 'deliberating, exercising control, and taking charge'. The soul is considered in terms of the different aspects of living in the moral sense unique to man. The soul is a complex whole. Each of its three aspects, reason, spirit and appetites, has its own distinctive function in relation to the overall function of the soul as living. Each aspect, like the soul, is complex and has its appropriate desires, pleasures and satisfactions which it realizes when it does its appropriate task (580d, 586d–e).

The signal importance of this division of the human soul into three aspects is the way in which it confirms and expands Socrates' initial functional definition of man so that all men are naturally equal in having as their distinctive human function, their function as men, the condition of justice. Plato made it clear that every individual, regardless of any aptitude or knowledge of the forms, had the same three aspects as any other man. Every man, then, in displaying these three aspects of soul had the same potentiality for expressing the unique human function that was realized in the just condition of the soul.

Once Socrates had established that the individual soul did have three aspects similar to those of the state (426a–41c), he applied the insights he received from finding the nature of the justice of the state to the justice of the individual. These characteristics or generic parts are present in different degrees in the souls of the citizens with one characteristic naturally predominating in the performance of tasks. These characteristics, both in the state and the individual, have a natural (in Plato's sense) tendency to be under the guide of the rational characteristic. But just as in the state those characteristics which naturally should predominate do not, so with the characteristics in the individual soul; the rational characteristic should predominate in all individuals but, as a matter of fact, it may not.

The generic parts or characteristics, then, of the individual have two different ranges of application. They reveal one respect in which the individuals as citizens display them in differing amounts thus making up the justice of the state and accounting for a certain inequality in social aptitudes. But these same characteristics are, in a different respect, the ground for the virtues of the individual. Reason, spirit and the appetites in the individual are the basis for the virtues in the individual, but they bring about an equality in justice among individuals rather than an inequality in social tasks as does justice of the state. Justice of the individual signifies the fundamental equality that man *qua* man has with his fellows in the capacity to acquire inward justice. For when reason rules the individual soul, it can do so only in the same way for all; either reason rules or it does not. On a different level, individuals are unequal in terms of the social kind of task they can do. This, then, brings out the underlying differences between justice of the state and that of the individual.

The natural working of these characteristics of the soul in terms of performance of the state's functions results in an inequality in ability among the citizens, because the principle of justice of the state is realized through such inequality. The achievement of justice of the individual presupposes that every individual acquires justice in the same way through the correct organization of the three aspects of his soul. The basis of the difference between the two justices is that in the justice of the state one of the three characteristics as applied to social functioning predominates in the three different groupings of citizens. Hence justice of the state requires the achievement of a kind of social inequality, but justice of the individual requires that within each individual the same characteristic, reason, should predominate.

What distinguishes the application of these characteristics is their context. The characteristics as applied socially are inter-individual; individuals from the appetitive order display talents appropriate to their order, those from the spirited aspect reveal their military aptitude, and so on. Applied to the individual's own justice these characteristics are intra-individual. To achieve their own justice all individuals order their souls in the same way, unlike the differences they display in doing their social abilities. So that although the same characteristics are in play in achieving the justice of the state and that of the individual, they have different areas of application which provide the distinction between the justice of the state and that of the individual. As Socrates himself noted in the statement of the analogy, a similarity or likeness rather than an identity of form exists between the justice of the state and that of the individual.

The link between the justice of the state and that of the individual is the form or eidos of justice: 'Then a just man . . . will not differ at all from a just city in respect of the very form of justice, but will be like it' (435a–b). But here, of course, eidos or form does not mean content. Socrates, surely, does not mean that the justice of the individual is the same as that of the state, each citizen doing his appropriate social function. 'Eidos' also means 'form' or 'shape'. Socrates noted this when he remarked that the just man will be like, not identical with, the just state. Now the eidos or character of the justice of the state and of the individual taken as 'form' or 'shape' is the same, 'the doing of one's own', but it does not follow that two wholes are identical because they have the same shape or form. This identity of form or eidos stems from the principle of the specialization of function. Both wholes, that of the state and that of the individual, have the same eidos in that the generic parts or aspects of the whole are arranged in their natural (what ought to be), hierarchical order with the rational aspect ruling the whole. It is in this way that 'the just man will not differ in any way from the just state in respect of the very character [eidos] of justice'. The phrase 'but will be like' shows that the just individual and the just state are not identical, but like or similar. For the generic parts or aspects of the individual soul are only like those of the state because they are intra-individual; those of the state are inter-individual. As justice of the individual arranges the aspects of the soul in their proper order and relationship, so justice of the state attains the proper functioning of the three aspects or classes of the state. But the 'parts' of the soul are not the same as the 'parts' or classes of the state.

The virtue of wisdom displays a similar identity of form and difference of content when applied to the individual and to the state. The eidos or form of wisdom is the ruling of the whole by the rational part, with reason ordering inwardly the whole of which it is a part, and directing its internal and external activities (428c–d). This eidos or form of wisdom is identical in both state and individual (442c). The difference in content, again, is due to the difference of the medium in which the eidos of wisdom is applied, and in the basis of such wisdom. Applied to the state, such wisdom requires the philosophers and their specialized knowledge of the forms. Applied to the individual living within the ideal state, wisdom concerning the direction of his internal and external affairs can be acquired through what I call 'educated right opinion'. Such 'wisdom' is calculative or deliberative as the use of to logistikon, the rational aspect of the individual's soul, implies (441e).

Temperance of the state and of the individual occurs when the generic, appetitive part of the individual and the generic, appetitive 'part' of the state, the artisan class, are each 'doing its own' under the guidance of their respective rational generic aspects. In doing its own, each rational aspect (of the state and of the individual) agrees to rule the whole and the other two aspects agree to be ruled. This harmony or agreement between the natural aspect on the one hand and the spirited and appetitive aspects on the other as to who rules and who is ruled constitutes the identity of the eidos of the temperance of the soul and that of the state (432a, 442c–d). The differences between the individual and the state account for the different content in the temperance of the individual and that of the state. The rational part of the individual rules over the spirited aspect of the appetites which contribute to the satisfaction of his different individual needs; the philosopher rulers direct the activities of the auxiliary and appetitive orders in meeting the economic needs of the whole society.

Courage of the individual occurs when the spirited aspect keeps to the 'rule handed down by reason' as to what pains and pleasures ought to be feared and what ought not to be feared (442c), just as the courage of the state is won when those citizens constituting the spirited characteristic of the society preserve the conviction of what ought to be feared and what ought not to be feared that had been handed down by law through education (429c–d).

Socrates completed his analysis of the justice of the state and of the individual by reviewing the process from the definition of the justice of the state to that of the individual.

> Finished, then, is our dream and perfected—the surmise we spoke of, that, by some Providence, at the very beginning of our foundation of the state, we chanced to hit upon the original principle and a sort of type of justice ... It really was ... which is why it helps, a sort of adumbration of justice, this principle that it is right for the cobbler by nature to cobble and occupy himself with nothing else, and the carpenter to practice carpentry, and similarly all others. But the truth of the matter was, as it seems, that justice is indeed something of this kind, yet not in regard to the doing of one's own business externally, but with regard to that which is within and in the true sense concerns one's self, and the things of one's self—it means that a man must not suffer the principles in his soul to do each the work of some other and interfere and meddle with one another, but that he should dispose well of what in the true sense of the word is properly his own ... (443b–d)

In this final summation on the problem of justice Socrates showed how the eidos of justice, the doing of one's own in relation to the whole, when applied to the state, was an image or symbol (eidolon) of the justice of the individual. The 'truth of the matter', the justice of the individual, is like the justice of the state, but different, in that the 'doing of one's own', as a man, is internal, not external, and 'concerns oneself, and the things of oneself'. By the use of eidolon, Socrates did not mean that justice of the state is any the less real than that of the individual. Just as the state, because of its size, is the individual 'writ large' and enabled us to find the eidos of justice, so the justice of the state, with its emphasis on doing one's own in some external way as a citizen in the visible context of the state, is a symbol or image of the justice of the individual. Since the inquiry which brought on the political analogy concerns the nature of the justice of the individual, the 'truth of the matter' is that the 'doing of one's own' as a man is not with regard to one's social function, which is of course the 'truth of the matter' for the justice of the state and for the citizen, but with regard to 'oneself and the things of oneself'.

Once the definition of justice of the individual has been completed, the problem remains of seeing the range of its extension. To whom does the justice of the individual apply, to all individuals in all three orders, or as is widely believed both by friends and enemies of Plato, only to the philosopher rulers? My contention is that justice of the individual is indeed to be acquired by the citizens of all the orders of the state (Hall, 1963, pp. 170–1; Vlastos, 1971, pp. 92–3; Guthrie, 1975, p. 539). This provides a new slant on the relation of the individual to the state in that rather than the individual being subordinated to the state, the state in a way can be said to be subordinated to the individual. For in accord with the refutation of Thrasymachus' claim that justice is the interest of the rulers, Socrates maintained that the art of the ruler and of ruling was the benefit of the governed. The only true benefit possible for the citizens was justice as the excellence or arete of man's distinctive function.

Let us review the evidence. Early in the *Republic*, Socrates provided a functional definition of man that applied to all individuals. Any man as man can potentially achieve the excellence of the distinctive human function 'of taking charge of the soul, management, rule, and deliberation'. The nature of the excellence of this distinctive human function is spelled out in more detail as the correct, natural functioning of the three aspects of soul had by all men, with the rational aspect ruling the appetitive and spirited aspects in a unified whole that produces justice of the individual and its accompanying virtues of wisdom, courage and temperance. The context of this final definition of justice of the individual provides no warrant for restricting it to the philosopher. Standard English translations, as well as the Greek text, make it clear that the referent of just man is any individual in the just state (Skemp, 1960, p. 37). The just man, according to Socrates, can be entrusted with a deposit of gold or silver, does not commit adultery and does not neglect his parents (442 3b). Obviously these characteristics could not apply to the rulers. They have no parents in the ordinary sense that they could neglect, nor have they wives to whom they could be unfaithful. They would not be guilty of embezzling funds for the simple reason that they are not allowed to have anything to do with gold and silver. These qualities of the just man, therefore, could only apply to the ordinary individual.

Perhaps the most telling point in support of a univocal theory of justice applying to all individuals of the ideal state is that only if the members of the appetitive order are inwardly just can it be certain that they will do their tasks and obtain the justice of the state. Socrates noted that only if the citizen were inwardly just could he do his appropriate social task. The just man

> having first attained to self-mastery and beautiful order within himself
> . . . and made of himself . . . one man instead of many, self-controlled
> . . . should then and then only turn to practice if he find aught to do
> either in the getting of wealth or the tendance of the body or it may be
> in political action or private business . . . (443d–e)

Justice of the individual is the only way in which the effects of the ambivalent nature of the knowledge of techne can be avoided. Plato's contention that knowledge of an art may be applied to achieve ends contrary to the appropriate ends of an art is well known (*Lesser Hippias*, 367c; *Rep.*, 333e–4a; Moreau, 1939, pp. 105–6). The doctor, for example, can kill as well as cure. Only inward justice guarantees that the doctor, or any craftsman, will not misuse his craft. Without this guarantee there could be no assurance that the justice of the state could either be secured, or if secured, maintained. For if the craftsman should for one reason or another misuse his art or aspire to reach to another order beyond his ability, the principle of the justice of the state would be violated. And one aspect, of course, of the virtue of temperance is that in agreeing to the rule of the philosophers and of the auxiliaries, the members of the appetitive order agreed to do their own work, so that this virtue would also be denied the state.

The rule of reason in the just individual in no way results in asceticism for Plato. On the contrary, the individual realizes the diverse aspects of his nature only when he is just. Each of the three aspects of the soul, reason, spirit and appetites, has its own appropriate desire and pleasure. These are best realized under the direction of reason, in the sense that the pleasures of the appetite are most satisfactorily realized with no tendency towards excess and imbalance within the soul when it is led by reason.

> May we not confidently declare that in both the gain-loving and the contentious part of our nature all the desires that wait upon knowledge and reason, and pursuing their pleasures in conjunction with them, take only those pleasures which reason approves, will, since they follow truth, enjoy the truest pleasures so far as that is possible for them, and also the pleasures that are proper to them and their own, if for everything that which is best may be said to be most its 'own'? (586d–e)

This condition of the soul is attainable by the ordinary individual of the ideal state who also has justice within. Although I can not go into detail here, I would add that the entire argument of which this is a part, that the just life is superior to the unjust from the standpoint of the ordinary criteria of happiness (576b–80d), from the account of the three lives (580d–3b) and from the superiority of its pleasures (583b–8a), applies to the ordinary just individual of the ideal state as I have stated elsewhere (1963, pp. 174–7; 1968, pp. 221–4).

What appears as the chief stumbling block to the acceptance of the univocal view of justice as attainable by all individuals in the just state is the supposed condition that because the wisdom and justice of the state require knowledge of the forms, so the wisdom and justice of the individual also require such knowledge (Strauss, 1963, p. 21; Cross and

Woozley, 1964, p. 126; Cooper, 1977, p. 152). The ordinary citizen of the ideal state, of course, has no such knowledge of the forms. But do wisdom and justice of the individual require knowledge of the forms? As we have seen, as far as the political analogy is concerned the nature of the wisdom of the state is not carried over to that of the individual. The difference between the wisdom of the state and that of the individual is in its content, and consequently its function, which is a change in its nature. The analogy between wisdom of the state and that of the individual is in the fact that the rational part directs the whole, whether state or individual. But the difference lies in the function performed by each kind of wisdom. The individual is to rule himself by his wisdom, the ruler the state by his knowledge of the forms. The discussion culminating in the definition of justice of the individual is not so much of an analysis of the nature and basis of the knowledge that constitutes the wisdom of the state as it is of the knowledge and wisdom appropriate to the individual. Socrates himself suggested something of this sort when in the course of his discussion concerning the three parts of the soul he conceded that by their present methods, he and his companions would never find the truth about the problems under consideration:

> we shall never apprehend this matter accurately from such methods as we are now employing in discussion. For there is another longer and harder way that conducts to this. Yet we may perhaps discuss it on the level of our previous statements and inquiries. (435d)

Now what exactly is discussed in Books II and IV which seem to constitute the shorter road implied here? Socrates discussed the nature of the virtues of the individual and of the state, but from what standpoint? The definition of the virtues of the state by analogy illuminates the virtues of the individual. As far as the ordinary citizen is concerned, his virtues are those discussed in Book IV. What we know about his virtues is that for him 'just and honorable action' is 'that which preserves and helps to produce this condition of soul and wisdom the science that presides over such conduct' (443e–4a). And this, I think, is fundamentally all the citizen needs to know to acquire his justice, concerned as it is with control of the soul by reason and the consequent external activity. But wisdom of the state has to be concerned with the external and internal affairs of the state. While the shorter road may be adequate for the explanation of the virtues of the ordinary individual, a more penetrating account must be made of the bases of these virtues. For the ordinary individual can acquire these virtues only if he is living within the right kind of society, that ruled by the philosopher. Although we know what the ordinary individual's virtues are, we still must take the longer road to understand fully the basis of the virtues in the forms and to see how the ability of the philosopher to rule is grounded on knowledge of the forms. The contrast between the shorter way and the longer way can be made in terms of the contrast between 'educated' right opinion and knowledge of the forms. Knowledge of the forms is the condition of the philosopher's rule, and it is only on the basis of his knowledge that the individual can acquire the necessary know-how to be just through receiving educated right opinion.

An accustomed interpretation of Plato's thought based on the Fifth Book of the *Republic* is that there is a necessary and unbridgeable gap between knowledge and opinion (Sabine, 1959, pp. 50–2; Cross and Woozley, 1964, p. 169). The Fifth Book of the *Republic* is the conventional source for this view (474b–80a). The distinction between knowledge and opinion of the Fifth Book occurs in the existing society, not in the ideal state. The lover of sights and sounds has mere opinion, his objects are of 'what is and what is not'. Socrates here distinguished between those whose pretensions to knowledge were no more than opinion, and those few who knew the forms and were, therefore, most suited to be rulers. Part of the reason for the unfavorable contrast of opinion with knowledge stemmed from Socrates' concern to convince the people that the rule of philosophers was genuinely desirable. For he did not believe that the philosophers could become kings forcibly but only through persuasion (432a–b, 499e–500a, 501c–e). The distinction between ordinary empirical opinion and knowledge was not Plato's final word, that the ordinary person was forever condemned to the murky miasmic mist of opinion while the philosopher ascended to the contemplation of ultimate reality.

The concept of opinion with its empirical character as stated in the Fifth Book is not the basis for the overall view of right opinion in Plato's thought (Gulley, 1962, pp. 13–14). The *Meno* emphasized that right opinion could become knowledge when 'fastened down' with knowledge of the causes (*Meno*, 98a). Although in the *Meno* Socrates admitted that knowledge and right opinion were different, they were equally successful in attaining useful results (98c). In this sense right opinion was on a par with knowledge, although it cannot be maintained with the same stability as knowledge. That the right opinion in the *Republic* connotes only a knack of acting or supposing rightly without any basis is clearly denied by Socrates. Socrates had already rejected 'courage' based on mere right opinion without education. Indicating his distaste for 'mere right opinion', opinions divorced from knowledge, Socrates scorned them (506c) as 'ugly things'. But the opposite of mere right opinion is not knowledge of the forms but 'educated right opinion' brought about by education. Socrates provided a new dimension to the theory of educated right opinion when he indicated that it has a sphere of objects more akin to that of knowledge than of mere opinion, which was concerned with 'what is and what is not'. In Book IX of the *Republic*, a right opinion far different from that of Book V was described, along with reason and knowledge, as partaking of 'true essence'. Such right opinion, I suggest, is the product of education, and is assimilated by Socrates to knowledge and reason, and belongs to 'things that are more excellent' (585c).

Two well-known similes in the *Republic*, the divided or the broken line (509d–11b) and the cave (514a–21b), provide additional support for the concept of an 'educated right opinion' and, of course, justify the rule of the philosopher in the ideal state. No real agreement exists among scholars on how these similes are to be interpreted and how they are related to each other (Cross and Woozley, 1964, pp. 196–228). In giving the main outlines of these two similes I shall follow the 'standard' or 'orthodox' interpretation of the line and the cave and their interrelationship (Cross and Woozley, 1964, pp. 208–9). According to this view the line presents the four states of mind and their corresponding levels of reality or objects in the *Republic*'s theory of knowledge. The cave is an illustration of these different levels; its topography contains different levels within and outside the cave that correspond to the different states of mind depicted in the line. The two similes differ in that the line affords an analysis of the different levels of cognition, but the cave is concerned with the development of mind from its lowest to its highest state. Both similes have a moral and political as well as an epistemological significance.

Initially the line (usually viewed as vertical) was divided into two unequal segments. One, the 'upper line', stands for the intelligible world, the other, the 'lower line', represents the visible world. Each segment is further divided in the same ratio into two parts to depict four states of mind and their corresponding objects.

The lowest state of mind is imagining (eikasia) or conjecture. Its objects have a correspondingly low degree of reality and are described by Plato as images or shadows, reflections on water and on bright, smooth and dense surfaces (410a). Some scholars (Cross and Woozley, 1964, pp. 220–2) have attributed a political and moral connotation to imagining. For although people at times may interpret distortions, shadows and the like at face value without being aware of their originals, their perception can not always be of this sort. They do, after all, see objects as they are in the sensible world. But their moral and political perceptions may be the distortions and shadows of the originals. The people are bombarded on all sides by the distorted and shadowy moral and political values of the Sophists, orators and statesmen. Young Sophists like Thrasymachus preached that injustice was a sign of arete, an obvious distortion of the common belief that injustice, regardless of its consequences, was an evil (358e).

Higher up on the lower part of the line is the second state of mind, belief or opinion (doxa or pistis). Opinion grasps not only the original physical things but also the moral and political beliefs that were the originals of the distortions that were the objects of imagining. These originals were 'legal and deliberative decisions', and the conventional notions of current morality (Cornford, trans. *Republic,* 1978, pp. 179–81) and are now grasped as the objects of belief. Belief perceives the individual that cast the shadow of the principle that justice according to popular belief is valued as a good (612d) and not according to its distorted image, a mark of a fool or simpleton (349c).

In his account of the vertical ascent from the lower to the upper line, Plato passed from the visible to the intelligible world. But just as imagining, the first state of mind, does not see its objects as clearly and as fully as opinion, so thinking or understanding (dianoia), the first state of mind of the upper line, does not have as clear and as complete a comprehension of its objects as dialectic, the highest state of mind, possesses of the very same objects, mathematics. Dianoia displays two conditions that limit or restrict its intelligibility. Thinking uses assumptions in its demonstrations that it takes for granted and never proves. Yet, its conclusions are dependent on the validity of these assumptions. Secondly, thinking must use diagrams or images in its proofs. These diagrams or images used by thinking are the 'originals' of the shadows and other distortions of imagining. Thinking has to use a diagram of a circle that is an image of a circular physical object that caused the shadow that was the object of imagining. Thinking is not concerned with the particular diagram of the circle but with the nature of the circle itself, not however as a form (which can only be the object of dialectic) but as a unitary concept (Hall, 1974, pp. 77–8). As the highest state of mind, dialectic achieves complete intelligibility. It employs the assumptions whose validity was taken for granted in the proofs constructed by thinking as hypotheses to arrive at the unconditioned first principle, the idea of the good. Then the dialectician proves each one of the hypotheses in the light of his knowledge of the form of the good. Secondly, he dispenses with diagrams using in his studies only the forms themselves.

Dianoia or thinking in the line is preparatory to the study of dialectic. Yet, it has political and moral implications like the other states of mind. Gulley (1962, p. 16) showed that educated right opinion (in my sense) is akin to, if not identical with, dianoia in its acceptance of unproven assumptions. There is no difference between the objects of dianoia or of educated right opinion and those of knowledge; to opine the things that are is to possess the truth (413a). But thinking and 'educated right opinion' have a lesser degree of clearness and completeness than knowledge has of these objects. The objects of educated right opinion could be ethical or political as well as mathematical (Gulley, 1962, p. 19). Such educated right opinion can be brought about in the souls of the citizens of the ideal state by instruction, through formal education, laws, the arts and religion. With such educated 'right opinion', the individual will know how to obtain what is good for himself internally and for himself and others in external situations (441e, 442c; Hall, 1963, pp. 178–81).

The simile of the cave in the standard interpretation parallels the broken line in presenting differing degrees of states of mind and of corresponding objects. The outlines of the description of the cave are simple, although as with the line the interpretation of these details has been intricate and complex. Prisoners are seated facing a wall in a cavern so chained that they can only see the wall. Higher up in the cave a fire is burning and behind the prisoners people are walking on a parapet carrying various objects whose shadows are cast on the wall facing the prisoners. The cave is really an odyssey of the mind's development from imagining to knowledge of truth. And Plato clearly intended to bring out the extreme difficulty of breaking out of preestablished attitudes and beliefs, especially the moral and political. Seated as they are, the prisoners take them as assumptions upon which mathematics and moral and whatever they hear from the people carrying the objects behind them. When the prisoner is released from his bonds and is turned around, with extreme difficulty he perceives the individual objects as they are. This scene in the cave is of course parallel to the lower line.

Going out of the cave into the sunlight the prisoner is so dazzled by the light that he can only view the heavenly bodies at night. Finally he is able to see the sun and the other heavenly bodies in daylight. Of course here the conversion of the individual is complete. Looking at the sky at night is parallel to thinking which is not able to comprehend mathematics or moral values in the full light of the comprehension of their bases but must take them as assumptions upon which mathematical and moral and political actions are based. The individual seeing the world in the full light of day is the philosopher who has grasped the unity of the forms, their nature and relationship to the idea of the good.

Obviously the two aspects of the cave, the inside and outside, correspond to the upper and lower lines in their levels of knowledge and reality. But the cave represents the stages of development in the conversion of the soul from illusion to knowledge of the mind while the line presents a static account of the levels of reality and the corresponding states of awareness.

The moral and political character of the simile of the cave, then, suggests a radical conversion of the individual from viewing the moral and political shadows, distortions and mere opinions of existing society to the clear apprehension of the truth of the world of forms, especially the moral and the political, and the form of the good. With such knowledge the philosopher is equipped for his necessary return to the cave. The initial return of the philosophers to the gloom of the cave (520a) implies that the people have finally been persuaded to accept philosophers as their rulers. But subsequent references to the return of philosophers to the cave after the completion of their training (539a, 540b) have caused some to think that, as before, the people live in the same cavern of the mind and have as states of mind only imagining and opinion (Murphy,

1934, pp. 211–13). But surely these later references to the return to the cave have a different meaning than the initial return. They indicate that after the completion of his education the philosopher as a member of society performs that social function for which he is naturally suited. Surely, if the citizens have acquired inward justice they do not just have mere opinion or imagining. According to our interpretation through the rule of the philosopher, they have acquired an educated right opinion of moral and political values that is akin to dianoia or thinking. For only in this fashion can the individual realize man's distinctive function of deliberating, taking charge and maintaining control over himself (353d).

While Socrates acknowledged that the philosopher's wisdom was based on knowledge higher than the wisdom of the just individual, still the wisdom of the latter was all that was necessary for justice of the individual, and constituted a kind of 'educated right opinion'. Although both entail awareness of 'true essence', 'educated right opinion' does not have the full awareness and certainty possessed by knowledge of the forms. 'Educated right opinion', like the 'thinking' (dianoia) appropriate to mathematics, has assumptions underlying its conclusions, while knowledge of the forms, dialectic, has understanding of these same assumptions in the sense that it can demonstrate their truth. This difference between 'educated right opinion' and knowledge of the forms certainly fits in well with the distinction mentioned earlier between the shorter and longer roads. Books II–IV provide by way of the analogy of the state and the individual an awareness of the virtues of the individual which he himself can secure through educated right opinion. The longer way (V–VII) is necessary not only to show the bases of the virtues of Book IV in the forms, but also to give an account of the education of the philosophers who, because of their knowledge, can rule the state. Thus, the shorter way and the longer way well bring out the fundamental difference and similarity of the analogical thinking of Books II–IV and the knowledge of Books V–VII. They both achieve the same result, an account of the virtues of the individual, but one with assumptions, the other with knowledge. Knowledge of the bases of these virtues is not for the acquisition of justice by the individual, but to enable the philosophers to rule and help the citizens to acquire justice.

In fact there are in the *Republic* two kinds of virtue applicable to the individual. One kind, the four virtues of the individual—wisdom, courage, temperance and justice—is entailed in the shorter way which apparently is concluded at the end of Book IV. The other kind of virtue is wisdom, not, as in Book IV, primarily knowledge of how to take charge of one's external and internal affairs, but as knowledge of the idea of the good, the result of the longer way of Books V–VII. The philosopher has both kinds of virtue, the ordinary individual only the four virtues as described in Book IV. But justice of the individual applies in the same way to both the ordinary man and to the philosopher since it is a univocal term. It is justice that constitutes the arete of the individual.

Prior to the simile of the sun in Book VI, Socrates again notes the difference between the relative imprecision and inexactness of the shorter way in comparison with the longer way, the way of knowledge of the forms (504d). He observes that there is 'still something greater than justice and the other virtues we described' (504d). Pointing out now the need for depth and completeness, Socrates affirms 'of these very things we need not merely contemplate an outline as now, but we must omit nothing of their most exact elaboration'. Here Socrates is distinguishing between the account of the individual's virtues in Book IV which has been adequate for the purpose of discovering the justice of the individual, and the need to discover the foundations of virtues in the forms so that the ruler may implement them in society. The knowledge of the idea of the good that the philosopher has is his wisdom, which differs from the other virtues of the individual, including wisdom, discussed earlier. Wisdom in the sense of knowledge of the forms should not be confused with wisdom of the just individual.

When Socrates at 517c remarked that no one can act wisely in private and public life unless he has knowledge of the idea of the good, he apparently was contradicting the claim made here that without knowledge of the forms the ordinary individual in the ideal state could acquire justice, and was in agreement with the earlier *Phaedo*'s claim (69a ff.) that true virtue cannot be without knowledge. It's possible that this passage in the *Republic* reflects Plato's inability to discard completely the earlier view of the *Phaedo* that true virtue requires knowledge of the forms. But the general character of the *Republic* does indicate a broadening of Plato's moral and political thought. Arete is no longer acquired in isolation but in the context of the state. Later dialogues concerned with Plato's moral and political thought also stress that arete can be based on something less than knowledge of the forms (*Pol.*, 309c; *Laws*, 689c–d).

But literal application of 517c presents its own problems. Since the would-be philosopher does not win knowledge until he is 50 years old (504a) what would be his moral condition until then? Would he not really be just like the ordinary individual? Finally the passage presents a problem all its own when it extends to *all* individuals the possibility of knowledge of the forms and of the idea of the good (518c). But just as it is more consistent with the whole of Plato's thought to uphold the inability of the ordinary individual to acquire such knowledge, so I think it more consistent and plausible to hold that in the *Republic* and subsequently Plato believed that under the proper political and social conditions, the ordinary individual could acquire justice or its moral equivalent, but of course not knowledge of the forms.

Again, analysis of the political analogy should keep the two sorts of wisdom separate, the wisdom of the polis and that of the individual.

Later, Socrates emphasized the wisdom which came from knowledge of the forms and the idea of the good as a higher virtue:

> the other so-called virtues [the virtues of Book IV including wisdom] of the soul do seem akin to those of the body . . . But the excellence of thought is certainly of a more divine quality. *(Republic,* 518e)

Here I suggest that Socrates was not decrying the virtues of Book IV, but striving to put the knowledge of the good in its most favorable light to justify the rule of those who had attained knowledge of it. Clearly, then, Socrates distinguished between the wisdom of the individual and the wisdom of the philosopher. No contradiction exists, since wisdom has different meanings in these two instances.

The wisdom of the individual brought about through 'educated right opinion' is distinguished from the special wisdom of the philosopher who in that respect has a higher wisdom but not necessarily a higher justice. Here there is an obvious anticipation of Aristotle's distinction between the moral and intellectual virtues, with justice resembling Aristotle's notion of moral virtue, and the special wisdom of the philosopher being akin to the intellectual virtues, especially the scientific, intellectual virtues.

Socrates drew a further parallel between the just state and the just individual when he averred against Thrasymachus' claim that the individual should be governed to his own detriment, that just as in the state the rule of intelligence governs the whole, so 'it is better for everyone to be governed by the divine and the intelligent, preferably indwelling and his own, but in default of that imposed from without . . .' (590d). Many scholars have taken this passage to mean that so far as the ordinary individual of the ideal state is concerned, he is governed not by his own reason, but 'by that imposed from without' by the philosopher ruler. But in the interpretation I have made in this chapter, clearly the ordinary individual would be ruled by his own reason since he is just, and as just he is wise in precisely the sense that reason is in control of his internal and external activities.

The description of the justice of the individual as 'concerned with oneself and the things of oneself' provides evidence of a morality of the individual apart from, though not unrelated to, the justice of the state. It justifies the view that there is an area of the individual, a vital area, which is distinct from and is not subordinated to the state (Hall, 1963, p. 184; Havelock, 1978, p. 322). That there is underlying the separate morality of the individual a personal reality distinct from that of the state, transcending it and uniquely constituting man's essence is glowingly illustrated in the great myth of Er which concludes the *Republic.* In that dramatic myth souls are depicted after their death on earth as being in heaven and choosing their next lives. The quality of choice is, for the most part, dependent on the moral nature of the life as lived on earth. A just soul chooses wisely, an evil soul foolishly.

No divinity shall cast lots for you, but you shall choose your own deity. Let him to whom falls the first lot select a life to which he shall cleave of necessity. But virtue has no master over her, and each shall have more or less of her as he honours her or does her despite. The blame is his who chooses: God is blameless. (617e)

However we take the literal meaning of the myth, Plato clearly implied that each individual was responsible for his moral condition. His fateful choice in the afterlife was made apart from his existence in the state, although the character of that life influenced the nature of his choice. It is all the more important, therefore, that the individual live in the right kind of society. Plato's concept of the justice of the individual and his intrinsic value as the fulfillment of man's arete or excellence is a significant innovation in Greek thought. It reflects his determination to break away from the prevalent view of his time that the value of morality depends on its beneficial consequences (Hall, 1963, pp. 34–54). In his definition of justice of the individual he has met the challenge of Glaucon and Adeimantus to show that justice is valuable for itself and for its consequences, but much more for itself.

The goal of the individual is, however, intimately linked with life within the right kind of state ruled by those who have knowledge of the forms. Thus morality is shown to have an intimate connection with political thought and epistemology. But it is also vital in understanding Plato's theory of the justice of the individual to keep the political analogy in its proper perspective by maintaining the separate, but related, concepts of justice that apply to the two distinct terms of the analogy, the state and the individual.

The analysis of the justice of the individual as the realization of man's distinctive, if not defining, function contrasts sharply with Plato's acceptance of slavery in the practical state of the *Laws*. Nowhere does Plato explicitly affirm slavery to be a natural distinction among men (Vlastos, 1960, p. 146), as Aristotle did later (*Pol.*, 1254a, 25–35). Nonetheless Vlastos has argued that Plato has implicitly made such a distinction based on the slave's ignorance of the good and his consequent inability for self-determination (1960, pp. 135–6). His argument incidentally noted a kinship between the slave and the ordinary individual of sharing in varying degrees a condition of slavery (but not of social status [pp. 136–7]) because they lacked logos, 'they do not know the Good, and cannot know their own good or the good of the state; their only chance of doing the good is to obey implicitly the commands of their superiors' (1960, pp. 135–6). The slave boy passage in the *Meno* only established a kind of empirical right opinion that Vlastos believed insufficient for the individual self-determination required by Plato's theory of moral virtue.

In a later paper dealing not with slavery but with justice in the *Republic*, Vlastos affirmed that there may be right opinions brought about by education. The ordinary individual of the Platonic state could acquire moral virtue through such right opinions (1971, p. 93, nn. 71, 76). Moral virtue did not require philosophical wisdom, the knowledge of the idea of the good. The rational aspect of the just soul, to logistikon, was able to deliberate and to choose appropriate courses of moral or just action as a result of right opinions brought about by education.

The implications of Vlastos' acceptance of the ability of the ordinary citizen in Plato's society to acquire moral self-determination suggested that for Plato slavery was not even implicitly by nature. If the slave and the citizen have a roughly similar rational capacity, then it is plausible to assume that theoretically the slave could acquire moral virtue in the same way as the citizen—through right opinion with education. Schlaifer's denial that the slave could acquire the self-determination of the worker in Plato's *Republic* (1960, p. 118) entailed a rejection of the kinship in rational ability between slave and citizen held by Vlastos. But Schlaifer has ignored the implications of the slave boy passage of the *Meno*. If through educated right opinions, the slave boy could gain an increasingly informed awareness about geometry, even leading to knowledge of the relevant forms (Vlastos, 1960, p. 134, n. 9), surely in the same way a slave could acquire a like degree of moral awareness. Socrates' use of the slave boy experiment was, in fact, to encourage his young companion Meno to undertake a similar kind of inquiry into the nature of virtue (*Meno*, 86b–c).

Although, then, Plato like most of his contemporaries accepted slavery as an institution that was not unjust and required no defense (Schlaifer, 1960, p. 127), he did not hold that some men were slaves because they had a natural deficiency in reason. Any rational deficiency blocking moral self-determination in the slave was due to the slaves not receiving the kind of education that would lead to their having right opinions about moral virtue and action. That kind of education would have kept the slaves from performing their intended roles in the practical state of the *Laws* (I share Levinson's minority view [1953, pp. 167–71] that no need for slavery existed in the ideal state of the *Republic* because its citizens performed all the appropriate social tasks). Plato's acceptance of slavery in the *Laws* reflected the prevalent view of his day that it was necessary for the economic and social well-being of the state, which for Plato would have included the moral virtue of the citizens (Schlaifer, 1960, p. 119). It is regrettable that Plato did not go beyond the attitudes of his age and consider the consequences of his theory of the justice of the individual for the existence of that institution. But we should not charge that omission to his acceptance of slavery as grounded, even implicitly, on a distinction among men based on nature.

An important pendant to the account of the justice of the state and the individual is Plato's analysis of the decline of the state and its parallelism with the analogous decline of the soul (Taylor, 1939, pp. 23–38; de Romilly, 1977, pp. 10–11). It is usually accepted that although there may be historical overtones in the description of the decline of the state, Plato's discussion (544a–69b) is analytic rather than historical. This analytic approach to considering the decline of the state is bolstered by its relationship with the decline of the soul which shows a logical or analytic development away from the just condition, a decline which is progressive until a complete inversion of the genuine well-being of the soul is achieved with the very worst of the passions ruling the whole soul, instead of the very best, the rational element.

Plato affirms that the different unjust constitutions line up with the different types of unjust individuals.

> Are you aware . . . that there must be as many types of character among men as there are forms of government? Or do you suppose that constitutions spring from the proverbial oak and rock and not from the characters of the citizens. (544d–e)

As I emphasized earlier the virtues of the state are not derived from those of the individual. So the vices or evils of the state are not derived from those of the individual. Rather the different kinds of injustice are derived from the way in which the primary or leading disposition or characteristic in a morally neutral sense is used. These generic parts, dispositions or characteristics, themselves neither virtues nor vices, are the bases for the virtues and vices of both the state and the soul. The three aspects, rational, spirited or appetitive, are in themselves ethically neutral. Depending on how these characteristics are used the state or soul can become just or unjust. If all of the characteristics or dispositions of the soul or state perform their natural function, then the appropriate virtue of each characteristic and that of the whole is attained; if not, then injustice occurs. The degree of injustice in both the state and the individual depends on which disposition is in charge of the whole soul or state. In the parallel decline of the soul and of the state, each stage of decline occurs when one characteristic not in itself good or evil takes over the role of leading the whole. If there is any sort of derivation in the state–individual relationship, it is that the dispositions or characteristics of the state are derived from those of the individual.

The decline of the state begins in a curious fashion. Through some breeding mishap a partial 'bad crop' of children is produced in the philosopher order (546a–e). This error, more fanciful than real since supposedly the philosophers are infallible, seems to be a device to begin the decline of the state. Two factors should be noted in Plato's account of the decline. The decline is presented as developing factionalism in the ruling class in the timocratic society, in which honor is paramount, culminating in the polarization of the state between the tyrant and those that he has oppressed, the people. This factionalism arises when some members at least of each order of the state no longer perform that task for which they are naturally suited. The factionalism, then, becomes more serious or divisive as the decline goes through its various stages since each stage represents a dominant faction which is further from the natural condition of the just society. Secondly, Plato gives us in his analytic account a picture of an inexorable decline in which apart from the just state itself which begins its decline fortuitously, each stage carries within it the seeds of its own metamorphosis to the next, lower stage.

The change in the ruling class of the just state lay in the rise to power of men who as rulers of the timocratic state regarded the citizens they ruled no longer as friends and supporters but as subjects and serfs. While professing an outward show of honor, military courage, readiness for combat rather than for peace, the rulers began to develop a desire for property and wealth and all that comes with it, nourished and enjoyed in secret (548a–b). The timocratic state changes into the oligarchic when the lust for wealth and property becomes the dominant characteristic of the ruling class instead of military prowess and courage. The possession of wealth and property rather than ability becomes the criterion for holding political office (551a–b).

The oligarchic state in fact becomes polarized into two states, the state of the rich and the state of the poor, with one plotting against the other (551d). Allowed by the wealthy to sell their property, some citizens become rootless with no social function to perform. They eventually join the swelling ranks of the many poor and unemployed while the few rich become richer. Two kinds of poor appear, those who accept their condition and those who are in revolt against the oligarchic order. The second kind often includes those who have been disenfranchised and thrown out of the oligarchy because they lost their wealth (555d). Joining the rich in warfare against a common enemy, the many poor realize how weak the rich have become through indolence and easy living (556d–e). Dissatisfied with their lot, and confident of their strength, the poor rise in rebellion and overwhelm their wealthy masters whom they exile or kill (557a).

The democracy comes about when all the citizens enjoy the rights of a full citizen and can hold office, usually one assigned by lot (557a). Plato's account of the rise of democracy through the revolution of the poor against the oligarchy is an interesting interpretation of the thesis that radical Athenian democracy came about through the demand of the thetes, the poor who manned the ships of the Athenian navy, for political rights commensurate with the importance of their role in making Athens a great and imperial power. Plato's portrait of the democratic state here is not necessarily drawn from Athens itself. Some of its features do not fit Athens, and it may be that Plato was primarily referring to other democracies of the time of which we know little (*Epis.*, VII, 326b–d). Democracy assigns a 'kind of equality indiscriminately to equals and unequals alike' (558c). The democratic city is 'chock-full of liberty and freedom of speech' and every man can do as he pleases (557b). It is this excessive if not lawless freedom, in Plato's eyes, which proves the undoing of the democratic constitution and abets the rise of tyranny (564a). What characterizes the democratic state is the absence of any moral or legal standards. The people come into conflict with the wealthy who are attempting to defend themselves against spoliation by leaders of the people who are trying to win favor with the demos. To defend their freedom the people find a champion who claims to look after their interests. Because of the intense opposition his defense of the demos has aroused among the wealthy, the people's leader asks for and receives a bodyguard or private army (566b). Having come to an agreement with some of his enemies and having executed or banished the rest, the leader of the people redistributes the land and cancels all debts (566e). Once he has attained power, the leader seeks to maintain such power by ridding himself of all possible opposition by oppression and by frequent wars which will remove many of his rivals and keep the people occupied in working to pay war taxes so that they will be less likely to plot against him (567a). At this stage the leader, now the tyrant, has become hated by many of the people but with his private bodyguard supported at the public expense he holds on to his power, and the people come to realize that their absolute freedom which knew no order or lawful restraint now has been exchanged for bitter servitude under a lawless tyrant.

Chapter 6

Law in the *Republic*, *Politicus* and *Laws*

Despite Plato's conviction that the decline of states was the result of lawlessness and the absence of law, a customary distinction between his principal political dialogues has been to characterize the *Republic* and the *Politicus* as advocating the rule of the wise statesman or philosopher in contrast to law, while the *Laws* abandons such rule of the individual for the rule of law (Barker, 1960, p. 39; Sabine, 1959, pp. 66–78, 75; Sinclair, 1959, p. 187). But relatively recent studies (Cairns, 1967, pp. 45–7; Hall, 1956, pp. 175–87; Morrow, 1960, pp. 577–84) have shown that although the scope of law may not be as broad in the *Republic* and the *Politicus* as in the *Laws*, it still has a significant role to play in these two earlier political dialogues. In fact, the importance of law provides an important focus of similarity rather than of difference among these political dialogues.

The *Republic* displays three ways in which law can be ascribed to the ideal state. The forms or ideas are the source of natural moral and political laws which underlie the constitution of the ideal state (Maguire, 1947, pp. 165–7). These moral and political forms function as a model for the philosopher ruler as he attempts to shape and preserve the just society and to make it possible for the citizens to attain their own justice.

A second use of law appears in the process of forming the ideal state as Socrates and his companions are acting as legislators (433a–b). Some of these laws appeared basic to the constitution of the ideal state and its well functioning such as the laws governing the education of the young (380c–d) discussed in Chapter 4. These laws were typoi or patterns for the form and content of poetry. Socrates also laid down laws concerning medicine (409e), and the denial of property rights to the guardians (417a). What seemed to be the item of basic legislation was the law relating to religion that stipulated that all religious affairs would be governed by Delphi, the traditional source of Athenian religious law (427b–d). Plato's discussion did not distinguish clearly between a written code of law and unwritten laws (which over the years in the ideal state could become ancestral laws) since nomos could refer to both kinds of laws. Unwritten laws, however, for Plato, as well as for the Greeks of his time, were as important as written law. Plato did recognize the significance of custom and tradition of his times (the early program of education was drawn from Athenian practice [376e]) in the constitution of his state, but they had to be of the right kind.

The importance of law in the ideal state was again shown by the making of further laws after the basic legislation was completed on such topics as festivals (459e), the holding in common of wives and children by the guardian order (453d, 457c), military honours (486b), war (471c), the place of mathematics in the education of the guardians (525b, 530c) and the role of dialectic in the advanced education of the guardians (534d–e).

The items of basic legislation were not sufficient to realize all aspects of the ideal state, but, if followed, they ensured that whatever further legislation required would be easily discovered.

> . . . if a right education makes of them reasonable men they will easily discover everything of this kind—and other principles that we now pass over, as that the possession of wives and marriage, and the procreation of children and all that sort of thing should be made as far as possible the proverbial goods of friends that are common. (423e–4a)

A third kind of law found in the ideal state is that body of law relating to the regulation of business, matters of judicial procedure, trade and commerce, and other matters not central to constitutional enactment. Socrates and his friends did not regard such laws and ordinances as unnecessary, but they did not think them important enough to be incorporated in the basic constitution of the state. For those with proper education and nurture (425d–e) would be able to enact all necessary laws and ordinances as the need for them arises 'provided God grants them the preservation of the principles of law that we have already discussed' (primarily the basic laws of the education of the young).

The importance of law in the ideal state is again shown in the way in which it is interwoven with the duties of the philosopher rulers. According to law (519e) the rulers are not to be concerned with the happiness of any one order of the state, but with the happiness of the whole. The rulers are 'guardians of the law' (421a, 504c), a phrase applied to an important body of magistrates in the *Laws*. The philosopher rulers themselves will obey the laws (458c). If they have received the proper education and nurture as youth the rulers, singly or collectively, will not 'alter to any extent worth mentioning the rules of the city' (445e). Although the philosopher rulers do have knowledge of the forms and the idea of the good, they are constrained by such knowledge to follow the laws enacted in the ideal state and in its constitution.

The *Politicus* presents a transition between the political theory of the *Republic* and that of the *Laws* by way of its emphasis on the sovereignty of positive law. At the same time, however, it upholds both the desirability of the rule of the individually wise man above the positive law, and its unattainability. What is forever to be contrasted with our age, the human age, is the age of Cronus when life was totally different (296b–71e). All races of creatures at the onset of this earlier change in the motion of the world stopped growing, and reversed the growing process until they disappeared. Later a race born from the earth emerged. This was an age when 'all things come without human labor'. The supreme ruler of the universe in this era of the cosmic cycle was God and there were lesser gods set over different regions and creatures. Here the natural condition was the opposite of that pictured by Callicles who envisaged the natural condition as constant struggle and war, 'savagery was nowhere to be found nor preying of creature on creature, nor did war rage nor any strife whatever' (271d–e). A god was ruler over men and there was no political constitution or private family. Men lived in a sort of idyllic garden of Eden where no serpent appeared. All the fruit they needed emerged spontaneously from the ground and the weather was such that they needed neither clothes nor bed, and the grass was soft enough for them to rest upon.

The present age reflects a change in motion when the gods released their control of the universe. All things followed the change in the universe and the earthborn returned into the earth. A new law presumably accepted as universal in the human era governing procreation, birth and development held sway. Now, as the Eleatic Stranger, Plato's spokesman in the *Politicus,* put it, not the gods but 'the universe must take sole responsibility and control of its course' (274a). Man came to his present condition aided by the gods so that he could develop arts and crafts; 'from these gifts everything has come which has furnished human life since the divine guardianship of men ceased' (274d).

The Stranger emphasized that in this present age the 'shepherd' of men was akin to men, not to the gods, both in training and nurture (275b–c). But although the subsequent but not final definition of the statesman was rejected, an important distinction was made between the rule of the statesman and that of the tyrant. The rule of the tyrant was imposed on the people and that of the statesman was consented to by people (276e).

Plato seemed to take a jaundiced view of law in the *Politicus.* Thinking of the age of Cronus, when there was no law or constitution and the gods were in charge, the Eleatic Stranger noted that the true statesman should be able to rule without law. Laws are inflexible; of necessity they cannot take into account individual peculiarities, or the flux of circumstances in issuing their injunctions as to what should or should not be done. True rulers, claimed the Stranger, must really have the 'scientific understanding of the art of government' (293c). If they have this understanding they must be free to do whatever their judgment recommends as long as their underlying principle of action is the following of justice and the betterment of the life of the state so far as possible. As long as the statesmen have the genuine knowledge of the art of government, it does not matter whether they are rich or poor, whether they rule with or without law, or whether their rule is over willing or unwilling subjects. All other constitutions are mere shadows of this one true constitution, although those that follow law are closer to the ideal than those that are lawless. The Stranger, however, does not deny, as the young Socrates seemed to think, that the true statesman rules without law. For even though law can not ever take into account 'what is best and just for each member of the community at any one time' (294b), the statesman must make law

> for the majority of his subjects under average circumstances. Thus he will legislate for all individual citizens, but it will be in a somewhat less refined manner by making a written code of law or by issuing laws that are unwritten but embody ancestral customs . . . How could any lawgiver be capable of prescribing every act of a particular individual and sit at his side all through his life telling him what to do? (295a-b)

There can be little doubt that for Plato the true statesman does rule with law.

> In one sense it is evident that the art of kingship does include the art of lawmaking. But the best thing of all is not full authority for laws but rather full authority for a man who understands the art of kingship and has wisdom. (294a)

What Plato meant is that on a practical basis law was unavoidable. But the written laws and ancestral customs should not be obstacles to prevent the true statesman from ignoring them or changing or adding to them whenever he thinks that society and its citizens will be benefited. What is final, or authoritative, is not law itself, but the scientific knowledge of the statesman which takes precedence over law. The true statesman, then, must not allow his knowledge of what is truly best for the society to be fettered by having to adhere blindly to existing laws and ancestral customs regardless of changed circumstances. Such inflexibility the Stranger complained, in a biting caricature of the extreme Athenian democracy, would make impossible a science of government (297e-9e). How could any science like medicine or navigation, or any other art, flourish, or even survive, if its practitioners were forced to follow undeviatingly the laws for their art set down by a popular assembly and if they were answerable to the assembly for their conduct as craftsmen after they were no longer practicing the particular art? The true statesman, then, in the exercise of his art does use laws but he, or others like him, must always be able to act in accordance with his scientific knowledge and not be bound by the existing law.

Consider for example, says the Stranger, the physician who prescribes treatment for his patient, and then goes away on a trip (295b-e). When he returns, he finds that his patient will be benefited by a change in the course of treatment. Whether the patient agrees or not, he orders him to follow this now improved course of treatment. The important factor in attaining the patient's health is not following a written prescription, but the knowledge the doctor has when applied to existing conditions of what would best restore that physical well-being. So it is with the true statesman.

> Imagine, then, the case of a scientific legislator. Suppose that by a written code or by unwritten legislation he has laid down what is just or unjust, honorable and disgraceful, good and bad for the several communities of the human flock who live in their cities as their appointed pasture, shepherded by the codes their legislators have provided. If this man, who drew up his code with the help of his art, wishes to amend it, or if another scientific legislator of this kind appears on the scene, will these be forbidden to enact new laws differing from the earlier ones? Surely such a prohibition would in truth appear as ridiculous in the case of the legislator as it was in the case of the doctor. (295e–6a)

If after he prescribes laws to the state, the statesman finds that its citizens will be benefited by change in the laws or by new laws, or even by a course of action not sanctioned and even against the existing laws and traditions, he will not shrink from such appropriate action even if he must coerce the citizens to obey. For rulers can do no wrong so long as they stick to the one all important principle

> that they must always administer impartial justice to their subjects under the guidance of intelligence and the art of government. Then they will not only preserve the lives of their subjects but reform their characters too, so far as that can be done. (297a–b)

Finally, the fact that the true statesman may rule by compulsion does not conflict with the earlier statement that the distinction between the rule of the tyrant and the rule of the true statesman was that under the latter the tendance of men is 'accepted freely' while under the former such tendance is by enforced control (276e). The basis of the state for Plato always lies in the willingness of the people to be ruled by the true statesman. Now and then, the true statesman may have to resort to compulsion implied in law to do what is best for the state and its citizens. A tyranny, however, reflects a continual compulsion underlying the tyranny and all that the tyrant decrees, which is only in his own interest.

In his discussion of the rule of the scientific statesman, the Stranger had nowhere repudiated law. He never claimed that law is evil. What is evil was the demand that the science of statesmanship must blindly follow the dictates of a popular assembly and be answerable to it for its actions.

In the absence of a scientific ruler, the code of laws should be followed. What was the worst possible situation in a state was the deliberate refusal of its rulers without knowledge of the science of statesmanship to follow the laws in order to gain what they considered their own advantage (300a). For the laws, both written and unwritten, were adopted by the people with the aid of 'counsellors'.

> The laws which have been laid down represent the fruit of long experience—one must admit that. Each of them incorporates the clever advice of some counselor who has persuaded the public assembly to enact it. Any man who dares by his action to infringe these laws is guilty of a wrong many times greater than the wrong done by strict laws, for such transgression, if tolerated, would do even more harm than a written code to pervert all ordered activity. (300b)

Law enacted in this fashion seemed to be acceptable to the Stranger, although of course the rule of the scientific statesman with or without law was preferable. States ruled by law rather than by the scientific statesman, though not genuine, imitate the true constitution fairly closely, but the others that ignore or circumvent the law are 'shocking caricatures of it' (293e). The salvation of states is to adhere to the already existing laws as the best possible. Any attempt to improve the law through change by those without the knowledge of the true science of statesmanship will result in a poorer imitation of the true constitution (300d–e). The Eleatic Stranger has said that of all constitutions besides the one ruled by the scientific statesmen 'some are more perfect copies . . . others are grosser and less adequate imitations' (297c). There appear to be two conditions for those more perfect copies of the one true constitution. The first is that the state has a well-founded code of written and unwritten laws or ancestral customs. The second requirement for a 'perfect imitation' of the rule of the scientific statesman is unswerving obedience to the laws by the rulers and ruled with no attempt to improve them through any kind of modification.

Actual constitutions, then, are distinguished by whether or not they follow the laws 'once they have been laid down and never transgress written enactments and established, ancestral customs' (301a). Ignoring the importance of the code of laws for the well-being of the state and its citizens, those constitutions which are lawless aim solely at the interest of the rulers. The states are lawless not necessarily in the sense that there are no laws, but that the laws if they were initially well grounded are ignored, twisted, changed or replaced by laws or decrees which serve the interests of the stronger, the rulers, and bring about the detriment of the ruled.

Among the lawful states the state ruled by one man, a king, is considered by Plato to be the best of the imitative constitutions that adhere to their laws. The king imitates the truly wise ruler. The Stranger makes no difference in name between the individual ruler guided by 'scientific knowledge' and the individual ruler 'guided by opinion and acting according to laws' (301b). Both are kings. When their rule adheres strictly to the enacted law, the rule of a few or of many is called, respectively, aristocracy and democracy. When law is not observed, the rule of the rich few is an oligarchy. The rule of the many is still styled a democracy. But when a man rules without observing the laws or the ancestral customs and falsely claims to be the scientific ruler who need not obey the written codes, then he is a tyrant. For he claims the mantle of the scientific ruler, not because he has knowledge of the statesman's art, but because of 'his passion and his ignorance' (301c).

Of the lawful constitutions the rule of the king is best. Of the lawless states, the tyranny is the worse because if one man as king can by observing the law provide the best actual constitution, one without knowledge acting outside the law will be 'the most grievous to have to live with' (302e). The rule of the few whether lawful or lawless is midway in value between the rule of one and the rule of many. If the few rule by law they have a 'middle' capacity for providing a good constitution, but if the few rule without law then their middle capacity is for evil. The many, whether observing the law or not, have the least capacity for doing good or evil. So democracy is the best among those constitutions flouting the law, but worst among those observing law.

Although Plato does not give his reasons for preferring the lawful monarchy and aristocracy to the lawful democracy, his probable reasoning seems clear (Taylor, trans. *The Sophist and Statesman*, 1961, pp. 236–7). In a democracy an unanimity of purpose would be hard to come by and, consequently, effective political action would be difficult. Assuming that the laws were being observed in a monarchy or aristocracy, a greater opportunity would exist for an agreement on political aims and for the ability to follow through with them. But just as greater numbers of the democracy rendered effective political action for the good more difficult, so they would make democratic action for evil in the lawless constitution more ineffective. Action contrary to the established laws could be realized more effectively in the oligarchy or the tyranny. Existing constitutions, then, are either lawful or lawless. Those who take part in them are not true statesmen but 'party leaders'. They are the Sophists of whom Socrates said in the *Gorgias* that they practice the sham art of legislation and try to give the people what they want rather than what is good for them.

The definition of the true statesman offered in the *Politicus* shows that his knowledge differs substantially from that of the philosopher king. The philosopher ruler of the *Republic* had all the knowledge necessary for running the state. He was legislator, general, judge and true rhetorician all rolled into one with a knowledge whose objects were the forms themselves. But those arts or sciences most allied with the science of statesmanship, the art of rhetoric, the art of generalship and the art of administering justice, do not form the content or substance of the true statesman's art. The expert in each of these arts is separate from the statesman, but he receives his instructions as to when he shall perform his art from the statesman. The art of rhetoric is an important art which tries to persuade the people to a certain point of view or course of action through the telling of imaginative stories rather than through coercion. Although the *Gorgias* spoke harshly of rhetoric as a sham art that sought only to please the people rather than to do what was good for the well-being of their souls, Socrates did allow that there was a good rhetoric which would have such a concern. In the later *Phaedrus* rhetoric became a normative art of the dialectical philosopher. With his knowledge of the like and unlike the rhetorician of the *Phaedrus* had as the chief object of his study the nature of the human soul and how best to persuade it (*Phaedr.*, 270a–1b). If he was indeed the dialectical philosopher who practices rhetoric in the *Politicus*, it was only under the direction of the statesman. With the aid of such an official expert in rhetoric, the true statesman brought about the moral well-being of the souls of his subjects which was his chief responsibility.

Generalship decides military strategy when a condition of war exists, but it is the scientific statesman who makes 'the reasoned decision' whether to fight or to settle a dispute on friendly terms (304e). The art of the judges does not go beyond the issues at litigation. The judge attempts to reach an impartial and unbiased decision on the merits of the case using as his standards for what is just or unjust the criteria 'set up for it and embodied in the legal rules which it has received from the kingly lawgiver' (305b).

Thus the important functions of the state are in the hands of specialists (Field, 1949, pp. 104–5) who act according to their specialized knowledge when ordered to do so by the statesman. It is his unique task to know when it is appropriate for beginning and 'setting in motion the most important matters in the state' (305d). This science of statesmanship is concerned with 'the laws and with all that belongs to the life of the state' (305e). It is the universal science which knows how best to utilize all of the arts within the community to weave all that is within the state in a 'unified fabric'.

In the *Politicus*, Plato found two opposing temperaments among men, courage and moderation. Domination of the state by those displaying courage resulted in an aggressive policy, which through many military adventures finally brought ruin to the state. But the state also faced ruin when dominated by the moderates for through their moderation they and those they influence would not resist aggression against themselves but would yield to aggression through appeasement (307a–8b). It is the task of the statesman to weave citizens with these disparate temperaments into a unified whole. The statesman hands over the youth displaying these diverse temperaments to the spinners and carders, the teachers of the young through games, formal education and the laws under the watchful eye of the statesman. These teachers make the youth ready for the eventual weaving by the statesman of the different threads into a unified fabric. Treating those with a courageous character as the firm warp and those disposed to moderation as the soft and supple woof, the statesman tries to weave these two diverse characters into a unified whole social fabric. He achieves this through linking the souls of the citizens with divine and human bonds. The divine link comes about

> When there is implanted in the soul of men a right opinion concerning what is honorable, just and good, and what is the opposite of these—an opinion based on absolute truth and settled as unshakeable conviction [real true opinion with confirmation, Campbell trans.]—I declare that such a conviction is a manifestation of the divine in a race which is in truth of supernatural lineage. (309c)

With this linkage to the divine, the 'educated right opinion' of the truth of the honorable, just and good, the man of courage will realize gentleness as a foil to his aggressiveness and be more amenable to righteousness. The moderate soul also infused with its grasp of the truth will be sufficiently 'prudent' to discharge its public duties and not be dangerously pliable. Thus through a sharing of 'sound standards and a sense of values' (Skemp, trans. *Statesman*, 1957, p. 97, n. 49) the statesman is able to effect a mixture within the souls of those having the opposed temperaments. Through these 'sound standards and shared values' each of the souls in which one of the two opposed temperaments predominates will receive an awareness of the temperament it lacks, so that it will engage in wise action. The human bonds come about when intermarriage occurs between men and women displaying the contrary types of character so that their offspring will naturally come to have a mixture of the two opposed temperaments (310b). In this fashion the true statesman is able to weave a unified and harmonious web of human society, making use of law or not as he sees fit to achieve what is truly for the benefit of the society and the citizens.

In the *Laws* Plato moved from the rule of the exceptional individual, whether the philosopher ruler of the *Republic* or the scientific statesman of the *Politicus*, with the aid of law, to the rule of law over citizen and magistrate alike. In the *Laws*, as in the two earlier dialogues, the laws were not directed towards merely preserving the order and stability of the state, but were ultimately charged with helping the individual to attain his arete or moral virtue. Despite an apparent concern for legislation and its details, the *Laws* was continuously concerned with the moral well-being of the individual citizen (Vanhoutte, 1954, p. 157; Hall, 1963, pp.

190-7). The Athenian Stranger who speaks for Plato in the *Laws* observes:

We should, of course, trust whatever the legislator tells us, but especially his doctrine that the soul has an absolute superiority over the body, and that while I am alive I have nothing to thank for my individuality except my soul . . . Our real self—our immortal soul, as it is called—departs, as the ancestral law declares, to the gods below to give an account of itself. (959a-b)

This profoundly moral ground of law implied in the *Republic* and the *Politicus* was the express object of the practical state of the *Laws*. The inability to acquire a moral basis to legislation was the cause of the relativity of moral and legal standards in existing states.

Now we can see why it is hardly surprising that rules and regulations fluctuate so much from state to state: it is because legislation has a different aim in each. Nor is it surprising that in most cases you find that some people think of justice as nothing but the subjection of the state to the rule of this or that type of person without regard to their vice or virtue, while others think of it as the opportunity to become rich, no matter whether they are thereby enslaved or not; others again are hell bent for leather on a life of 'freedom'. Some legislators keep both ends in view, and their laws have the dual purpose of securing control over other states *and* freedom for their own. The cleverest legislators of all (as they like to think of themselves) so far from aiming at one single end, look not only to these but all others like them, simply because they cannot identify any supremely valuable end to which all others ought . . . to contribute. (962d-e)

It is this supreme end, a moral end, which must never be lost sight of in considering Plato's theory of legislation in the *Laws*. Plato does not literally mean that morality can be legislated in the sense that the law can make the individual act with a certain inward condition of soul. The right kind of laws are designed to keep in view the whole of virtue, not only a part, as was the case with those states that emphasized as their object of legislation military courage (630d-e, 688a-b).

But to obtain this moral object, the problem remains of what kind of code of laws should be set up and what is the best way to do so. Plato's spokesman in the *Laws*, the Athenian Stranger, thought that the most appropriate way to embark on the right kind of legislation and constitution was to have a young autocrat who had self-control, a retentive memory and courage. If such a man came into contact with a distinguished legislator then there would be the most auspicious conditions for forming such a constitution and code of laws. Thus 'supreme power in a man joins hands with wise judgement and self restraint'; this was the birth, the

Athenian Stranger says, of the best political system and the best laws (712a). This was not to be taken literally, but was a fable or story to indicate the spirit and temperament that was at the basis of the right kind of legislation and the right kind of state (712a). Taking up the notion of this fable or fiction the Stranger and his companions, Megilius a Spartan, and Cleinias a Cretan, pretend that such circumstances are present, and that they are to make laws for a colony in Crete which Cleinias and nine others had been charged with founding (702a–e, 712b). They were to frame legislation from existing Cretan laws and other laws as well so long as they were superior. The Stranger welcomed the opportunity to erect such legislation and was confident of useful assistance from his companions since, in his opinion, both Crete and Sparta had laws that had been composed with 'reasonable success' (634d).

Plato in proposing legislation of the way things are, rather than under what could be termed the 'controlled' conditions of the ideal state of the *Republic,* realized that legislation is always affected by chance (tyche) and circumstances which equally ruin legislation or help bring about useful changes (709a–c). Wars may destroy constitutions and laws, disease or protracted inclement weather cause innovations so that if these examples be multiplied it might almost be said that human history 'is an affair of chance'. But granting the influence of chance and the working of God who is 'all', the skill of a true legislator can 'co-operate' with circumstances and depend on nothing beyond his own skill (709c–e).

At the beginning of a lengthy introduction or preamble to the entire code of laws the Stranger invoked the assistance of the God who was the basis of the state of the laws and its code of laws, as he made an imaginary address to the group of settlers who were to be citizens of the city whose legislation Cleinias was charged with formulating. The underlying theocratic nature of the state is seen in the Stranger's half serious suggestion that if the state was to be named after anything, it would be after God (713a). According to venerable tradition there was a God who

holds in his hands the beginning and end and the middle of all things . . Justice, who takes vengeance on those who abandon the divine law, never leaves his side. The man who means to live in happiness latches on to her and follows her with meekness and humility. (715e–16a)

God deserts whoever thinks that he has no need to follow justice. The unjust one associates with evil companions who like him are bursting with pride and self-importance and claims that he can be a leader of the state and of men. But soon he pays a deserved penalty to justice when he 'brings himself, his home, and state to rack and ruin' (716b). Any individual blessed with good judgment will seek to follow 'in the steps of God'. A man, therefore, becomes 'dear to God' when he attempts to be like God, for 'like approves like'. Through achieving temperance in his soul, man becomes like God, who is the measure of all things; 'the moderate man is God's friend, being like him, whereas the immoderate and unjust man is not like him and is his enemy; and the same reasoning applies to the other vices too' (716c–d). The emphasis on temperance and the individual becoming like God stresses the fundamental importance of the moral well-being of the citizen of the state of the *Laws*.

To understand the purpose and nature of the legislation of the *Laws*, some consideration of the nature of temperance would be helpful since temperance seems a significant goal. In its developed sense, temperance in the *Laws* means 'a conscious control of pleasurable feelings' (Saunders, 1962, p. 52). It is loving what one knows or judges to be 'fine and good' and loathing what one knows to be 'wicked and unjust' (689a). Temperance entails the agreement of the rational judgment, knowledge, reason or right opinion with the feelings of pleasure and pain. Such agreement is wisdom (sophia) (689d); lack of such accord (689a) is the worst kind of ignorance (amathia).

The temperate man of the *Laws*, then, was not wise in the sense of the members of the Nocturnal Council who had knowledge of the forms (963a), especially of the ethical forms in their unity and plurality, and participated in the cosmic nous or reason. The Nocturnal Council was the body charged with preservation of the laws in the practical state. Rather, the temperate man of the *Laws* knew how to keep his reason and emotions in their proper relationship, thereby establishing a harmony of the soul (689d) very much akin to the *Republic's* notion of the temperance of the individual (442d). In this sense temperance in the *Laws* was identified with the whole of virtue of all individuals, both the highest magistrates and the ordinary citizens.

> I call 'education' the initial acquisition of virtue by the child, when the feelings of pleasure and affection, pain and hatred, that well up in his soul are channelled in the right courses before he can understand the reason why. Then when he does understand, his reason and his emotions agree in telling him that he has been properly trained by inculcation of appropriate habits. Virtue is this general concord of reason and emotion. (653b)

The familiar notion of the unity of the virtues shared by Socrates and Plato alike was then present in the ethical doctrine of the *Laws*. Temperance appeared as a necessary condition for the acquiring of the other virtues of justice, wisdom and courage (696b–d). Temperance in its full meaning could not exist apart from the other virtues (696d). Just as in the *Republic* justice applied to all individuals in the ideal state, so temperance can be attained by all individuals in the practical state of the *Laws*. (Plato's use of aner [man or individual] and hekastos [each one or everyone] at 689b, for example, suggests that the individual in whom there is the worst discord can also be the one in whom there is harmony. But the extension of these two terms is indefinite and did not refer to any elite group, but to any citizen of the practical state.) As in the *Republic* where the philosopher rulers had a special knowledge of the forms which justified their rule, so the members of the Nocturnal Council had an additional knowledge, nous (963a ff.). Temperance also applied to the rule over self, the rule of the better part of the self, the rational, over the worse, the desires and the appetites.

> This . . . is where a man wins the first and best of victories—over himself. Conversely, to fall a victim to oneself is the worst and most shocking thing that can be imagined. (626e)

The theme of self-mastery or of the individual showing that his better part is stronger than his inferior, a central theme of the *Laws*, was vividly and memorably stated in the famous passage likening man to a puppet of the gods. Man was pulled by conflicting 'sinews or cords'; our inward affections cause internal conflict. The one pulling force we should follow is the 'leading-string, golden and holy, of "calculation", entitled the public law of the State' (645a, Bury trans.). Some have interpreted this passage as a whole to mean that the law with its 'helpers' or 'ministers' conquers the influence of the passions. But this is a self-conquest and not one imposed by the law. For the law and its ministers do not impose themselves on the individual but ensure that 'the gold in us may prevail over the other substances' (645a). The law of the state does not so much restrain our passions, but develops and nourishes our rational capacity so that our own reason can do the job of 'self conquest'. It is in this way that

> the moral point of this fable, in which we appear as puppets, will have been well and truly made; the meaning of the terms 'self-superior' and 'self-inferior' will somehow become clearer, and the duties of state and individual will be better appreciated. The latter must digest the truth about these forces that pull him, and act on it his life; the state must get an account of it either from one of the gods or from the human expert we've mentioned, and incorporate it in the form of a law to govern both its internal affairs and its relations with other states. (645b)

Thus the state seems to have an understanding expressed in its laws as to what forces moved the individual. Through its laws and preambles the state helped him to obtain moral virtues through his obedience to law which can be summed up as being like God. The injunction to become like God applied to all the citizens.

Plato's innovation of a preamble or an introduction to written laws attests to his concern with winning the informed consent of the people to individual laws and to the law itself. At the same time, the preambles were designed to aid the citizen in attaining his own excellence not only in obeying those laws that directly developed his virtue, but also in obeying those laws that constituted civic morality. For in obeying these laws with which civic morality was concerned for the right reasons as embodied in the preambles, rather than through sheer compulsion, the citizen furthered his own morality. Through the preambles, as well as through their content, the laws educated the citizens not only to become good citizens, but more importantly to become moral individuals.

The preamble was a justification of why the written law should be followed. The preamble and the law itself were two distinct items and constituted what the Stranger called legislation (722e). The law itself stated what must or must not be done, and the sanction for non-compliance. The preamble sought to win the hearts and minds of the citizens by persuading them to comply willingly with the laws. In the words of the Stranger, 'I should like the citizens to be supremely easy to persuade along the paths of virtue' (718c).

Clearly this was the effect the legislator should try to achieve in his legislation. Both the preamble and the law were the work of the legislator to bring about a willing and comprehensive obedience to the laws of the state, which ultimately sought to bring about the virtue of the individual citizens. Unthinking conformity would not help to bring about such virtue although it contributed to the maintenance of law and order in the state. But such conformity would not lead to the attainment of an inward morality in the soul. To illustrate how the law should be preceded by a preamble to encourage, persuade and to inform the citizenry, the Stranger contrasted the procedure of the slave doctor with that of the free doctor in his dealings with patients. The slave doctor made no attempt to explain to his patient the reason for the course of the treatment that he prescribed. Not the 'study of nature' but 'observation and practice' characterized his training. In contrast, the free doctor, who has learnt the art of medicine instructed his patient so that he would understand the nature of his illness, and how he was to be treated. The doctor hoped by so doing to enlist his patient's cooperation in the treatment. He sought

> to construct an empirical case-history by consulting the invalid and his friends; in this way he himself learns something from the sick and at the same time he gives the individual patient all the instruction he can. He gives no prescription until he has somehow gained the invalid's consent; then, coaxing him into continued cooperation, he tries to complete his restoration to health. (720d–e)

What is emphasized in this passage is the doctor's need for knowledge or science based on experience of the nature of that which the doctor was trying to prescribe to his patient, and some awareness of the same knowledge by the patient because of the instruction he had received. He would then be able to make a reasoned compliance with his doctor's prescription; so with the legislator and with the citizen. The legislator sought to convey to the citizens an understanding of why the laws were necessary and to win their willing and knowing compliance through the rational or emotional persuasion contained in the preambles. The need for the preamble is apparent when the Athenian Stranger at the end of the *Laws* urged that for the laws of a state to be preserved, its citizens must have grasped its laws not by mere habit, but by comprehension (951b). Rhetoric now was an art kindred to medicine rather than a part of flattery as in the *Gorgias* (466a). In the *Phaedrus* just as medicine must determine the nature of the body, so rhetoric must determine the nature of the soul if their practicers were to be scientific (270b). Knowledge of the nature of the soul was necessary if the legislator of the *Laws* wished to implant in the individual citizens the appropriate convictions and virtues. The purpose of the preamble, then, was for the legislator 'to make the person to whom he promulgated his law accept his orders—the law—in a more co-operative frame of mind and with a correspondingly greater readiness to learn' (723a).

The preamble was not a mere tale or fable designed to gain the hearers' acquiescence to the laws through charms and incantations which developed the proper attitude in the hearer. Some preambles, because of the character of the laws to which they served as an introduction, might appeal to the emotions of the citizen, and thus charm the citizen into obedience. But instruction also could persuade men's minds into obedience to law. Preambles usually employed argumentation; some contained logoi, arguments intended to give reasons why an individual should obey the law. The general principle of the preambles was to bring the citizen into a reasoned compliance with the law for which it was a prelude, and to give him some awareness of how it served towards the attaining of his morality. Preambles were 'intelligently persuasive; they are persuasion at the high level of rational insight suffused with emotion' (Morrow, 1960, p. 558).

This focus on the virtue of the individual and its unity with the obedience to law of the citizens is clearly apparent in the general preamble to the entire system of legislation that the Athenian Stranger and his fellow jurists were to set up. The scope of the preamble is vast and concerns 'how far a man should concentrate or relax the efforts he devotes to looking after his soul, his body, and his property' (724a–b). Here obviously are integrated the inward morality of the individual and external duties. That this preamble has a rational character is apparent when the Athenian suggested that both the makers and auditors of this preamble should 'ponder', or reflect on it, so as to 'perfect' their education 'as far as they can' (724b).

By far the most important thing that both legislator and citizen should 'ponder' on is the soul, for after the gods, 'of all the things a man can call his own, the holiest . . . is his soul, his most intimate possession' (726a). In the course of the preamble the Stranger laid out the further areas with which the preamble and subsequent legislation would be concerned: the body (728d–e), wealth (728e–9a), the proper treatment of children (729a–c), duties to relatives, friends, the state (729c–e), and foreigners (729e–30a), the nature of individual morality (730b–1b), the treatment of criminals (731b–d), selfishness (731d–2b), the control of the emotions (732b–e), and the relation between virtue and happiness (732e–4e). The rulers governing these areas were of 'divine sanction' and constituted what should be the right character of individuals and institutions. In discussing the rules of human origin the Stranger pointed out that the virtuous life entailed the pleasant life, although it was also intrinsically valuable as realizing the nature of man. But the importance of these areas stemmed from the direct or indirect effect they had on the well-being of the soul. We should not, for example, gain money by improper means. Such a breach of law reflected a misvaluation of the soul and an unconcern for the attainment of inward morality.

> A man who is seized by lust to obtain money by improper means and feels no disgust in the acquisition, will find that in the event he does his soul no honour by such gifts—far from it; he sells all that gives the soul its beauty and value for a few paltry pieces of gold; but all the gold upon the earth and all the gold beneath it does not compensate for lack of virtue. (727e–8a)

Plato here gave his own interpretation of what was to be the later Christian adage, what profit it if a man gain the world and lose his own soul. At different places in the *Laws*, the Stranger stressed that the principal object of legislation was the moral well-being of the citizens. But at times he seemed to give priority to the good of the state, a legislator 'should frame his code with an eye on three things, the freedom, unity, and wisdom of the city for which he legislates' (701d). No real problem of reconciliation of the two apparently diverse aims of the moral good of the individual and the good of the state exists. Plato, in the *Laws*, viewed the good of the state as characterized by freedom, unity and wisdom and as a stage towards the fulfillment of the morality of the individual.

Prior to the introduction of the notion of the preamble, the Athenian Stranger and his companions stressed that the object of legislation should be the well-being of the soul of the citizens:

> when we examine the natural features of a country and its legal system, our ultimate object of scrutiny is of course the quality of its social and political arrangements. We do not hold the common view that a man's highest good is to survive and simply to continue to exist. His highest good is to become as virtuous as possible and to continue in that state as long as life lasts. (707d)

That the ultimate object of the laws is the morality of the individual, the realization of virtue by the citizens, is apparent in his criticism of the modern lawgivers' method of classification of laws. The Stranger complained that they classified laws according to the subject matter of their content, rather than according to the whole of virtue, which laws ought to promote (630e–1a). This is a vivid and telling way of showing that Plato considered the laws of the state as above all concerned with the moral well-being of the individual citizen. Finally, in a dramatic and seldom noticed passage, the Stranger contended that the sovereignty of law was not absolute; if the state and its laws frustrated and impeded the individual citizen's progress towards fulfilling his own moral virtue, the citizen should either revolt or go into exile.

> Our aim in life should be goodness and the spiritual virtue appropriate to mankind . . . Whatever the means, it's this aim we've described that we must all strain every muscle to achieve throughout our lives. No man, whoever he is, should ever be found valuing anything else, if it impedes his progress—not even, in the last resort, the state. Rather than have the state tolerate the yoke of slavery and be ruled by unworthy hands, it may be absolutely necessary to allow it to be destroyed, or abandon it by going into exile. All that sort of hardship we simply have to endure, rather than permit a change to the sort of political system which will make men worse. (770d–e)

There could be no clearer statement of the priority of the value of the individual soul over that of the state.

The supremacy of the morality of the individual as the aim of the legislation of the state of the *Laws* emerged early with the Stranger's pronouncement that of the two products of the laws, the divine goods and the human, the human depended upon the divine.

The Stranger had noted that such laws should have the production of two kinds of benefits: the divine or moral virtue and the human goods, those goods ordinarily valued by society, health, beauty, strength and wealth accompanied by sound judgment (631b–d). The highest divine good attainable by man was good judgment, followed by the self-control of a rational soul, justice formed from a mixture of self-control and courage. The human benefits were dependent on the divine, and had them as their end. Thus the morality of the individual had priority over the merely human goods, a priority embodied in the laws, both written and unwritten.

Of prime importance in the constitution which the Stranger and his friends were setting up was the role of unwritten law or ancestral customs. These unwritten laws were not laws of nature but something like our notion of common law. They were customs which reflect years of habit which, however, did not take hold through an unconscious assimilation as with the common law, but which were instituted by the legislator and did have a beginning in time. Plato, without making unwritten laws on a par with written law, stressed their importance because they were the mortar of the social framework 'linking all written and established laws with those yet to be passed' (793b). Here, of course, the Stranger was making passing reference to the ongoing process of lawmaking. The unwritten laws were to operate like ancestral customs in 'being soundly established and instinctively observed' (793b), and so strengthen existing written law through the habit of obedience it engendered in the citizens. But these unwritten laws were not preexisting ancestral customs, for as the Stranger suggested, there may be wrong ancestral customs (Strauss, 1975, pp. 101-2). Rather, the Stranger was attempting to institute correct, unwritten laws, or his own ancestral customs founded on the way things really were (793c-d). He remonstrated, for example, with the custom of treating the right and left hands as though they were fit by nature for different tasks whereas he would affirm as unwritten law that the hands were by nature equal in capacity (794e-5a). These unwritten rules dealt with topics important enough in their own way but which did not admit of precise regulation. They were advice and instruction that became habitual through education. He regarded these unwritten rules as halfway between admonition and law (822d-e). They constituted suggestions which should not be formalized into law, yet they embodied what the legislator thought was or was not respectable, or worthy or not worthy of approval. The good citizen should, then, obey these unwritten rules even though they were not codified as law.

The same realism which Plato displayed in realizing that the ideal state and ruler could not be achieved in this world carried over into his recognition that laws, both substantive and procedural, were subject to revision, amendment or addition. Although permanence of law may be an ideal to strive for, surely the Stranger's recognition of the influence of chance and circumstance on the constitutions of states suggested that he realized the need for change in the laws. The Stranger graphically expressed the notion that changes would be made by likening the legislator's activity to that of a painter (769a-d). A painter wishing to produce an immortal and enduring canvas would realize that he needed successors who could 'repair the ravages of time' by touching up his painting and taking care of any gaps or shortcomings in his work. The analogy from the painter, then, suggested that not only was law subject to the 'ravages of time', that is, to chance and circumstance which might require change in the laws or addition to them, but also to unavoidable shortcomings in the work of the legislator, however impressive his overall accomplishment might be. The continual monitoring of the laws required that it be performed by members of the body charged with overseeing the laws, the guardians of the laws. Not only did the guardians oversee the laws, but they trained their younger associates also to be lawgivers as well as law-guardians (770a).

In addition to the legislative activity of the guardians of the law, another separate body, the Nocturnal Council (951a–2b) which includes the ten senior guardians of the law, was a continuous study body which could recommend changes or additions in the law. Unlike the scientific statesman of the *Politicus* who could implement any changes he thought desirable, the council could not implement such changes. Only through the initiative of the guardians of the law in their function as overseers of the law, not as members of the Nocturnal Council, could actual changes come about through being presented and voted on favorably by the people (772c–d). Such changes would be especially prominent in judicial procedure (846b–c, 855c–d, 957a–b), and in laws relating to songs, sacrifices and dances (772a–b, 835a–b).

Some have argued that Plato did believe laws could acquire an immutability (Morrow, 1960, p. 570). While passages could be taken to suggest such absence of change, once perfection of the laws has been realized, I think it more plausible to take Plato to mean progress towards an ideal which may be achieved now and then, but not in terms of legislation as a whole (772c). The ultimate moral purpose of the laws remained unchanged, the attainment of virtue by the citizens. Since motion or change, as Plato realized in the *Sophist* (248 ff.), was an aspect of reality, laws also were subject to alteration and addition.

> even when you have achieved or gained or founded something you have never quite finished. Only when you have ensured complete and perpetual security for your creation can you reckon to have done everything that ought to have been done. Until then, it's a case of 'unfinished business'. (960b–c)

While this might suggest a complete end to legislation, it also implied a certain 'open-endedness' to legislation indicating that complete security from change was never possible for laws in this world of motion and change, no matter how skilled the legislator. What was required for law was a procedure for amendment and innovation that ensured continual legality and rightness. The Stranger intended not so much to keep the content of laws irreversible as the notion of the rightness of the laws and their continual concern for the moral well-being of the individual citizens (960d). The realization of these goals would constitute the 'firm foundation' of the laws (960e). Surely the fact that the Nocturnal Council was charged with a continuous examination of the adequacy of the laws and ways to improve them strongly implied that Plato did not expect even good laws to be impervious to change. What Plato did think to be the unchanging aspect of law was its being grounded on mind or nous and having the moral well-being of the citizens as its ultimate aim (630c, 631c–d, 963a–e). The Nocturnal Council was charged with preserving what might be called this spirit of the law. Change or addition to the content of the laws in the face of different conditions might be required in order to preserve this spirit of the laws.

The comparison of the function of the council to the activity of generals and the deployment of their armies and to doctors concerned with keeping the bodies of their patients 'safe and sound' seems to confirm that the Stranger did not expect laws to be unchanging (961d–2c). Rather he wished to control change as much as possible and to make it change for the good, whether of the army, body or the state. Those charged with the preservation of the laws had to deal with changing circumstances and chance by refurbishing, amending and making new laws to preserve the integrity of laws as a whole, and the constitution as the salvation of the state (961e–2b). If law in the practical state ever became completed, finished in its legalistic nature, what need would there be of the council? Rather the state would be like those imitative constitutions of the *Politicus* where, once made, those laws were to be followed invariably. The chief difference would be, supposedly, that in this case they would be the right laws. But part of the meaning of having the right laws seems to be the ability to deal in whatever way necessary with law to meet changing situations. Of course for Plato the basic nature of man, what constituted his arete, and what influenced him for better or worse, the representation of the good or imitation of the bad, never changed.

Plato's preoccupation with laws based on nous as the salvation of the state and his charge to the Nocturnal Council to act as a permanent body of legal research and improvement stressed the sovereignty of law in his practical state. Sovereignty of law in the *Laws* is usually assumed to indicate Plato's coming to terms with reality. He realized the impossibility of the philosopher ruler of the *Republic* and the scientific statesman of the *Politicus*, and replaced the rule of the wise man with the rule of law. But the sovereignty of law is not necessarily absolute. Plato totally rejected the positivist view of law, that law was whatever the leaders of the state say it was, assuming that it had been enacted in accordance with the appropriate law-making norm of the state. The genuine sovereignty of law meant that law must in its enactments reflect the valuation by the legislator of the supremacy of the divine goods mentioned earlier over the very existence of the state and its laws. The object of the laws, as the preamble of the entire code of legislation for the practical state tells us, was the well-being of the soul of the individual citizens. At the conclusion of the legislation projected by the Stranger and his fellow jurists, the criterion of the law that was sovereign, that was 'the rule of law in the souls' of the citizens and 'the preservation of the laws themselves' (960d), depended on the great principle that earlier they took as the 'right one' that 'every detail of our legislation ought to have a *single* end in view, and the proper name to call it was . . . "virtue"' (963a).

The Stranger rejected law as viewed by positivistic theories as 'bogus' or as not true (714b–15d). Such law was bogus because it was based on a definition of justice that maintained that the purpose of legislation was directed towards preserving the interest of the established political power whether it be the rule of one man, a few or the people; and towards ensuring that it was not overthrown and held power permanently. Because the main interest of such constitutions was the preservation of their power as long as possible, the only concern was that law be 'just' in the sense of furthering the aim of permanent power.

The entire driving force of such laws was to ensure the continuance of the *status quo*. Such legislation was false because it did not have the interest of the state as a whole but was enacted for a particular section of the community, the ruling power and its supporters. When offices were filled through competition the winner took all, but the losers and their followers and descendants had no share in power. The ascendant power in the government filled all its offices with its supporters and created a dangerous split in the state between the 'haves' and 'the have-nots' of political power. It was in this sense of a constitution with 'bogus' laws that the division in the *Politicus* was made between lawful and lawless constitutions. The lawless constitutions, of course, had laws but they were directed towards the well-being not of the whole society, as in the case of the lawful states, but of the rulers. The enactors of such laws were 'party-men' and, continued the Stranger, 'people who say those laws have a claim to be obeyed are wasting their breath' (715b). The Stranger contended that the positivistic thesis concerning the nature and function of law, as the interest of the class in power and the maintenance of that power permanently, was the ruin of the state.

Where the law is subject to some other authority and has none of its own, the collapse of the state, in my view, is not far off; but if law is master of the government and the government is its slave, then the situation is full of promise and men enjoy all the blessings that the gods shower on a state. (715d)

The sovereignty of law reflected the working of reason or nous and was addressed to the reason within the citizens who were to obey it. To bring out the necessarily rational character of law that was to be sovereign in the state, the Stranger referred to the Myth of Cronus familiar from the account of the *Politicus* (269b–74e, although in the *Politicus* no laws were used during the time of Cronus). Law in the age of man was to replace the role of the gods in the mythical age of Cronus. In that age the result of divine attention to man and his needs was 'peace, respect for others, good laws, justice in full measure, and a state of happiness and harmony among the races of the world' (713d–e). Now, during their time, the Stranger remarked, the rulers of the state were men, and not a god. People, therefore, 'have no respite from toil and misfortune'. But today, urged the

Stranger, we should follow as closely as possible life in the age of Cronus. This above all entailed that we should 'run our public and our private life, our homes and our cities, in obedience to what little spark of immortality lies in us, and dignify these edicts of reason with the name of "law"' (713e–14a). The Athenian Stranger was urging the citizens to obey in themselves and in the laws of state, 'reason, the immortal element' within them.

Chapter 7

The States of the *Republic* and *Laws*

The relationship of the ideal state of the *Republic* to the practical state of the *Laws* can be fruitfully explored in terms of the somewhat anomalous aspect of the metaphor of the philosopher as an artist or craftsman. The philosopher ruler has as his model the world of forms, especially the moral forms, to which he refers as a standard for creating the proper social conditions for the just society and the just individual (500b–1c). The ideal state of the *Republic* serves as a type or model which is to be approximated by the practical state of the *Laws*. The practical state, however, does not duplicate the institutions of the ideal state, but approximates in its own constitution the principles underlying that state: unity and fellow feeling, wisdom and freedom.

The philosopher in the *Republic* uses the forms as his model in making a copy of it in this world, just as the artist copies his ideal on canvas. But unlike the ordinary artist or the demiurge of the *Timaeus,* and indeed unlike any craftsman, the philosopher has perfect material to work with (Cornford, trans. *Timaeus,* 1957, pp. 36–8). The philosophers in initially creating their city 'would refuse to take in hand either individual or state or to legislate before they either received a clean slate or themselves made it clean' (501a).

If anything indicated the ideal quality of the ideal state it would be this claim to have a perfect material to work within, which is, of course, practically impossible. The later suggestion in the *Republic,* that the rulers make a clear canvas by rusticating or sending all the population over 10 years of age into the country is, from a practical point of view, too improbable to be taken seriously (541a).

If Plato deemed it impossible in some way to implement what he took as the fundamental principles of his state, then the state of the *Republic* would be a never-to-be-realized ideal. But if he meant that a beginning could be made with an existing society that would consent to having philosophers rule them, there might be some possibility of the realization of the ideal state.

> Is it possible for anything to be realized in deed as it is spoken in word, or is it the nature of things that action should partake of exact truth less than speech, even if some deny it? (473a)

Plato was not suggesting a split between theory and practice. In fact, he thought there was a continuity between theory and practice. The ideal state could be realized. It was not merely a theoretical, abstract, forever unrealizable model that tantalized us with its impossibility. After describing the model in words, Socrates asked how it could be realized in deed as well (Bosanquet, 1925, pp. 201–2). The single change that would bring about a realization in deed of the words of Socrates and his companions would be the inauguration of the philosophers as the rulers of the state. With this knowledge of the forms they would know how to order the state and bring about justice in the state and individuals to the fullest ideal extent 'until they have done all in their power to make the moral character of the men as pleasing as it may be to God' (501c, my trans.).

Arendt (1968, pp. 107–8) has raised an objection to the feasibility of realizing the ideal state. She implies that the difference in the powers of mind between the philosophers and the other citizens of a state was so great that the latter would be unable to know whether their would-be rulers had the necessary knowledge to rule. While the few rulers may be 'coerced' through their apprehension of the objective truths of the forms, the many people would lack such an awareness.

Plato admitted that it would not be easy to convince the people of a society that they should be ruled by philosophers. But he thought this due to the bad name given philosophy by the Sophists and others such as Isocrates, who emphasized in his school an embellished, ornate and rhetorical style with no real philosophical substance (498d–e). Plato seemed to think it possible that the masses would listen and not be harsh to the true philosopher (499a–500a). In the *Laws*, the Athenian Stranger observed that ordinary individuals and even the wicked could tell a good or virtuous man (950b–c), so it would be possible for the many to recognize and accept the rule of the true philosopher.

Arendt raises a spurious difficulty in her supposition that because they lack the knowledge of the philosopher the people would be unable to realize that the philosophers have such knowledge. Her objection depends on positing a difference in kind between the philosopher and the ordinary man along the lines of a master-slave relation. But Plato stressed that despite their differences of social function all men had reason and that all members of the society were kin to one another. Further, as the *Meno* revealed (82b–5e), all individuals, even slaves, had within them right opinions that could be brought to light through the proper kind of education. The true philosopher employing the good rhetoric mentioned in the *Gorgias* (503a–b) would be able to arouse those right opinions latent within individuals so that they could recognize the capabilities of the philosophers and willingly accede to their rule. Plato's belief in the *Republic* that the many could be persuaded to accept the rule of the philosophers contrasts sharply with the historical Socrates' gloomy view in the *Apology* that the true philosopher who attempted to participate in politics in a democracy would be destroyed by the people (31d–e). Plato changed his mind in the *Laws* about the feasibility of the political rule of the philosopher not because he thought the philosopher would not be accepted by the people, but because he did not think that such an extraordinary individual could be found: 'such a character is nowhere to be found' (875d), perhaps because of the 'general weakness of human nature' (854a).

Although the failure of Plato's attempts related in his Seventh Letter to help in the founding of a constitution after his own principles in Syracuse may have had some influence in his abandoning the possibility of the unfettered rule of the philosopher, it is more plausible that underlying changes in his metaphysical or ontological outlook were more influential in forming the mixed constitution of the practical state of the *Laws*. What took place was that the formerly static nature of reality was broadened to include the principle of motion; to 'that which is perfectly real' (*Sophist*, 248e) belonged life, soul and wisdom, a familiar position to readers of the *Timaeus* and *Laws* Book X. There was a cosmic reason from which the individual soul derived its reason (Hackforth, trans. *Philebus*, 1958, p. 50). This notion of soul or mind directing the universe as a whole for its true good had a profound impact on Plato's view of what kind of state could be realized and how it was to be realized, the state of the mixed constitution of the *Laws*.

This state applied the principles of society ideally realized in the *Republic*—unity and fellow feeling, wisdom and freedom—to the realities of man's nature and social existence. The mixed constitution reflected a tendency towards the concept of mixture as a basic feature of Plato's later thought that attempted to show how the notion of soul, intelligence or mind shaped unformed, unshaped matter, and underlay both the cosmic and political order (Morrow, 1960, pp. 536–7).

The ideal state was a 'pure' state, reflecting the imposition of an ideal model on an ideal matter or canvas through approximation. If details of the model could not be fully realized it was not because of the recalcitrance of the matter of the state in receiving the form, but because words could never be fully realized in deeds. It did not matter whether they were written deeds like the dialogues or projected events such as the realization of the ideal state.

The ideal state of the *Republic* was a type of model for the practical state of the *Laws*. In both words and execution a close similarity, although not an identity, existed between the words and their realization in the deeds of the ideal state. But in the practical state of the *Laws*, the stuff upon which the state was to be constructed was no longer the clean canvas, the *tabula rasa* of the *Republic*. The problem became one of the founders of a state taking people and political institutions as they were and could be in society and attempting to effect a measured and balanced mixture through the application of nous or reason in the laws. The mixture, a compromise between monarchy and democracy, was the practical state of the *Laws*. The monarchical character of the state did not refer to the rule of one man, but to the existence of important offices of the state endowed with the power and authority to govern the state effectively. The democratic aspect of the constitution obviously signified the meaningful participation of the people in the workings of the constitution. Either the monarchic or the democratic aspect could dominate the constitution. The result would be the tyranny of the oligarchic rulers over the people, or the lawless anarchy of a people intoxicated by their possession of absolute power. The object of legislation was a 'compromise between a monarchical and a democratic constitution, which is precisely the sort of compromise a constitution should always be' (756e–7a). To this meaning of mixed constitution, Plato added a further restricted sense of its being 'a system of checks and balances' among the various offices of the state (von Fritz, 1954, p. 78).

Appropriating the terminology of the *Politicus* (309b–c), the Stranger presented the two elements of the constitution as the warp and the woof. According to the Athenian Stranger, the warp, the agencies of the state, should be 'strong and firm' while the woof, the people, should be 'softer and suitably workable' (734e–5a). In the mixed constitution, the authority of the rulers and the freedom of the people was to be blended in the right way with neither one going to extremes. The extent of Plato's political achievement can be seen in comparing how the three principles of the state—unity and fellow feeling, wisdom and freedom—have each been implemented in the ideal or near ideal circumstances of the *Republic* and in the actually existing conditions of the *Laws*.

The unity of the ideal state of the *Republic* was as close an approximation as possible of the adage, friends have all things in common (424a). This unity was fostered by the having of all things in common by the guardians, the equality of the sexes and the sense of community and fellow feeling engendered by each citizen doing his particular task for the good of the whole.

Those guardians selected to be rulers were to have all things in common. They were to have no families, no gold or silver, no property, and were provided their food and shelter by the other citizens in lieu of annual cash wages (416d–17a). The sense of unity among the rulers would be further strengthened by the institution of common meals and dwellings (416e). The commonality of life among the male and female rulers was not intended to breed promiscuity, but rather in carefully regulated unions at specified times to produce the best possible offspring through careful eugenic procedures (458e–60a). Through the abolition of the family and of private property among the rulers, Plato hoped to intensify the sense of oneness and unity among them through a community of intensely shared feeling and loyalty to their group and the state. The best-ordered state,

Plato thought, would be that one in which this sense of duty or oneness of fellow feeling applied to the widest number (462c). Although relations among the rest of the citizens of the ideal state might not be as intensely communal as among the rulers where 'mine' and 'not mine' were not used and all shared the same pleasure or pain (462e), there was still a sense of community that exceeded a mere sense of civic loyalty or pride. The citizens considered the rulers not as masters as in tyrannies or oligarchies, or as the government in democracies, but as 'their saviors and helpers' (463b). The rulers regarded the people as those who supported and maintained them in their service to the state and as their fellow citizens (463a–b). The laws embodying the abolition of family and property and of the sharing of an intense fellow feeling and communal spirit not only guaranteed unity among the rulers but also ensured unity of the entire state.

> Then in all cases the laws will leave these men to dwell in peace together . . . and if these are free from dissension among themselves, there is no fear that the rest of the city will ever start faction against them or with one another. (465b).

The sense of unity among the citizens as a whole also arose from the justice of the state itself. It signified that each individual was doing the job for which he was naturally suited, making the state a unified whole and removing any source of friction and imbalance that would dissolve the state.

> The purport of all this was that the other citizens too must be sent to the task for which their natures were fitted, one man to one work, in order that each of them fulfilling his own function may not be many men, but one, and so the entire city may come to be not a multiplicity but a unity. (423d)

Graphic representation of this unity was provided by the allegory of the metals (414c–15d) and the quasi-organic analogy of the state to a statue, with each aspect of the statue having an appropriate function to play in the depiction of the whole (420b–d, 462d–e). Each part of the statue was to be in its proper or natural proportion in relation to the whole.

The unity and fellow feeling of the guardians was a necessary condition for the unity of the entire state. Social unity was assured by observance of the law that stipulated that the well-being and unity of the state as a whole took precedence over that of a part (519e–20a). But concern for the whole did not mean that genuine good of the individual citizen was secondary. A significant factor in ensuring the spiritual unity of the state was ridding the state of the extremes of poverty and wealth. For these extremes would create two states within the same geographical unit, the state of the rich and the state of the poor that were always conspiring and plotting against one another and destroying any sense of unity or fellow feeling (422a–3b). The unity of the ideal state was further enhanced by the guardians ensuring that its size and population did not exceed what was consistent with maintaining a sense of unity and friendship among the citizens (423c–d).

But although the unity of the state was stressed, it did not conflict with the true well-being of the individual. The justice of the individual, as Plato said, was 'not the doing of one's own business externally, but with regard to that which is within and in the true sense concerns one's self, and the things of one's self' (443c–d).

The good of the state, its justice, was distinguished from the good of the individual citizen, his own justice. Both goods were the object of the ideal state, and they complemented each other. The justice of the state was not an end in itself, but a means to the justice of the individual citizen. To foster the necessary unity implicitly required by the justice of the state, Plato would have women equal with men in every way as being in accord with nature.

Plato, of course, affirmed that women as well as men could be rulers of the ideal state, but it is not generally realized that the equality of the sexes was maintained in the state as a whole. Justice of the state required that every individual have some social occupation: 'each one man must perform one social service in the state for which his nature was best adapted' (433a). Wives were, it is implied, to engage in social occupation. Socrates emphasized that for purposes of distinguishing between the kinds of social functions open to both men and women, classification of differences and similarities between the two sexes did not depend on the fact that the 'male begets' and the 'female bears', but on what was 'pertinent to the pursuits themselves' (454d–e). Socrates meant, for example, 'that a man and a woman who have a physician's mind have the same nature' (454d). Plato clearly intended women to participate in the social functions necessary for the state. There were no sexual differences that would bar women from doing the same kind of social task as men. References to women's differing abilities with regard to war, athletics and music also testify to the range of different occupations for which women were naturally suited (455e–6a). Although Plato considered that men were generally superior to women in various occupations, he nonetheless contended that 'many women . . . are better than many men in many things' (455d). Among these 'many things' were those qualities of high spiritedness and wisdom that qualified a woman who had both to be a guardian (456a–b). But obviously the 'many things' in which many women were better than many men also included crafts and skills, not merely child care and familial concerns (433c–d). Such equality of the sexes, then, added greatly to the sense of unity prevailing in the ideal state.

In the *Republic,* Plato did not explicitly emphasize as he did in the *Laws* the importance of religion as a source of unity and fellow feeling among the citizens. He accepted the existing religious law as the arbiter of religious customs and behavior (427b–c). He did insist, however, that God (or the gods) was to be represented as the source of good only, as simple in nature and as no deceiver of men (378a–83c). This understanding of the nature of God was a vitally important aspect, it may be assumed, of the education of all the youth (Cornford, trans. *Republic,* 1978, pp. 67–8). The sense of community in the ideal state would obviously be enhanced by all its citizens sharing the same conception of God's nature, and the same religious customs, rites and festivals (427b–c).

In the *Laws* as in the *Republic* the overriding concern was how to attain unity in the state. But the unity of the practical state of the *Laws* was to be achieved in a different manner from that of the *Republic.* In an exaggerated reference to the holding of all things in common as true for the state as a whole rather than for the guardians (739b–c) the Stranger singled out the approximation of this unity as the object of legislation and the producer of the happiness of the citizens of the ideal state.

> To sum up, the laws in force impose the greatest possible unity on the state—and you'll never produce a better or truer criterion of an absolutely perfect law than that. It may be that gods or a number of the children of gods inhabit this kind of state: if so, the life they live there, observing these rules, is a happy one indeed. And so men need look no further for their ideal; they should keep this state in view and try to find the one that most nearly resembles it. This is what we've put our hand to, and if some way it could be realized, it would come very near immortality and be second only to the ideal. (739d–e)

The implementation of this ideal of unity, as well as the two others of wisdom and freedom, resulted in quite different political and social institutions in the *Laws* from those of the *Republic.* What underlay these different institutions in the mixed constitution was Plato's combination of the principle of authority or of kingly rule with that of the democratic principle, of freedom and popular participation in the affairs of state. There was to be a system of checks and balances among the various sources of authority in the state so that no one source would dominate the others.

To drive home the need for a mixed constitution for the right kind of state, the Stranger presented an account of the evolution of society to the states of his time that was partly speculative and partly historical. He attempted to isolate what laws were responsible for the rise and fall of states (676a, 683b). For as the Stranger noted, all the features of contemporary states developed from these beginnings: the laws, political

systems, technical arts, vices and virtues (678a). Plato's treatment here of
the evolution of society resembled the analytic approach he used in the
Republic to discover the conditions necessary for the coming into
existence of the ideal state and what principles underlay the progressive
decline of states from the ideal condition.

The Stranger succinctly described the development of society after a
great flood (a catastrophe that has been repeated countless times before in
other ways) in four stages (678c-93e). The only survivors of the flood
were those men who live in isolation on hill and mountain tops to whom
were lacking all the technical and cultural achievements, virtues and vices
of the civilization that had vanished in the flood. In this initial stage in the
development of society men were 'loving and cherishing one another'
(678c-80e). They had sufficient resources to supply their needs for food,
shelter and clothing. They had neither gold nor silver and were not
wealthy enough to produce envy and jealousy among themselves. Fear
prevented them from going to the plains below them. Here were
'produced the finest characters', who were good because of their
simplicity. This was the society of paternal autocracy. No need existed for
written law because people lived under the ancestral law as set down for
the family by the father, who bequeathed such authority to his eldest son.

As families moved from their isolated position in the hills and
mountains and engaged in agriculture, they evolved into a community of
families (680e-1d). The heads of the various family groups appointed
representatives from their kinfolk to select from the ancestral laws,
religious and social customs those rules that would govern their
community. These family representatives, in effect, became legislators
and the customs and ancestral laws they selected became the first
legislation. These representatives also appointed from the people the
community leaders who became members of what was a developing
aristocracy.

People apparently had forgotten about the flood that had occurred
many ages ago. Leaving the foothills, they settled on the plain and formed
cities like Troy. In this third stage of the development of society all the
possibilities of differences in constitutions and social and political change
exhibited in actual states were present (681d). Cities and peoples
increased, men lost their fear of the water and began to sail the seas. Some
of these cities launched by sea an expedition against Troy. During the ten
years of the Trojan war domestic matters in the cities of the men who were
besieging Troy grew so bad that upon their return from Troy the
victorious troops were forced into exile. As exiles from their cities, these
troops became known as Dorians after Dorius who grouped them
together. They founded the cities of Sparta, Messene and Argos in the
Peloponnese.

The fourth stage in Plato's historical survey was a consideration of the
Dorian League and the laws that were responsible for the League's failure

as well as for the continued well-being of its surviving member, Sparta (683a–93b). Here, the Stranger thought his investigation into the origins of constitutions was on firmer ground than before because it was being conducted on the basis of actual facts rather than of conjecture (683e–4a).

The League began with great promise. Collectively the kings and peoples of the three states exchanged oaths agreeing to abide by previously established laws that defined the limits of sovereignty and what was expected of the allegiance of the people to their kings. The kings swore never to expand their authority beyond the limits set by the laws, and the people promised that so long as the kings did not overstep their legal authority, they would neither revolt nor allow others to overthrow the kingship (684a–b). The kings would help both kings and peoples when they were harmed and the people would assist both the kings and peoples when they were in danger. The most important principle agreed upon by members of the League was that two states would war against the third when it disregarded the laws delimiting the scope of sovereignty and of allegiance (684b). The League was also intended to protect the Greek world from external aggression by the Assyrians (685b–d). Equal distribution of land in the three states gave their citizens hope of internal stability since there would be less opportunity for economic discontent among the citizens (684d).

Despite great expectations among the people of the League's success, it failed. The constitutions of Argos and Messene were destroyed. The cause of the League's failure was attributed to the rulers (683e) who showed the 'worst kind of ignorance [amathia] about mankind's vital concerns' (688c). Such ignorance preferred what it knew to be wicked and unjust over what it knew to be fine and good. Regardless of their other abilities, rulers afflicted with this kind of ignorance should have been disqualified from rule, even if 'they have worked hard at every nice accomplishment that makes a man quick-witted' (689c–d). Wisdom was synonymous with temperance and good judgment, in having the good sense to have one's preferences accord with what is right and good. To those who were wise in this sense of temperance should be entrusted the offices of the state (690b), even if in terms of the old adage the Stranger quoted 'they cannot read, they cannot swim' (689d–e).

The kings of Argos and Messene failed to have reason, control their appetites and desires and to act only in accord with what they knew to be right and good. In their zeal to take for themselves what belonged lawfully to the people, they flouted Hesiod's maxim that the half is often greater than the whole (690e). They were not content with the power they lawfully had, but attempted to gain more, and as a result, lost their sovereignty. Their moral and political failure resulted from their lack of wisdom, which caused them to be 'infected by the acquisitive spirit in defiance of the law of the land' (691a). They had not lived up to the kingly oath to observe the legal limits of sovereignty. This again reflected their ignorance in preferring their own advantage to the legality and sanctity of the original oath between kings and peoples.

Although he recognized that the immediate cause of the League was the greed of the rulers, the Stranger probed deeper into the underlying cause. The initial legislators should have realized that oaths alone would not have restrained youthful kings inflamed with arrogance and power from developing into tyrants (692b). They neglected the rule of due measure (691c) and blundered by giving power to the kingship without ensuring that there was a system of checks and balances to prevent a youthful or unwise king from excesses (693b).

According to Plato's reconstruction of Peloponnesian history, Sparta alone of the members of the Dorian League survived. Early in her history, wise legislators did foresee the need for the rule of due measure or proportion (691d–e). The result was the 'mixed constitution', a system of checks and balances in the sources of sovereignty as well as a blend of the monarchic and democratic aspects of the state. A balance of power existed among those in authority (691e–2c). The royal power was limited by having two kings instead of one. As counter to or check on the kings' authority, a council of twenty-eight members, the gerousia, which included the two kings, was created supposedly by Lycurgus. Because the other twenty-six members had to be over 65 years of age, they acted as a curb to the kings should they happen to be young and impetuous. The council was equal to the king in the greatest matters (692a). Although elected by the people for their virtue, they were not chosen from the people for their lifelong reign, but from the nobles. To counter the monarchic-oligarchic character of the state, five ephors were selected by lot from the people as a whole to represent the interests of the people. They had considerable power. The ephors were charged with watching the conduct of the king, and were able to indict him, to make him appear before them and to levy punishment. But restraints were placed on the ephors; they held office for only one year, could act only as a group and were examined for their conduct in office. The Spartans thus achieved a 'mixture of the right elements' in the constitution that brought about the stability of the state. The Spartans succeeded where the two other states failed because they had set up a constitution with a system of checks and balances in their government that in significant ways represented both the aristocrats and the people. Although Plato did approve of the stability of the Spartan constitution, he rejected its single-minded dedication to courage to the exclusion of virtue as a whole (630d–e).

The Athenian Stranger summed up the reasons for the failure of the Dorian confederacy by concluding it had not achieved the aim of legislation which was that a 'state ought to be free and wise and enjoy internal harmony' (693b). To avoid the example of the Dorian confederation, a state established by law should neither have a government 'great' in having unlimited power or have an unmixed constitution. For all forms of states or constitutions were derived from either monarchy or democracy, the two 'mother-constitutions' of government (693d). The good state whose laws were laid down by the wise legislator was a blend or mixture of monarchy and democracy. A constitution that had only one of these 'mother-constitutions' was doomed to failure in realizing the true goals of the state. The Athenian Stranger clinched his argument by an analysis of the excesses of monarchy in the constitutions of the Persian empire and of the Athenian democracy. Both states he believed had been better served in the past with constitutions that were more of a blend of monarchy or democracy than had been true recently (693e–4a).

The good beginnings in the fortunes of Persia made by Cyrus and by Darius (who was able to repair the damage caused to his state by the ineptitude of Cyrus' sons) were brought about by a balance between freedom and subjection among their own subjects and those that they had conquered (694a–b, 695c–e). The two rulers introduced among their subjects an equality, freedom and a sense of fellow feeling that under Cyrus' rule encouraged the more intelligent of their subjects to offer useful advice on advancing the common cause of the Persian state (694b).

According to the opinion of the Stranger, the subsequent rulers of Persia did not receive the right kind of education that would have enabled them to preserve the empire (695e–6a). The Persian legislators had made no laws that governed the proper distribution of honors and dishonors among the people of the state. The proper scale for evaluating such distribution was to put first the spiritual goods accompanied by temperance, followed by bodily goods and advantages, and finally by material wealth and prosperity (696e–7c). The Persian leaders were unfit to rule because of their ignorance of this scale of values. They preferred what was evil and unjust to what was accepted as good and right (698a). The leaders ignored the people and concentrated their efforts on increasing their power in the quest for royal wealth to the exclusion of public well-being and freedom (697c–8a). The communal solidarity and fellow feeling of their subjects nurtured by Cyrus and Darius were destroyed by the excesses of subsequent kings. The vast armies of the empire lacked the will to fight and had to be either replaced or supplemented by foreigners or mercenaries (697d–e). Once again, lack of due proportion in the constitution that resulted from the extreme authoritarianism of the rulers of the state adversely changed the fortunes of the Persian empire.

The Athenians, too, complained the Stranger, allowed disproportion of another sort (698a–b) to squander away their fierce sense of fellow feeling and community that had been won in the lonely and magnificent victory against the power of Xerxes at Salamis. What acted as an insidious and enervating force, weakening the sense of solidarity, was a gradual turning away from the notion of 'voluntary slavery' to the old laws, and a development of freedom from external restraints and values other than those imposed by the individual on himself (700a). Without implying that music was the causal factor of the development of a lawless freedom, the Stranger described how changes in music, as Plato had already suggested in the *Republic* (424a–c), could set an example for harmful innovation in other areas. Music had contributed to the decline of respect for the old laws and the rise of an excessive freedom (700a–1d). Musicians of talent but 'ignorant of the correct and legitimate standards laid down by the muse' (700d), and overcome by frenzied and excessive lust for pleasure, introduced the notion that music had no standards of right and wrong. The criterion of value in music was simply the pleasure of the listener. Regardless of their musical training people began to believe that they were fit judges of what was good and bad in music. If it applied only to music such democracy would have been tolerable. But the notion took hold that any free individual was able to judge the good and bad not only in music, but in anything. Because they arrogated knowledge for themselves of any and all subjects, people were freed from all restraints. They ignored their magistrates, their parents, their laws and their religion (701a–c). It was this excessive freedom that resulted in the misfortunes of Athens during and after the Peloponnesian war. Again the Stranger underscored one of the most important points of his historical survey, that the legislator should have not only freedom, but also understanding, unity and fellow feeling as the goals of his laws (701d). To neglect any one of these as the object of legislation was to bring about that disproportion that the Athenian showed to be the ruin of previously mixed constitutions (701e).

The lesson taught to aspiring legislators by Plato's historical interpretation of the fall of the Dorian League and the decline of the Persian and Athenian empires stressed the need for a unity and fellow feeling of the state that could be brought about only by the right balance or mixture between the monarchic and democratic aspects of society. The preservation of such a balance depended, in turn, upon a similar balance in the individuals making up the society, including the rulers. They should display a balance between the rational and emotional aspects of their souls, keeping their likes and dislikes in accord with what they knew to be right or valuable and wrong or not valuable (689a–c). Argos and Messene came to ruin because their rulers failed to observe the appropriate balance within their souls, which led to their disregard of laws they had sworn to uphold. In their greed to gain more wealth and property the kings of Argos and Messene exceeded the authority they originally agreed to in the pact with the people. The Persian kings also became too authoritarian and grasping, and unbalanced their kingdom by restricting the freedom the people enjoyed under Cyrus and Darius. Athens, in its days of empire, neglected due balance by putting the will of the people above the established laws through their decree-making powers in the assembly. The excessive freedom shown here, and in the other areas already indicated, resulted in a split in the Athenian state between those inclined to lawlessness and those who wished to be ruled by law. Many among the people preferred to do what each one individually considered to be to his advantage rather than what was to the benefit of the people as a whole. Lost to these states were the wisdom, freedom and fellow feeling and unity that the Stranger repeatedly asserted were the aims of legislation.

As legislators for a new state, the Stranger expected that the reasons for the decline of Argos, Messene, Persia and Athens would not be lost on him and his companions. The principle of proportion or balance must be present in two senses in terms of the state as a whole. The constitution should be a mixture of the monarchic and democratic aspects of the state. What Plato further brought to the concept of the mixed constitution, as noted earlier, was a system of checks and balances in the state to preserve the unity and friendship of its people. Such a system preserved Sparta from the fate of Argos and Messene. The introduction of checks and balances in government was to keep any one individual or body of officials from having complete power, and thus causing an imbalance in the organs of government that would destroy the proper mixture of the constitution. Complementing the Stranger's analysis of the rise and decline of constitutions was his account of how such a mixture could be achieved, the number of offices of the state and how they would be organized, what powers and duties they would have and how officials would be elected or appointed (751a–b). But before these aspects can be discussed, we must see what would be the principal features of the proposed state for which the Stranger and his companions drew up legislation, the state of Magnesia (702b–e).

The proposed site for Magnesia was on rugged terrain in Crete and was about 10 miles from the coast (704b–d). The Stranger considered this site a fortunate choice on the whole because the many problems associated with a coastal city were absent (Morrow, 1960, pp. 95–100). There was no danger of sea invasion nor any tendency to build a maritime and naval force as Athens did, which in Plato's opinion developed into a ruinous maritime imperialism. By keeping out foreign influences more readily, this landlocked character would facilitate the observance of good laws. The state itself would be able to supply all its necessities of existence, but would not produce enough to engage in trade and to bring in a large number of aliens engaged in commerce. Society would have an agricultural rather than a commercial base (743d) which would ensure greater stability and uniformity among the population.

There were to be 5,040 households or families on as many plots of land (737e). The criteria used to arrive at this number were the requirements for economic self-sufficiency and defense of the land (737c–d). The number 5,040 could be divided into many consecutive divisions useful for organizational, administrative, collection and distribution purposes during war and peace (738a). The number of households was to remain constant (740b–e).

Instead of following the principle that 'friends shall have all things in common', Magnesia's stability entailed the continued existence of private families on the household plots. The plot of land was inalienable and was given to the son designated as his heir by the father. The daughters were to be married. Fathers without sons were encouraged to adopt them to have an heir for the family plot. Overpopulation would be dealt with by sending out colonists, and underpopulation by the immigration of new citizens (740e–1e). Travel abroad would be restricted to citizens over 40 years of age who were on official business (950d ff.). Only visitors meeting certain requirements set down by law would be allowed in Magnesia (952d–3e). Plato restricted travel to and from Magnesia because he believed that the introduction of novel and bad customs from poorly run states would harm the citizens living in a state like Magnesia with good laws (950a). Even the 'educated right opinion' that was the basis of the morality of the citizens of the practical state could 'run away' (*Meno*, 97d) and be overwhelmed by the development of the wrong kind of desires and appetites within the soul.

The city was to be placed near the center of the country on a favorable site (745b). The land would be divided into twelve parts with the citizens similarly divided (745d–e). One-twelfth of the citizens would have one-twelfth of the land, with each of the twelve groups having about the same amount of private property other than land. The quality of land allotted to each of the twelve groups would be approximately the same. These twelve groups were the twelve tribes of the state; they would have an administrative importance and form the basis for the selection of some of the state offices. Each plot of land of the 5,040 households was to be divided in half. One half would be near the city and the other half near the border. Every lot holder had two houses, one on each of his lot halves (745e, 775e–6a). There was further division of the citizens into traditional associations and local administrative units (746d), but it did not appear to assume any importance in Plato's analysis.

As the citizens engaged only in agriculture (743d–e), the trades and crafts, including the teaching of music and gymnastics, would be carried on by aliens (804d, 919d–20a), who must by law observe the principle that each alien should practice only one art or craft that was necessary for the well-being of the society (847a). The citizens of Magnesia would not be employed in the usual crafts, trades and commercial activities of contemporary Greek states because Plato believed that the 'vocation' of citizenship demanded 'a great deal of time and study' and was not a 'job for part-timers' (846d). Such enterprises, he felt, would arouse in their practitioners an uncontrollable desire for profit that ran counter to the citizen's moral and civic responsibilities (831c–e). Slaves could belong to the state, to the citizens or to aliens. The slaves belonging to the citizen were not to engage in any trade (846d). They either were to work in the field (806e) or take care of the house (808a) and serve their master and his family (763a, 808e). The holding of slaves was to be regulated by law. Currency regularly in use would be of the land, not of the sort that would be considered as of any value by foreign countries. The state would have Hellenic currency to use when needed (741e–2a). There would be no credit and no lending on interest (742c).

The new inhabitants of Magnesia would come with differing amounts of private property. The population would be divided into four classes based on differences of wealth (744a–5a). The fourth class had the least wealth, but its members would have a sufficient yield from their plots to maintain themselves in good health and as good citizens and moral individuals (743d, 744e). The wealth held by the fourth class provided a standard for the amount allowed the other property classes. The third class would have double, the second class three times, and the first class four times the amount that the fourth class possessed. Any surplus beyond the amount allowed to each of the property classes was to go to the public treasury. Membership in a property class depended on the individual's ability and enterprise (Taylor, trans. *The Laws*, 1960, p. 126, n. 2). The state afforded 'equality of opportunity' (744b) to the citizens (cf. Morrow, 1960, p. 132, n. 115). Depending on how successfully he handled his property, anyone could change from one property class to another.

Property differences were a factor in what Plato thought should always be the object of the good legislator, proportional or geometric equality (cf. *Gorg.*, 508a; Dodds, 1959, pp. 339–40). Proportional equality distributed in unequal amounts to the citizens of the state the rewards, honors, offices and burdens such as fines, taxes and financial assessments on the basis of what was appropriate or due to them (757b–c). In contrast arithmetical equality assigned the same amount in 'measures, weights, numbers' (757b) of whatever was being distributed to the citizens. But for Plato property was only one of several factors in assigning privileges, offices and duties (744c). There were no property requirements for any of the important offices such as the guardians of the law, the court of the select judges, the chief education officer and the board of audit. Some minor offices required talents that could be best filled by those whose membership in the wealthier classes attested to their skill and experience in dealing with finances and the supervision of lands, buildings and equipment (759e–60a, 763e). Any citizen could nominate candidates for these positions, and all had to vote for them.

Plato wished to realize proportional equality as much as possible in the practical state. It was a means for bringing about the genuine friendship and equality among the citizens that was so necessary for the unity of the state (757a, 771d). But arithmetical equality always 'fills a state with quarrels among its citizens' (757a). Both kinds of equality were necessary for the ordinary person would be angry if he were deprived of the 'equal chance of lot' (757d–e). They were to be applied in 'a rather rough and ready way' if factionalism was to be avoided. This 'rough and ready way' of applying the two different equalities was apparent in the procedure for most appointments for officials. These were made 'partly by election and partly by lot' so that use of both democratic and non-democratic methods would 'produce the greatest possible feeling of solidarity' (759b).

Plato devised a procedure for elections that tried to wed the principle of securing the most able individuals as judged by his fellow citizens with the arithmetical equality of lot. Initially those involved in the electoral process (either the people in assembly or a group of officials) chose a list of nominees. From a particular number of those citizens receiving the greatest amount of votes in the preliminary election, the electors voted for a shorter list of candidates. If necessary this winnowing process would be repeated until the desired number of candidates was achieved. From this final pool of candidates, the final selection would be made by the drawing of lots. The successful candidates then underwent a scrutiny of their moral fitness, the validity of their citizenship and the adequacy of their performance of civic and familial obligations (759c). But going beyond what was basically the Athenian procedure of scrutiny, Plato would also have the successful candidate's fitness for the position tested (765b, 766b; cf. Morrow, 1960, pp. 217–18). For us voting on a list of previously selected candidates would seem quite in accord with what we understand as democratic principles, but for the Athenians of Plato's day it was aristocratic. For them the essence of democracy was the use of lot. But in his insistence that the offices of the state be filled by those individuals the people thought most competent, Plato instituted an election from a list of candidates eventually followed by the use of lot that selected a certain number from a pool of candidates who the people thought by their votes were equally qualified for the positions.

The constitution of the practical state effected a 'compromise' (756e) between its monarchic and democratic aspects. After the monarchic aspect had been realized through the selection of those citizens the people judged would be the most authoritative and able for office, the equality of lot (judged as the essence of democracy by Plato's contemporaries) was used in deference to a deep-rooted need of the people. But these equalities together should not be confused with the mixed constitution. They referred to the distribution of honors, offices, taxes and so on to individuals under different constitutions such as the ideal state of the *Republic* or the extreme Athenian democracy, not to a blend, mixture or mean of the monarchic and democratic constitutions (Harvey, 1965, pp. 104–5, n. 12). Both equalities were to be used in Plato's practical state, the democratic as little as possible, but they were to be applied as separate equalities.

The assembly was made up of all citizens who served in the military forces. Plato did not explicitly mention women as members of the assembly, but since they participated in military activities and other civic duties it may be assumed that women also were members of the assembly (804e–5a, 805c, 814c; 785b). The primary function of the assembly appeared to be voting on the filling of many of the different offices of the state. Every citizen had to vote in any final selection of candidates for which he was eligible or pay a fine proportionate to his property class membership and be stigmatized as a bad citizen (763e–4a). The assembly also participated in cases where the public good was threatened by the actions of any citizen (767e–8a). Only the two highest property classes were required to attend the ordinary meetings of the assembly or else be fined. Members of the third and fourth class could attend assembly meetings but were not required to do so unless a special assembly meeting was called (764a–b).

The council in Plato's state probably performed more or less the same functions as in the Greek cities of the times. It called and dismissed the assembly in regular and special session. The constituency of the council represented not simply the wealthy element of the society as was often the case in Greek states, but all four economic classes so that there would be a representation of all interests of the society in the council. The election procedure reflected this combination of the democratic and monarchical principles.

The election of the council took five days (756b–e). On the first day each citizen had to nominate one member from the first property class by listing his name on a ballot. This procedure was repeated on the second day for the selection of nominees from the second class. The penalty for not voting was a fine whose amount varied depending on the property· class to which the citizen belonged. On the third day the first three property classes were again required to vote in the same way as before for nominees from the third class. Only the first two property classes had to vote on the fourth day for nominees from the fourth class. The penalty for not voting on this day was proportionally higher for the two highest property classes than it had been for the previous days. On the fifth day from the result of the previous days' elections all citizens had to select by ballot 180 nominees from each class. Presumably each citizen again listed one name on his ballot for each class and the 180 nominees from each class who received the most number of votes formed a final pool of 720 candidates for the council. From these 180 finalists in each class ninety were selected by lot to form a council of 360. The heavy fines levied against members of the first two classes who failed to vote on the fourth day was to ensure that the members of the council would be nominated by all the citizens.

In a society whose members were supposed to be full-time citizens why was attendance at regular assembly meetings and at nominations for council members from their own ranks required of the three high property classes and optional for citizens of the fourth class (members of the third class were not required to vote for nominees from the fourth class)? I think a probable explanation lies in the application of the principle of proportional equality. To be a full-time citizen did not necessarily require the attendance of all citizens at all civic functions. Since no pay was given for any form of governmental service, including attending the assembly (unlike the practice in democratic Athens), it is plausible to assume that some of the citizens would have preferred to spend more time consonant with their civic obligations in their fields. Members of the higher property classes would be expected to participate more fully or pay the appropriate penalty. Privileges and duties, then, in these voting procedures were distributed in accordance with what was appropriate to the citizens. One factor in determining what was appropriate was the citizen's economic status. Those citizens not required to vote, of course, could vote if they desired. Plato may also have thought that since there were probably many more citizens from the fourth property class than from the others, enough of them would vote for nominations of their fellows to have an adequate selection of nominees from their property class.

Like the Athenians' practice, Plato considered that the council as a whole would be too unwieldy to run the state on a daily basis. In a state that was usually taken to deprive the individual of any private concerns, Plato stipulated that it was necessary most of the time to let the council members be 'free to live their private lives and administer their own establishments' (758b). The council was divided into twelve groups and each group had daily charge of the affairs of state for one month (758b). This executive council had to be available to deal with questions concerning foreign relations and queries from individuals arising from within and without the state (758c). It was also to watch carefully for any of the frequent innovations that occurred within the state and was to deal with them (758c–d). The executive council also was in charge of convening and dismissing regular meetings of the assembly in accordance with law as well as extraordinary sessions (758d). It cooperated with other officials in its continual watch over the state (758d).

Plato's assignment of duties to the assembly and council bore some resemblance to the traditional functions of these bodies in the Greek states. From what Plato has written elsewhere (cf., for example, Ep., VIII, 356d) the assembly and council together would probably deal with questions of peace and war, treaties with other states and changes in legislation as indicated in the Laws (772d). Though not as important a deliberative body as the guardians of the law, the assembly and council jointly could be considered as a deliberative body of the state (Morrow, 1960, pp. 175–8). Plato, however, probably with an eye to what he considered the excesses of the radical Athenian democracy limited the power of assembly and council in several ways. He instituted a board of audit that was separate from the assembly and council (945c–d). The function of this board was to conduct an examination of the official conduct of governmental officials during and after their term of office and to assign appropriate penalties for misconduct. Although the people had an important role to play in private suits (which included both criminal and civil cases), the final appeal was out of their hands and rested with the court of select judges which was independent of direct popular control (767a). Cases calling for the death penalty were referred to a special court (855c). Finally, the lawlessness as seen by Plato in his account of the reasons for the decline of Athenian democracy (698a–b, 699e–701c) and Aristotle (*Ath. Const.*, 41, 2) brought about by the disposition of the Athenian demos to allow decrees that conflicted with established laws to prevail was avoided by having the guardians of the laws responsible for revising and adding to the laws (768e–72b) with the advice of the Nocturnal Council.

The guardians of the laws constituted one of the most important bodies of the state. While sitting in continuous session the guardians had many duties including what would be legislative, executive and administrative, and judicial functions. The first responsibility named by the Stranger indicated the primary responsibility of this body, the supervision of the laws (754d–e). The second named duty of the guardians was to see that the law regulating the registration of property was observed. Any citizen disobeying this law by retaining more property than was allowed could be brought by any one to trial before the guardians of the laws. This judicial role of the guardians was their third duty listed by the Stranger. But there were many more duties, in keeping with the Stranger's comment that as 'the legal code is extended, every new law will give this body of men additional duties to perform, over and above the ones we've mentioned' (755b). The supervision of the laws was carried out by the guardians' continually examining the way in which the various magistrates performed their official responsibilities and how they conformed to the laws governing the operation of their offices (762d). Supervision of the laws also included keeping watch over other offices as they were created along with their relevant laws (755b). The guardians in collaboration with the officials concerned were charged with revising and adding to the laws (768e–72b), with the final adoption of some, if not all laws, depending on consent by the people and the other officials and the approval by divine oracles (772d). In addition to their legislative function they were also magistrates in their own right. Among their duties as magistrates were supervising foreign trade and deciding what goods to import and export (847c–d). The guardians were concerned with family law (924b–c, 926e, 928a, 929e, 932a–b) and actions of private citizens (775b, 969d–e). As magistrates the guardians could fine citizens for various offenses set down in the law (775b, 960a–b). They also exercised some judicial capacities (767a) involving family and property (754e). They belonged to courts concerned with accusations against high officials, notably members of the court of select judges (767e), and were part of the court trying members of the board of audit (948a). In overseeing the magistrates, the guardians were not allowed to punish, discipline or fine them in any way. They could charge them before the courts or inform the board of audit about any misconduct (Morrow, 1960, p. 198). Thus, they seemed to have been able to peer into every nook and cranny of every official's conduct, but they themselves could not take action against any official. This was a significant limitation on the possible abuse of power.

The guardians were thirty-seven in number. They had to be at least 50 years old to hold office and had to retire at 70 years of age. The procedure (753b–e) explained in the *Laws* for electing the guardians of the laws was for the original group of guardians. Subsequent elections would be held only for replacements due to retirement, death or malfeasance in office. These elections of the guardians of the law would probably follow the same procedure (Morrow, 1960, pp. 204–9). The election took place in the assembly. Each citizen selected his nominee by written ballot. The 300 with the largest number of votes were put up for a second selection. Out of these, 100 were selected and a final election gave the position to those thirty-seven candidates with the highest number of votes who had successfully undergone scrutiny (753d). This office had immense powers, but was subject to other checks and was directly responsible to the people. For not only did the people elect the guardians of the laws, but a citizen could initiate prosecutions against a guardian for misconduct in office (928b).

Again, the character of the mixed constitution became apparent in the system of courts set up by Plato to have judicial decisions that were fair, equitable, intelligently arrived at and involving significant participation by the people. Plato spoke out against the enormous courts familiar to Athens that attempted to speed through the litigation before them. 'The point in dispute between the parties must always be made crystal clear, and leisurely and repeated interrogation over a period of time helps a lot to clarify the issues' (766d–e). He expressed dissatisfaction because the hundreds of judges, that is, the courts of Athens, were silent and did not interrogate the parties to the case. Such large courts could not arrive at good verdicts any more than small ones whose members were not able (766d).

Parties to a private suit initially brought their dispute before a neighborhood panel appointed by the parties to the dispute themselves. As friends to the contending parties the members of the panel knew them and had some understanding of the background of the dispute (766e). If both parties agreed to the verdict of the neighborhood court, then that was an end to the matter. The judgment of the neighborhood court in this instance was final (767a). But if one of the parties was dissatisfied with the verdict, he could appeal to a higher popular or tribal court (767a). This was again Plato's use of a principle that in its undiluted form resulted in large measure in the triumph of popular democracy, the domination of the courts by the people from whose verdicts there was no appeal. These tribal courts of appeal were made up of representatives from each of the twelve tribes of Magnesia, drawn by lot as the occasion warranted (Morrow, 1960, pp. 259–61). The members of these courts could be freer from the pressure of friendship than the neighborhood judges. If the tribal court was not able to present a verdict satisfactory to both parties, the dissatisfied party could appeal one step higher to the court of the select judges, a sort of supreme court (767a, 767c), Plato's important departure from Athenian tradition. Here was the transition from democracy in the courts, first in the neighborhood, then to the popular or tribal court and lastly to a more authoritative and select court. The select judges displayed an expertise and experience which probably was not available to members of the first two courts (although the latter could include magistrates who were no longer in office). Unlike the Athenian popular courts which allowed no appeal, the court system of Magnesia stipulated a final decision on appeal by specially qualified judges.

The court of select judges was chosen in the following manner (767c–e). On the last day of the year (like the Athenian year, the Magnesian year would begin in midsummer), the magistrates who held office for a year or longer assembled and selected each from his own board the individual he thought most competent and able. After passing a scrutiny conducted by their electors, the fifteen or sixteen who were chosen served for a year. Unlike the secret vote of the Athenian judges in rendering their verdicts, the members of the supreme court were to vote openly. Those officials who elected the judges were required to attend trials conducted by court. If they wished, the citizens could also attend. The court would be made up of those who had either completed their year as magistrate, or they would serve continuously as members of the supreme court and would continue as magistrates. Reelection was possible. The short terms, and probability of a large turnover of judges, made unlikely a concentration of power, but the turnover precluded a continuity in the court and the development of a judicial style and tradition. The court was made up of officials who were judged as the best of their group by all of the officials, and who could best function as jurists in the absence of a professional group of judges. Still, the annual replacement of judges would bring in new points of view that were always manifested by individuals of outstanding ability and experience. However, even a body like the court of select judges was not immune from prosecution. If anyone, not necessarily one who had appeared before the court, accused one of the judges of impropriety in rendering 'a false verdict', he charged the judge before the guardians of the laws. If found guilty, the defendant was fined double the amount awarded to the accuser, and any additional penalties were to be paid to the state or to the accuser (767e).

In addition to private suits that concerned civil or criminal injury brought against the supposed perpetrator by the injured party, an individual could charge any citizen with a crime against the state (767b–c). In recognition of the democratic demand that the man in the street play his part in judging the crime and the accused (768a), Plato believed that the people would be justifiably annoyed if they were unable to participate in judicial procedures involving the well-being of the state. Here, he followed the Athenian procedure where anyone charged with a crime against the state could be tried by the assembly, or upon its recommendation, by a people's court. Now the 'opening and closing of the trial' should be 'in the hands of the people' but the 'detailed examination' should be conducted by three of the highest officials agreed upon by both parties to the dispute or if no agreement was forthcoming, by the council (768a). This meant that the assembly decided whether the charge brought before it was worthy of further consideration. If it was, it was placed in the hands of the panel of three judges selected from higher officials, probably from the guardians of the laws, specially for this litigation. They made their investigation and findings based on it and made recommendations which presumably the assembly could accept or reject.

Here again was the working of the mixed constitution: the people could begin and conclude a suit directed against one accused of crimes against the state. But the actual interrogation and reaching of judgment were carried on by especially qualified individuals with experience in important posts. The ability of the people to participate decisively in such trials was supplemented by the judgment being given by those most qualified. At the same time, the final decision was in the hands of the people. They could accept, though of course they didn't have to, the informed opinion of the judges.

A final court considered in the *Laws* was that dealing with capital crimes punishable by death (855c–6a). It was made up of the guardians of the laws and the court of select judges. Their jurisdiction covered temple robbery, treason, subversion, sedition, intentional and attempted homicide and certain kinds of impiety. In capital cases Plato proceeded cautiously and emphasized in such life and death matters the need for trained and experienced judgment by seasoned and highly respected officials. It was characteristic of Plato's views on procedure in the courts that the final decision should be made by a small, highly competent court as it was in private suits and in crimes against the state where the examination was conducted by three special judges. Here Plato stressed the need for a thorough airing of the issues before the court. After the prosecutor and the defendant presented their positions, the senior presiding judge engaged in cross examination and continued 'until he has gone into the arguments in sufficient detail' (855e). The other judges followed through with an examination on matters with which either party to the dispute had left them dissatisfied by some kind of mistake or omission. They affixed their signatures to arguments that they endorsed as being relevant. After following this procedure two more times, they voted on a verdict, with the final decision being made by a majority. The obvious concern for calm, reflective judgment on the part of experts, with the opportunity for sober statement and cross examination, contrasted sharply with the circus-like atmosphere that seemed present in the large courtroom proceedings of the courts of Athens.

According to the Stranger, the education officer of Magnesia held the most significant of all the important offices in the state (765e–6a). The great emphasis placed on the importance of education in bringing about the temperance within the individual citizens and their leaders underscored the Stranger's evident concern to have the best possible man elected as the officer of education. He was to be at least 50 years old and the father of legitimate children. He should be the 'best all around citizen' in the state, knowing how to be ruled and to rule, which is the essence of education (643e). The minister of education was chosen from the guardians of the laws for a five-year non-renewable term. All of the officials except the council and the executive committee voted by secret ballot for that guardian they thought most capable. The guardian who gained the most votes was subject to a scrutiny of his qualifications by the officials who selected him. The guardians of the laws did not participate in that screening, however. The minister was responsible for the education in the state which included music and gymnastics (765d, 936a); he was charged with administration and with selecting education officials (813c). He chose the content of school lessons (811e) and acted as a censor for poetry that was to be heard publicly (936a–b). He greeted important foreign observers visiting the state (953d). He was also a member for life of the Nocturnal Council (951e).

The practical state of the *Laws* required provisions for priests and priestesses (759a–60a). The hereditary priesthoods in the state were for life. But as there would be need for additional temples and attendants in a newly founded state, there were to be new appointments of priests and priestesses aged 60 or older. In this case alone, Plato allowed the lot to select the priests because presumably God will 'express his wishes' and guide the choice. Still, all new appointees had to have a scrutiny (759c–d). Because of the theocratic nature of the state, the candidates were to be well versed in the details and rites of religion. But the man favored by lot had to be 'healthy and legitimate, reared in a family whose moral standards could hardly be higher' (759c). Though no mention was made of their explicit duties, the priests and priestesses probably were to take care of the temple and the holy areas, perform some sacrifices and meet with and look after visitors who came to observe the sights and the festival of the arts in Magnesia.

A second kind of religious official, and an important one, were the three religious examiners (759d-e). For the purpose of selecting the religious examiners, the twelve tribes of Magnesia were divided into three groups of four. Each citizen in each of the four groups was sent to the Oracle at Delphi which chose the three that were to be the religious examiners. Like the priests, the examiners were to be 60 years or older and their election was for life. Apparently the three individuals in each grouping of tribes whose names were to be sent to Delphi were scrutinized by the group of tribes that elected them.

The expounders were the interpreters of the laws on all religious matters emanating from Delphi and established thereby a code of laws for the priests. They were probably concerned with whatever topics were appropriate for religious law. This would include all of the property pertaining to religious rites and observances and services to the gods and lesser divinities such as demons and heroes; the religious aspect of marriage ceremonies; and purification, especially for homicides.

The relatively few references in the *Laws* to the process of scrutiny (759c, 765b, 766b, 767d), the presentation of an elected candidate's qualifications for office, probably stemmed from Plato's assumption that the process was familiar to his readers. That process as practiced in Athens focused more on whether the candidate was a citizen, his legitimacy of birth, piety, and his moral and civic character, all of which of course would be assumed in the process of scrutiny in the *Laws*. But Plato showed more concern for the merits of the candidate than for the office (765a-b). In the case of the scrutiny of the elected candidates for the supreme court, the electors appeared to be the ones who conducted the scrutiny based on the candidate's qualifications for the office itself. Presumably the other criteria had already been established in their selection of him. Candidates for other positions not expressly undergoing scrutiny by their electors were probably examined for their fitness by the guardians of the laws. With their long and detailed experience in vital aspects of the state's administration, guardians of the laws were uniquely capable of considering the qualifications for office of the candidates elected for the different magistracies (Morrow, 1960, p. 218).

Just as candidates for office were examined for their qualifications prior to taking the office for which they were elected or selected, so after their tenure they were to be examined or audited for any malfeasance or injustice committed during their period of office. Plato laid great emphasis on the board of audit as a means for preserving the unity of the state. The board of audit was 'the single most crucial factor determining whether a state survives or disintegrates' (945c-d). Here Plato thought that the very source of the unity of the state was in question, the trust and fellow feeling that integrated the fabric of society and prevented its unraveling. For if those elected to high office became 'crooked' and violated their trust, there had to be some way of conducting an investigation with impartiality and integrity. A state could survive misconduct of a high official if he were brought to a proper accounting for his actions, and could even flourish and prosper. No investigation, or a poor one, would fragment the state into different interest groups or splinter states. Filled with divisive party strife, the unity of the state would be destroyed.

What Plato was referring to was the fear and suspicion that dissolved what he called the sense of justice that united all the magistracies into one and directed them towards a common end. Again this brings out the familiar Platonic notion that the destruction of the state began in the action of its rulers. Any tendency towards injustice could be curbed if the men who oversaw conduct were of unimpeachable moral integrity so that it was absolutely vital that their moral standards should be 'exemplary' (945e). Hence, of course, it was of the first importance to select the right kind of men for the board of audit since upon them depended the preservation of the well-being and unity of the state.

Plato reinforced the special importance he placed on the board of audit by affirming that its members were to be priests of the Sun and Apollo. The chief priesthood was an annual position given to that one of the three newly elected members of the board of audit with the highest number of votes (947a–b). Plato thus underscored the close relationship between religion and one of the most important political offices of the state.

The wise choice of experienced, competent and virtuous members of the board of audit was clearly vital for the moral well-being and unity of the state. In recognition of the need for popular participation and support for so vital a group of officials, Plato would have the entire state assemble at the beginning of the new year after the summer solstice for the election of the board (945e–6a). Although at the beginning of the state, twelve members of the board of audit must be elected, the procedure for the annual election of three would be followed here. Each citizen proposed a person, excluding himself, over 50, whom he believed to be 'perfect in every way'. Of the list of candidates proposed by the initial vote of the people, the half with the greatest number of votes went on to a second stage of election. The halving process was repeated until three candidates were left with differing numbers of votes. These constituted the board of audit and they were to hold office until they were 75. The selection, then, was made on the basis of whom the people as a whole considered to be the most capable of handling this important position. Initially the board would divide the magistrates, judges and other officials into twelve groups with one-twelfth of their number watching each of these groups. Of course in later years the board of audit would be larger than the twelve original members and there would probably be a different division of the offices it observed. Unlike the Athenian process of audit, then, the members of the board were on

continuous service. When, either individually or together with their
colleagues, they found an official acting unjustly, they as a group were to
post a written notice fixing the penalty or fine that was to be sustained by
the guilty official (946d).

In keeping with Plato's scrupulous concern for the reality as well as the
appearance of justice, he stipulated that the accused official, if he thought
that he was unfairly judged, could bring the board of audit before the
select judges (946d–e). If judged innocent, he could accuse the auditors
of misconduct. If his appeal failed, he had to pay double the original
penalty, unless that was death.

Believing that no one was necessarily free from possible corruption,
Plato allowed an examination of the propriety of the official conduct
of the auditors during as well as after their term of office (947e–8b). It
was necessary that such an important group of officials be above board in
its function of ensuring the permanence of the important feeling of
justice and fair play among the citizens that unified the city. Any citizen
could bring the auditors to trial for what he thought was misconduct in
office. The members of the trial court were the present and retired
members of the board of audit, the guardians of the laws and the select
judges. If the prosecution were successful, the auditor was stripped of his
office and honors, which were considerable because of his exalted
position. But if the defendant prevailed, the prosecutor was fined heavily
in proportion to his wealth and to the property class to which he
belonged.

Although there were other offices in the Platonic state, these were the
most important ones. Some of the remaining ones were concerned with
the defence of the land, both internally and externally: the generals and
their lesser military officers (755b–c), wardens or policemen for the city
(763e, 764b), marketplace (763c–e) and country (761d–3b). What is of
interest in the generalship is that the office, unlike that in Athens, was
purely military. Reelection was possible, but it did not allow the
incumbent general to participate directly in public affairs, as at Athens.
An effective system of checks and balances is apparent in this account of
the principal offices of the mixed constitution. Despite long terms of
tenure important officials such as the guardians of the laws were subject
to continual scrutiny for their conduct by the board of audit. Members of
the board, in turn, were liable to trial by a special court for wrongly
finding an official guilty of misconduct in his office. Although the verdict
of the supreme court was final, their members individually could be
charged before the guardians for an unjust verdict and would probably
be tried by the board of audit. A citizen, of course, at any time could bring
before the assembly or a suitable board of officials charges against any
magistrate, high or low.

In the *Laws,* as in the *Republic,* Plato forged another aspect of the unity
and fellowship of the practical state through his insistence that women be

treated equally in all respects with men despite the fact that women tended to be 'secretive and crafty' (781a) and were inferior to men in their 'natural potential for virtue' (781b). Although the Stranger here was only expressing the need for women to join in communal meals as did the men, for the welfare of the state, he would regulate all institutions for both men and women in common (781b): 'In education and everything else, the female sex should be on the same footing as the male' (805d–e). Without the equal participation of women in all of the civic activities open to men, the state would only be half a state with only half of its potentialities and strengths developed (805a, 806c). Thus, any genuine unity and happiness (781b) of the state and the existence of fellow feeling depended on making women as equal as possible to men in the performance of civic functions.

Plato realized the uniqueness of his position on the equality of women with men when he attacked contemporary views that relegated women to the home and domestic concerns as being based on 'almost universal ignorance' (794d, Bury trans.). Plato was especially insistent that women would be able to fight in defense of their homeland (814a–b). Towards this end, young girls, if custom and their parents allowed, would at 6 years of age receive training in horse riding, archery, javelin throwing, slinging and weapons (794c–d). Compulsory education in cultural and military subjects applied to girls as well as to boys (804d–e).

Women were to have the same training in athletics and gymnastics as men, not only to develop their physical well-being so that they could produce healthy children, but also to prepare themselves for battle (814c). Along with children, women were to participate in military exercises under the same rules as men (829b–e). As bearers of arms, women were citizens (814c) and members of the assembly. They had the right to hold office (785b) and could participate in civic duties as far as possible (805c–d), and when deserving were to receive the same awards as men (802a).

A principal means of ensuring unity and a spirit of fellowship in the practical state of the *Laws* was through religion. Only through a kind of civic religion could the state achieve the overall unity and fellowship which Plato thought was vanishing from Athens and the other city-states. This came out clearly in Plato's attack on the physiologoi. For it was due to the different beliefs about the gods that there occurred a decline in moral standards (Reverdin, 1945, pp. 12–13). For if the gods were nothing but artificial concepts based on conventions in differing societies, then it was not surprising that the 'true natural life' was 'nothing but a life of conquest over others', and not 'one of service to your neighbors', which was required to promote the sense of unity and of fellow feeling so necessary to the health of the state (889e–90a).

The importance of the gods appears in every aspect of the state, and is, as in the *Republic*, based on customary Athenian religious law. Children are born as offspring sanctified by the gods (773e–74a). The young were introduced through family rites to worship of the divinity through respect for their ancestors and elderly relatives (717b–d, 729c). Through monthly religious festivals of their local districts and tribes, the young will come to know each other intimately. They will then later be able to fulfill the principle of proportional equality more effectively by assigning honors, offices and legal verdicts to those who deserved them (738e). Not only would the people of the city gain divine favor in this way, but they would also 'promote fellowship among ourselves and mutual acquaintance and association of every kind' (771d, Bury trans.).

Religion and the gods permeated and ordered every aspect of daily life. A divine basis existed for maintaining the integrity of the family unit (880e–2c) and the family lot (843a), ensuring the stability of the social order. Duties and correct action towards strangers (718a, 730a), contracts between citizens and artisans (921a–d), the sanctity of oaths (936e), all these had a divine sanction. The gods alone oversaw the workings of agriculture (782b). The gods were always upright and honest and never engaged in deceit or trickery. No lawbreaker was friend to the gods (941b).

In carrying out the Stranger's injunction noted earlier that he who was temperate was like God, and therefore dear to him, the good man

> sacrifices to the gods and keeps them constant company in his prayers and offerings and every kind of worship he can give them, this will be the best and noblest policy he can follow; it is the conduct that fits his character as nothing else can, and it is his most effective way of achieving a happy life. (716d)

Man became like God through using and hearing the right sort of dance and music for they are pleasing to the gods.

> What, then, will be the right way to live? A man should spend his whole life at 'play'—sacrificing, singing, dancing—so that he can win the favour of the gods and protect himself from his enemies and conquer them in battle. (803d–e).

Music and dance were to present noble and beautiful doctrines which helped the individual to attain his virtue by stressing that 'the gods say the best life does in fact bring most pleasure' (664b). This theme was to be sung by all the age groups of citizens: children, citizens under 30, and finally the elderly citizens who though 'no longer up to singing . . . will be inspired to tell stories in which the same [virtuous] characters will appear' (664d).

In the *Laws* piety did not consist in mere ritual, but in a moral and intellectual attitude towards the gods (Reverdin, 1945, p. 20). Such an attitude held that there were gods; that they cared for man; and that they could not be deterred from their purpose of meting out justice by prayers, sacrifices or entreaties of any kind (885c–907d). In the *Laws* Plato sought to create in his city a popular religion through which each citizen has a proper awareness of the majesty and perfection of the gods. It spurred him on to the fulfillment of his moral and religious vocation, in a fusion of morality and religion (Reverdin, p. 23). The central importance of the existence and providence of the gods for the unity and fellow feeling of the state helped to explain, if not justify in our eyes, Plato's severe treatment of atheists (907d–9d).

In the practical state Plato brought about a political and social order that he thought strengthened its sense of community and fellow feeling by avoiding the extremes of wealth and poverty. This sense of solidarity among the citizens was further bolstered by assigning to women as citizens the same civic duties and responsibilities as men. The religious and moral faith of the citizens capped their sense of community. They were unified through devotion to a common religion and participated frequently in religious rites and festivals of the state and of the family. Through their worship and attempts to be like god by being temperate, the citizens followed God as 'the measure of all things' (716c), in direct contrast to the Protagorean dictum 'man is the measure of all things' (*Theaet.*, 152a) that led ultimately, Plato believed, to the loss of unity and the rise of relativism in states.

Despite this sense of unity and fellow feeling, as in the *Republic*, the individual was not submerged in the whole. In fact, a true concern for the public interest would bring about the genuine good of both community and the individual (875a). This benefit would include the individual's material as well as his moral well-being. Plato dramatized this congruence of private and general good on a cosmic level in the Stranger's reply to one who was skeptical of the gods' concern for man:

> you have forgotten that nothing is created except to provide the universe with a life of prosperity. You forget that creation is not for your benefit: *you* exist for the sake of the universe . . . you don't appreciate that your position is best not only for the universe, but for you too, thanks to your common origin. (903c–d)

The importance of the moral well-being of the citizen as an individual not only in the afterlife (904b–c, 959a–b) but in this life was to be conveyed to the people by the legislator (959a). For it was this aim, 'the goodness and the spiritual virtue appropriate to mankind', towards which all men should strive that justified the very existence of states (770c–d).

Obviously wisdom played a crucial role in any attempt to realize the ideal state. Wisdom of the state came about when its rational aspect was, in fact, ruling the whole. With their knowledge of the forms and of the idea of the good (473c–e), the philosophers as rulers constituted the well functioning of the rational aspect of the state. The context of the discussion suggested the knowledge the philosophers exercised as rulers was practical and deliberative. It entailed the ability to calculate and counsel not 'about some particular thing in the city but about the city as a whole and the betterment of its relations with itself and with states' (428c–d). This primarily practical knowledge how to conduct the internal and external affairs of the state in the best possible fashion depended on the rulers' previously acquired knowledge of the forms that served as moral and political standards to be implemented in the society. After having served as rulers, philosophers would again be able to resume their study of the forms for its own sake. With their knowledge of the 'science of statesmanship' and how best to realize it in their society the philosophers as rulers were able to induce the citizens themselves to realize their own justice as individuals, and to have some awareness of it and of the conditions of just action.

Although the wisdom of the state was explicitly due to the well functioning of its rational aspect, the philosopher rulers, some sort of wisdom or 'state of mind' was shared by all citizens of the state. For temperance of the state occurred when both the rulers and the ruled were 'of one mind' (doxa) or belief as to who ought to rule and be ruled (431d–e). This implied an informed or reasoned acceptance by members of the appetitive order to be ruled by members of the other two orders. For surely the one mind (doxa) shared by the citizens had to be of the same quality. The quality of the state of mind held by the citizens of the appetitive order could not have differed significantly from that of the other citizens if indeed they were of 'one mind'. From Socrates' refusal to put courage of the state on an instinctive or fortuitous basis (430b) it would plausibly follow that the 'one mind' all citizens shared that made the state temperate would, *mutatis mutandis*, be one that was produced by education. Surely all the citizens would have at least an 'educated right opinion' (the rulers undoubtedly would have knowledge) as the basis of this 'one mind' as to who ought to rule and be ruled.

The way in which Socrates suggested the ideal state could be realized added support to the notion of an informed popular consent based on 'educated right opinion' to the rulers' authority. For as we saw, Socrates would attempt to persuade the people to accept the rule of the philosophers. His persuasion was based not on propaganda or on the notorious noble lie or fiction discussed earlier. The agreement of the people to the philosphers' rule would be through what Socrates called persuasion accompanied with knowledge or intelligence (*Gorg.*, 454e).

The people, Socrates thought, would willingly accept the rule of the philosophers when the definition of the philosophers, their nurture and function had been explained to them several times in the way Socrates and his friends discussed these same matters (499e–500a); this was a way of acquiring right opinions that had an obvious parallel with the way in which Socrates said the slave boy could acquire some knowledge of geometry (*Meno,* 85d–e). In agreeing to be ruled by the philosophers the people were persuaded to have a true belief with knowledge or intelligence about the nature and role of the philosopher. True belief in this sense was associated with knowledge, and intelligence as an excellence of mind (585b–c). Obviously the informed consent based on 'educated right opinion' displayed by the people in initially agreeing to the rule of the philosophers would be continued by them and their descendants in maintaining the temperance of the state.

The wisdom of the practical state was explicitly embodied in the laws (nomos) whose meaning Plato thought was derived from reason or nous (957c–d, 714a) and the Nocturnal Council who were the 'true guardians of the law' (966b). All of the members of the council were to have knowledge of the laws and their foundations rather than the true opinion that characterized the awareness that some of the guardians of the law possessed (632c). Plato did not mean to downgrade the importance of the governmental body of the guardians of the law whose functions were just discussed. But the preservation of the rule of law within the souls of the citizens and of law itself (960d) required a body composed of the wisest men, young and old, of the state whose sole occupation would be to reflect, meditate and consider in detail (951d) the underlying principles of the state and of legislation that would enable it to be the 'sheet anchor' that preserved the state and its institutions (961c). At early morning meetings (951d, 961b) the council was to confer on all matters relating to the legislation of the state and any insight gained from outside sources that would have an important bearing on this prime topic of concern. Studies in subjects that would clarify and illuminate otherwise murky and difficult points in their study of legislation would be made by the council. Its younger members were to pursue diligently those studies 'sanctioned' by their older colleagues (952a).

To advance the level of its civilization and to discover what good laws should be strengthened and inadequate laws revised in the state, especially qualified citizens 50 years or older should be permitted to travel abroad for as much of a ten-year period as they wished providing they had not reached their sixtieth year. Upon their return they would report to the council on what they had observed in their travels as good and bad in men, institutions and laws. They would provide any useful information that others had passed on to them in their travels on legislation, teaching and education. They were encouraged to present their own insights as well (951c–d). Without such research and investigation of a competent kind, no state 'will stay at the peak of perfection' (951c). No state could preserve its legislation without grasping the ground or bases of its laws. For the laws of the state had to be followed by its citizens with understanding not merely accepted as habit (951b).

The Nocturnal Council, then, appeared as primarily a research and educational group and was not an official governmental group exercising the powers usually associated with sovereignty. It had no parallel in Greek institutions of Plato's day. Although the council appeared to have only an advisory capacity, its evident importance as the sheet anchor and salvation of the state suggested that its advice and recommendations would be heeded by the important governmental boards and state officials. Its composition included both members of the important governmental boards and state officials. The membership of the council included the ten most senior guardians of the law, the present and past directors of education, priests (members of the board of audit), citizens of special merit and achievement, and the observers or travellers (951e-2a, 961a-c). Those observers who had impressed the council with their reports and were uncorrupted by their travels would become members of the council after passing a scrutiny conducted by their electors. Each regular member of the council was to bring with him to the meetings a young man between 30 and 40 years of age whose education and natural talents he thought qualified him to attend the council meetings. If his colleagues agreed and the candidate passed the scrutiny he was admitted as a junior member until his fortieth year. If the council did not find the candidate worthy of membership, his sponsor was reprimanded and no one, especially the candidate himself, was to know that he had been considered for council membership. Although these junior associates had to leave the council they could return to it later if they could qualify as senior members.

Together the junior and senior members of the council constituted the wisdom of the state. The Stranger likened their role in the state to the head of the wise man. Because of their ripe maturity in years and wisdom in the most important matters of state, the senior members functioned as the intellect. With their sharpened senses, the junior members would scan the state and report to their elder colleagues all that occurred. The younger members would give advice and counsel to the senior members during their debates and deliberations. The relatively frequent turnover of these young, associate members who were half of the council's membership would result in a continual infusion of fresh and different points of view in matters with which the council dealt. Through these junior associates or senses of the state the senior members would constantly see things in a new light and not simply be hidebound to tradition. Together they would effect the salvation of the state (965a).

This combination of reason and of the senses that constituted the Nocturnal Council had, then, the preservation of the laws of the state as its aim. To realize this goal, the Nocturnal Council had to keep constantly before it the nature of its political aim, how it was to be attained and what laws and men could assist it in such endeavors (962b-c). Usually states have had different political aims or targets. Some have as a standard of justice the single aim of the rule of a few without any concern for their virtue, or of wealth without any care for freedom from foreign domination. Some states sought freedom or a combination of the two aims of freedom and the domination of others. Finally, those states that considered themselves the wisest of all have all of these aims and others like them as targets of rule without singling any one of them as the most authoritative (962e). But there is only one aim or target of true statesmanship. That aim which would assure the salvation of the state was virtue (963a; cf. 770d–e).

The fulfillment of this aim would require that the council members received during their tenure an education going beyond that of the ordinary individual. They would appear to have had a knowledge of dialectic. Although the Stranger provided no explicit statement of this need, his observation that a really skilled guardian would not only have to see 'the many individual instances' of a thing but 'also to win a knowledge of the single central concept', and then to 'put various details in their proper place in the overall picture' (965b), seems an obvious reference to the study of dialectic. The members of the council were to be trained to make a sort of induction from many particular and different instances to the one notion that united all the instances. To ensure the salvation of the state, the council members were to see how virtue was in itself, and in its different manifestations of justice, courage, temperance and wisdom. Wisdom the Stranger considered the especially important virtue that characterized the Nocturnal Council as it did the philosopher rulers of the *Republic*.

Dialectical knowledge of the virtues was necessary for the council's deliberations on the effectiveness of the laws in realizing the basic political aim of the state. Such knowledge would be necessary in their role as moral educators of the state. They had to explain better than any one else the real nature of moral and immoral actions to those such as criminals who especially required such instruction (964b–c).

The moral focus of the wisdom of the members of the Nocturnal Council again was apparent in their second primary subject of study, a dialectical study of beauty and the good (966a–b). They were to know what beauty and the good were in themselves, how they were related to each other and to actions (966b). In their educational studies, the Nocturnal Council was to study more intensively the subjects in which the ordinary citizen was educated: arithmetic, geometry and astronomy (818a). The council members had to know what the sciences had in common and be able to apply sciences such as astronomy to morality and human conduct (967e).

In keeping with the Stranger's injunction that the council members should be able to prove all that could be proven (967e), these true guardians of the law had to have knowledge of the third subject of study and one of the fairest, the nature of the gods, their powers and the proofs of their existence (966c). Just as their grasp of moral principles required a knowledge of astronomy, so their understanding of religious truth would demand studies of the soul as well as of the place of reason in the universe. Soul, the oldest and most divine of things in Plato's estimation, was the source of becoming in this world. Reason directed the order of the heavenly bodies and arranged all things for the best. God, soul and reason, if not identical, were closely related and seemed to be the source of being and order in the visible universe as reason by implication was in the intelligible. Knowledge of the existence and nature of the gods as well as the two truths dealing with soul and reason provided the underlying metaphysical basis of the virtue of the practical state. They were the only way of preserving its stability and permanence because they presented unchanging principles which would serve as criteria for good laws.

For some (Barker, 1960, p. 349; Sabine, 1959, pp. 84–5), the institution of the Nocturnal Council in the closing pages of the Laws seemed a return to the rule of the philosopher king and thereby nullified Plato's emphasis on the rule of law in the practical state. 'The state must be entrusted' to the council, affirmed the Stranger. After being carefully selected and educated the members of the council were to reside in the citadel of the state and would have become 'guardians whose powers of protection we have never seen excelled in our lives before' (969c). Although law was not absent from the ideal state the philosopher rulers had complete sovereignty in their own hands in a way never intended by Plato to be exercised by any group of officials in the practical state. One important meaning of the mixed constitution of the state of the Laws was a separation of the powers of sovereignty and a system of checks and balances among the important state offices. No one official body of officials was to be able to have untrammeled sovereignty of the state.

The Stranger's remarks on the great importance of the council for the state are quite consistent with his portrayal of it as an advisory legal and philosophical research group. If the laws were the primary way of implementing virtue as the goal of the state then such a body as the Nocturnal Council would be necessary. But the council did not seem to have any sovereign powers. It did not, for example, have the power to assign penalties: these were handled by the courts (952c–d). Once it was formed, the members of the council would determine what laws would regulate its affairs. But they would be under law, not above it. Further, the members of the council would be accountable for their conduct. Although it would be an open question whether those of the council who were also governmental officials could be held responsible in their governmental capacity for their actions as council members, they and other members of the council could be charged by any citizen for endangering the safety of the state (767e–8a). Far from contradicting the rule of law in the state, the Nocturnal Council and its role made it possible by ensuring a continuous examination of the laws of the state, how they can be improved or revised to maintain virtue or arete within the state.

In a sense, wisdom or reason also applied to the citizens as a whole. If virtue and more specifically wisdom was the object of the laws, surely it would be expected that to some extent the ordinary citizen would have wisdom of a morally prudential sort. Along with freedom and unity or fellow feeling, wisdom was one of the three objects of legislation in the ideal state. Wisdom of this sort should be applicable to the ideal state of the *Republic* in its definition of temperance (431e–2a). 'One should always remember that a state ought to be free and wise and enjoy internal harmony, and that this is what the lawgiver should concentrate on in his legislation' (693b).

Wisdom in this sense was having the right relationship between our knowledge of what is right and wrong and our likes and dislikes. The citizens should like what they knew to be good and dislike what they knew to be evil. And the greatest ignorance was to know what was right and wrong and to prefer the wrong to the right. It was this concord in the citizens between knowledge of good and bad and their preferences that constituted wisdom of the state, for this kind of harmony was instilled in all the citizens through the rule of their reason (687e–8b, 689a–e). Education produced this concert between the preference for what was known to be right and noble, and the dislike for what was wrong and ignoble through bringing about in the souls of the citizens the rule of the rational principle by either knowledge or opinion. In the ideal state, all the citizens could achieve justice through 'educated right opinion'. Similarly in the *Laws*, Plato used interchangeably knowledge and opinion so far as it related to the acquisition of virtue by the citizens (688b). In this context of an association with knowledge or understanding, opinion and right opinion mean what I have earlier called 'educated right opinion' (see also Hall, 1963, p. 199). Virtue is to be acquired by the system of education in the *Laws*.

Some account of the education and curriculum that the citizens should follow would be helpful in assessing the sort of wisdom that was applicable to maintaining the agreement between what one knew as good or bad and what one liked or disliked.

> I call 'education' the initial acquisition of virtue by the child, when the feelings of pleasure and affection, pain and hatred, that well up in his soul are channeled in the right courses before he can understand the reason why. Then when he does understand, his reason and his emotions agree in telling him that he has been properly trained by inculcation of appropriate habits. Virtue is this general concord of reason and emotion. (653a–b)

The Stranger noted that at times this concord or agreement 'wear off'. One purpose of the religious festivals was to restore the harmony within one's soul (653d). A principal means for maintaining this harmony between reason and emotion was the right use of the arts. All 'young things' were innately disposed to movement 'being fiery and mettlesome by nature . . . unable to keep their bodies or their tongues still . . . always making unco-ordinated noises and jumping about' (664e). Only man was able to achieve a sense of order and rhythm in both voice and body. The choric art, the correct training in dance and music (with gymnastics falling under dance), nurtured the concord between reason and emotion in childhood. Rhythm was the imposition of order upon motion or movement, and harmony imposed order on voice. Together harmony and rhythm combined to form the choric art. Almost instinctively the children were to like good music and dance and dislike the bad. Later understanding would provide them with some basis for their preferences.

Good music and dance afford pleasure, but the judge of such music (or of any art) is not any chance person or even the majority of people, but the best and most highly educated men who know music, especially what music copies or represents, how correctly it has been copied, and the moral value of the rhythms, melodies and language (669a–b). The criterion of the 'fine arts', including music and dance, is 'correctness', the representation and 'successful reproduction of the proportions and characteristics of the model' (668b). As representative arts, music and dance were to display the doctrines that strengthen the individual's arete and concord of reason with desire by reiterating that the best life is also the happiest (664b). Such nurture or informal education was a process of attraction, of leading children to accept the right principles as enunciated by the law and endorsed as genuinely correct by men who have high moral standards and are full of years and experience (659d).

Between the ages of 10 and 13 children would be taught to read and write. Between 13 and 16 years of age they would receive training in the lyre. Presumably during these years the youth would also have been trained adequately enough to fight a war and run a house and administer a state (809c). An elementary knowledge of astronomy to enable the citizens to read the calendar would be necessary (809d–e). The citizens would study literature of the morally edifying sort like the Laws itself (811c–e, 858e). They would also have a rudimentary acquaintance with arithmetic, geometry and astronomy (817e). Astronomy was of particular importance in the education of citizens, for the citizens were to learn enough about the subject so as 'to avoid blasphemy, and to use reverent language whenever they sacrifice and offer up their pious prayers' (821c–d). The right conception of the heavenly bodies was that they did not wander erratically despite appearances but that 'each of them perpetually describes just one fixed object' (822a).

The injunction to all citizens to be like God in the Stranger's opening preamble to the Laws (716c) underscored the need for every citizen to have an elementary training in the proper astronomical knowledge. God's nature was to make circular motions conforming to his nature. Although God was invisible, the heavenly bodies were visible. With the proper astronomical understanding the citizens would be able to follow the movement and order of the planets. The citizen would seek to bring and keep his own soul in a like order, approximating the divine nature of God. For all men of 'good will' place God 'at the centre' of their thoughts (803c).

> The motions akin to the divine part in us are the thoughts and revolutions of the universe; these, therefore, every man should follow, and correcting those circuits in the head that were deranged at birth, by learning to know the harmonies and revolutions of the world, he should bring the intelligent part, according to its pristine nature, into the likeness of that which intelligence discerns . . . (*Tim.*, 90c–d)

Freedom was the last of the three principles that underlay both the ideal and the practical states. Few readers of the *Republic* have ever considered freedom as meaningfully realized in the ideal state. Because of the obvious control and censorship of education, art and literature, no purpose would be served, it seems, by an inquiry into its concept of freedom. The rulers might be free, but the citizens seemed to be mere pawns to be ordered about on the chessboard of the state according to the wishes of the philosopher kings and queens.

Our assessment of whether the ideal state displayed any meaningful concept of freedom depends on what we mean by a freedom as it may apply to the state and to the citizens. The distinction drawn between negative and positive freedom is a helpful means of arriving at what kind of freedom would be relevant to the ideal state (Berlin, 1970, pp. 118–72). Negative freedom implies that freedom as such is the absence of any control or obstacle outside of the individual that would prevent him from doing what he wants. Negative freedom is the ability to do what one wants where such action does not violate the laws of the state. The state exercises a policeman's role in maintaining security and order so that the individual can without fear of interference from others do what he will so long as he is law abiding (Berlin, 1970, pp. 121–4). Law has nothing to do with the fulfillment of personal aims or of the attainment of personal morality. It should be emphasized that negative freedom has no necessary relation with political democracy. An autocratic government could allow a wide area of negative freedom, while reserving to itself the reins of the state, or a political democracy could restrict more than such an autocracy the negative freedom of its citizens. Although there was no clear-cut articulation of the concept of negative freedom in classical Greece, something like it did exist in both fact and idea. In their struggle to preserve their independence from Persia and Athens in the fifth century and from Sparta in the fourth century, the Greek states surely exhibited a

negative freedom in their attempts to avoid foreign domination. Each of
the Greek states wanted to be free from control of its actions by another.
The primary sense of negative freedom appeared clearly in Pericles'
funeral oration (*Thucyd.*, II, 37, 2): 'we do not feel resentment at our
neighbor if he does as he likes'. Although a citizen was free to live as he
pleased in his private life, he was held to strict accountability in his public
life.

Positive freedom stresses the source of control over the individual. The
individual is ruled by himself; he has self-direction or autonomy (Berlin,
1970, pp. 130-1). Usually it is the rational or 'better' aspect of the
individual that exercises such control over him and his desires and
appetites. With this notion of positive freedom, we can arrive at some
understanding of what kind of freedom was envisaged for both the ideal
and the practical states, although its manifestation was somewhat
different in the two states. Positive freedom was the control of the rational
aspect of the soul over its spirited and appetitive side, but it did not entail
the deprivation of the natural and necessary desires and appetites of the
soul. Indeed these emotional and conative sides of human nature were
best realized under the direction of reason, when positive freedom existed
in the individual's soul. Such self-rule by reason was obviously the
definition of the individual's justice or morality, which was concerned
with the inward functioning of the three aspects of the soul under the
direction of reason. This sort of freedom was necessary so that all of the
citizens so far as possible may be 'equal and friendly' (590d). This notion
of positive freedom represents the realization of a morality which could
be fostered and developed by law, but had to be imposed upon himself by
the individual through doing well his proper function as man.

In the *Republic* Plato linked the notion of positive freedom, the soul as a
whole being directed by one's reason, with a certain measure of negative
freedom. For positive freedom meant that the individual would not be
dominated by the passions, whether all, a few, or the one or two worst.
The just individual would have no excessive or wrongful desires to
prevent him from achieving what he naturally aimed at, his true good.
The absence of such obstacles connoted a negative external freedom.
Negative freedom as presented by Berlin seems to be primarily an
external condition because he regards obstacles to doing what an
individual wants as being outside in the guise of a physical impediment or
the will of another person. Berlin associates negative freedom with a
unitary notion of personality or self which can only be a slave to or
frustrated in its aims by some agency other than itself. But Plato's analysis
of a soul or personality with parts or aspects hierarchically ordered
according to nature allowed one aspect to dominate the soul. If the
rational aspect was in charge of the soul, then a sort of negative freedom
existed in the soul since it was free from control by the appetites. What
uniquely characterized Plato's view of such freedom was that it enabled

the individual to pursue what was his true good (an objective good which is in accordance with man's nature) as grasped by his rational aspect through 'educated right opinion'.

Negative freedom also existed in the ability of the appetitive order to have property and money, and engage in trade and commerce. Finally, as Cornford observes, an important notion of political freedom is realized (Cornford, trans. *Republic*, 1978, p. 125, n. 1) in the willingness of the auxiliaries and artisans to be ruled. This is not a meaningless gesture, for the willing consent of the ruled to such rule is a constant and necessary feature of temperance that is an indispensable requirement of the justice of the state.

Not surprisingly, the view of freedom maintained in the *Laws* resembles that of the *Republic*; the internal control of the soul was by the rational judgment, intelligence and right opinion (689b). Such freedom comes about through the maintenance of temperance and values recognized by the individual through reasoned judgment or educated right opinion (689a–b). Without temperance the individual would not attain the other virtues of courage, justice and wisdom (696b–e). Positive freedom, then, in the *Laws* was in terms of the mastery of the individual over his appetites and desires. It stemmed from his temperance or the harmony between what one knew to be good or bad, and what one preferred and disliked, and in that way was like the *Republic's* concept of freedom.

Yet, although as in the *Republic* the primary notion of freedom is that of positive freedom, negative freedom did exist, Plato thought, in Magnesia more truly than in any other state. The Stranger posited that the citizens of the practical state live 'free of interference from each other', and that 'these laws of ours are quite unlikely to turn them into money-grubbers' (832d). In Magnesia negative freedom existed among individuals in the sense that they were not forced by the desire for profit to coerce either themselves or others into ways of behavior incompatible with the moral life. Usually, notes the Stranger, in other states a citizen's 'ruling passion is his daily profit and he's quite incapable of worrying about anything else. Everyone is out for himself, and is very quick off the mark indeed to learn any skill and apply himself to any technique that fills his pocket.' The result is that 'naturally decent folk are turned into traders or merchant-venturers or just plain servants, and bold fellows are made into robbers and burglars, and become bellicose and overbearing' (831c–e).

The citizens of Magnesia, then, had a negative freedom in two senses. In the first place, internally the individual was free from the tyrannical control of his desires and appetites. Secondly, being free internally from the domination of the appetites and passions the citizen was not inclined to use force or to interfere with others in ways that would benefit him. Plato explicitly attributed negative freedom to the citizens of Magnesia when he stated that the laws would prevent them from having to become money-grubbers and would do all they could to keep the aliens or foreigners engaged in trade and commerce from corrupting themselves or the citizens (919c, 920a). Plato's concern for a negative freedom of the citizens of Magnesia is apparent in his explanation of why the council of the state of the laws was divided into twelve parts, with each part to serve as an executive committee for one month of the year. Not only would the whole body of councilors be too unwieldy to transact its affairs, but more importantly, said the Stranger, 'most of the time we have to leave the majority of council members free to live their private lives and administer their own establishments' (758b).

Other constitutions, democracy, oligarchy and tyranny, were really instances of 'party rule' (832c). The rulers ruled for their own interest and did not really receive the consent of the ruled. But because there was not in the practical state the intense competitive drive after wealth, power and fame that existed in other constitutions, each citizen was free from interference from his fellows and his rulers in order to realize his own true well-being and excellence. Citizens were also free to increase their movable property within certain limits through their own efforts (744c).

Finally, the individual citizen has a measure of political freedom which goes beyond the political freedom of the *Republic* which was confined to the consent of the ruled to have the philosophers as rulers. Theoretically any citizen of Magnesia could stand for almost any of the important state offices, provided he was judged worthy of it by his fellow citizens. The citizens had an important role to play in judicial proceedings and deliberations. A citizen could call into question the conduct of any official, high or low, a safeguard unnecessary in the *Republic* because of the incorruptibility of philosophers. Plato regretfully concluded that such incorruptibility was not possible within the state of *Laws*, given the tendency towards corruption that human nature possesses. The political stability and freedom of state and individual depended on the observance of the mixed constitution, especially in the narrower sense given by Plato of its being a system of checks and balances within offices of government.

These three principles underlying the state, unity and fellow feeling, wisdom and freedom, display an interconnectedness and near identity. The state which was free in Plato's sense of freedom was based on the consent of the citizens, not upon their forced compliance with party rule. The citizens were not interfered with in their lives and goals by those seeking their own profit. They were free to develop their true moral well-being as seen by Plato. Linked with such freedom was the unity of the state achieved by the willingness and consent of the citizens to be ruled and the rulers not to exceed their authority, but to rule for the genuine moral well-being of the citizens. Fellow feeling arose from this unity through the rational aspect of the soul ruling the individual, giving him the awareness that the rulers were not concerned to advance the well-being of the part of the state, but of the whole, which meant that of each and every citizen.

The fellow feeling was enhanced by each citizen contributing towards that well-being of the whole. Participation of the citizens in communal activities of various kinds fostered a spirit of intimacy and fellow feeling buttressed by the awareness that neither state nor any individual was attempting to exploit them for the benefit of others. Freedom and unity and fellow feeling presupposed a certain wisdom in the state. The rulers or the highest officials had knowledge of the moral and metaphysical reality which should underlie the state and its institutions, and which they were able to apply to the state. They also had an accord of rational judgment with their desires. This wisdom or temperance prevented them from overstepping their authority and destroying the unity and fellow feeling and freedom of the state; the checks and balances would prevent any abuse. In the ideal state of the *Republic*, presumably the philosopher rulers are incorruptible. The citizens of the practical state, too, have such a concord brought about through an 'educated right opinion' whose production is the object of the preambles to the laws, the arts and the educational and religious institutions of the state. In a sense, as Plato indicated, these three principles were one, for they seemed to entail each other (693b–c).

The purpose of a state that manifested these principles was not simply the preservation of its power. Through its institutions and leaders the state was to lead the citizens to realize their most important concern as individuals, the true well-being of their souls through the attainment of arete. The soul represented an aspect of the individual that was most truly his own and was divine and not to be injured by earthly institutions. The individual soul had a value and existence enduring beyond the citizen's life in society which was the ultimate justification of the state, its laws, its education and other institutions, provided the state was the right kind, the state of the *Republic* or *Laws*.

Chapter 8

Plato's Political Heritage

Plato's plan for the reform of the state and of its underlying principles was never achieved, but his influence on Western political thought has been lasting. His contribution to the development of natural law is now being recognized by scholars (Solmsen, 1942, pp. 161-73; Maguire, 1947; Morrow, 1948; Wild, 1953; Rommen, 1979, pp. 3-16).

Natural law in a general sense provided man and society with legal, moral and political standards based on reality. These standards served as criteria for continually evaluating what was the good state and what were valid laws and moral principles in a world apparently caught in an ever-present relativity of legal, moral and political principles.

Although Plato never used the expression 'law of nature' in its traditional sense and developed no explicit theory of natural law, some of the principal concepts found in many theories of natural law originated with him, such as a reality that was prescriptive as well as descriptive, an egalitarian theory of man's fundamental nature and a compatibility of the good of the whole state with the good of each individual citizen. Through much of the history of natural law, the influence of Plato and the Platonic tradition (Klibansky, 1939, pp. 36-7; Armstrong, 1967, *passim*) was pervasive.

With some qualifications, Aristotle's theory of natural law or right shows a resemblance to Plato's views. Unlike Plato, Aristotle explicitly affirmed the fundamental inequality of man. He believed that by nature some men were slaves (*Pol.*, 1254a 18-55a3). His conception of natural right also lacked the transcendent basis of Plato's forms. Natural right for him, in fact, was political right (Strauss, 1953, p. 156). Still, for Aristotle the state or society was natural, for man was by nature social. Natural or political right emerged from Aristotle's asking what was the ideal nature of the state or of man (Ritchie, 1952, p. 28), questions Plato also asked independently of his theory of forms (*Rep.*, 353d-e; *Gorg.*, 503e-4e). Like Plato, Aristotle saw that the attainment of the good of each individual required living in the right kind of state.

The Stoics usually have been credited with being the originators of natural law. But almost every significant aspect of Stoic natural law as presented by Cicero was either implicitly in Plato's thought or was a natural development from it, revealing the normative aspect of 'nature' as a synthesis of being and value. Cicero's *Republic* and *Laws* bear more than a nominal similarity to Plato's works of the same name. The Stoic view expressed in those works by Cicero of a divine providence or reason guiding the world and uniting all aspects of the cosmos into one whole (*Rep.*, I, 56) was Platonic in its origin. This divine reason or mind 'rules the whole universe by its wisdom in command and prohibition' (*Laws*, II, 8). Thus for Cicero the divine reason with the law it embodied was the basis of justice (*Laws*, I, 19) and the arbiter of valid and invalid law as made by man (*Rep.*, III, 33; *Laws*, I, 44). The Stoic doctrine of the immanence of natural law in man's right reason (the correct use of reason in fulfilling the needs and tendencies of human nature) parallels the Platonic principle that when reason was functioning according to nature in the soul, the wise individual had an awareness of what should be done for his own well-being (*Rep.*, 441e, 442c). Strongly reminiscent of Plato's description of man's unique function of rational deliberation and self-control (*Rep.*, 353d) was Cicero's predication of reason to all men. Otherwise, there would be no definition applicable to all men, 'there is no difference in kind between man and man . . . and indeed reason . . . is certainly common to us all' (*Laws*, I, 29–30). And, claimed Cicero, there is no man who could not attain virtue through the development of reason if he could find a guide (*Laws*, I, 30). The production of such virtue and happiness was the proper object of the statesman (*Rep.*, V, 8). The state existed for this purpose by nature and was not simply a means for individuals pooling their resources and abilities to overcome the inadequacies of their living in isolation.

Cicero's concept of natural law as a criterion for just and unjust positive law though familiar to them was not used by the Roman jurists until the end of the second and the beginning of the third century. Even then, their use of natural law was casual and perfunctory, serving as window dressing for analyses in accordance with Roman positive law (Kunkel, 1973, p. 100). Daily the Roman lawyers and jurists were confronted with cases whose decisions through generalization formed the main principles of Roman jurisprudence. These practically minded jurists never invalidated positive laws because they conflicted with natural law. Most references to this function of natural law in Justinian's Digest (AD 533), a compilation of the principal theories of Roman law developed during the Principate—the so-called Classical Period of Roman law (27 BC–AD 305)—are thought to be post-classical interpolations (Schulz, 1963, p. 137) or modifications of the compilers. Following Justinian's instructions to make the work harmonious and consistent (presumably with the contemporary jurisprudence's emphasis on natural law) the compilers were to 'remove all superfluities, supply what is lacking, and present the entire work in regular form' (Justinian/Scott, 1973, Vol. 2, p. 181).

But the concept of natural law as it evolved from Plato played an important role in the formation of Roman law. Plato's notion that a thing had a nature which not only described what it was but also prescribed appropriate ways of action was adopted by the jurists in seeking out what would be the natural or proper condition of legal concepts within their own sphere of legal research and inquiry (Schulz, 1963, p. 137; Pound, 1954, pp. 10–11). The Roman jurists employed the principle of dialectic as the collection and division of 'kinds' or genera in Plato's dialogues (*Sophist*, 253d; *Phaedr.*, 265d) as it was developed in the Platonic tradition. They made a systematic analysis of legal genera and species to arrive at the principles underlying them as a means for dealing with individual cases (Schulz, 1963, pp. 62–6). In this fashion the Roman lawyers erected a system of law that was unrivaled in its simplicity, unity and symmetry and served as a model for other legal systems.

Drawing upon the tradition of Greek philosophy, including Plato's thought and Platonism, as well as, of course, the Stoics, St Paul and the other New Testament writers, the Church fathers (from about the second to the sixth century) constructed a theory of natural law that was to last until modern times (Carlyle, Vol. 1, n.d., *passim*). They adopted, from what was in part derived from Plato, the concept of a transcendent-immanent God who providentially ordered the world and gave it and man a purpose and direction. These Christian writers used Plato's contrast between an ideal, unchanging realm and an imperfect, transitory world. They agreed with his affirmation of the importance and permanence of spiritual values based on an external objective reality (Coplestone, Vol. 1, pt 2, pp. 247–8).

Plato's injunction in the *Laws* that the individual should as far as possible become like God or assimilated to him became extremely influential in the Christian political and social thought because it offered an object of Christian striving. Derived in part from Plato's thought and the Platonic tradition was the Christian doctrine of a divinely based natural, moral law which governed the moral and political order and had as its goal man's development to realize his true nature with the grace of God.

The Church fathers equated man's natural condition with his existence before the fall. In that state of primal innocence, man was good and held property in common with his fellows. Man's fundamental equality was compatible with rank or hierarchy in this primal society, but there was neither government nor slavery, inasmuch as both entailed the subjection of one man by another (Carlyle, Vol. 1, n.d., p. 117).

Because he was overcome by his evil passions and inclination, man fell and lost his natural innocence and freedom. The state and its repressive character, slavery, private property and legal subjection to the rulers became necessary and were designed by God to hold in check man's passions and inclinations, and to punish man for his original sin. The purpose of the state was not merely repressive or punitive. The state was God's way of dealing with man's corruption, but it was also a way of gaining and maintaining justice for the benefit of the people through laws that agreed with the law of nature (Carlyle, Vol. 1, n.d., p. 161). A ruler who acted unjustly did not deserve the name according to the Church fathers, but it is not clear that they would sanction rebellion against such a ruler (Carlyle, Vol. 1, n.d., pp. 170–4). Despite the repressive nature of legal subjection, imprisonment and slavery, men were still equal and free by nature.

St Augustine (354–430) gave classic expression to this view of the state, especially in *The City of God*, completed in 426 (*City of God*, XIX, 15). Although the state's existence and repressive character were in response to man's sin, St Augustine still thought it exhibited a kind of well-ordered 'earthly' justice which fell far short of true or 'perfect' justice in God's realm (*City of God*, XVII, 14). It provided an order and peace that allowed the citizens to acquire some modicum of well-being or happiness although man's highest good could only come through the grace of God (*City of God*, XIX, 13, 14; Deane, 1963, p. 125).

The repressive aspect of the state appeared to be held by most of the Church fathers until the thirteenth century. St Thomas Aquinas (1225–74) then presented what for some (d'Entreves, 1965, pp. 38ff.) was a more reasonable view of the nature and origin of the state. Utilizing the thought of little-known predecessors of his century and riding the crest of the rediscovery of Aristotle's thought, St Thomas argued that the state existed by nature and aimed at the common good of its members (*ST*, 1a, 2ae, 90, 2). All that was good and rational stemmed from the divine or eternal law which nourished and sustained its imprint, the natural, moral law (*ST*, 1a, 2ae, 91, 1–2).

Although he was still in sin, man became aware of his own innate, generic tendencies and inclinations towards the objective good of his nature (*ST*, 1a 2ae, 94, 2). Reflecting on his condition, any man could through his reason grasp these natural tendencies and inclinations peculiar to man, become aware of the dictates of natural law and act according to virtue. These dictates of natural law were to be implemented in just positive laws, laws in harmony with natural laws (*ST*, 1a 2ae, 95, 2) that were promulgated by those in authority (*ST*, 1a 2ae, 90, 4). The state and its institutions were designed to bring about the common good conceived in a temporal sense as the well-being of the state (*SCG*, III, 80, 14). This good would take precedence over the good of the individual when that latter good would be in the same class as the former, but not when there may be a nobler higher good, such as the moral welfare of the individual or his ability to work for his final salvation (Bourke, 1960, p. 229). Man's final well-being could be realized only in the afterlife through God's grace (*SCG*, III, 147; *On Princely Government*, XIV).

Underlying St Thomas' theory of man and his relationship to the state was, of course, the ethical and political thought of Aristotle. Aristotle's thought also provided the metaphysical structure which St Thomas adapted to the needs of his own synthesis of philosophy and theology. Although Aristotle's metaphysical thought differed significantly from that of Plato, much of his moral and political thought was similar to that of his great teacher.

Thus, it is plausible to assume that some of the principles of Aquinas' theory of natural law and morality attributed by him to Aristotle originated with Plato. In the notes to his translation of the treatise on law from the *Summa Theologiae* Gilby (Vol. 28, 1963, p. 10, n. d) for example, observes that Aquinas' affirmation under certain conditions of the supremacy of the happiness of the community over that of the individual (*ST*, 1a 2ae, 90, 2) 'derives from Plato', presumably from *Rep.*, 420c, although it is Aristotle, not Plato or Socrates, who was mentioned in the context of this passage from the *Summa Theologiae*.

Grotius (1583–1645) undoubtedly thought of himself as within the tradition of Christian or scholastic natural law. His *De Jure Belli ac Pacis* (1625) set the stage for the transition to modern natural law or natural rights theory (d'Entreves, pp. 50–4). The explicit statement of the divine origin of natural law (*Prol.*, para. 12) is orthodox Christian natural law doctrine. But Grotius' attempt to demonstrate the necessity of natural law avoided any divine ground. Grotius thought that the necessity of natural law could be demonstrated with a near mathematical rigour (I, i, x) revealing a Cartesian clarity and distinctness (*Prol.*, para. 39).

Modern natural law as it emerged in the eighteenth century has been regarded both as a continuation (McIlwain, 1932, p. 115; Troeltsch, 1957, pp. 205–9) and as a decisive break with the Platonic-Stoic-Christian natural law tradition (d'Entreves, 1965, pp. 48–62; Becker, 1959, pp. 33–70; Rommen, 1979, pp. 75–109). Whether or not modern natural law or natural rights theory was a continuation or a departure from the classic natural law tradition depends on what is essential to the theory of classic natural law. If the basis of positive law is divine law and revelation, the providential ordering of the world by God, if a generic human nature with tendencies and inclinations as the ground of natural law, if the intimate relation between morality and law (the state), and if the natural basis of society and man's morality were considered essential to natural law, then, the modern development of natural rights was a distinct change from the past conception of natural law. But if the true well-being of the individual, along with his equality, freedom and friendship with others were stressed as essential to the traditional natural law, then there was a continuation of classic natural law in modern natural law. To be sure, these terms meant something quite different in the two traditions, but in both traditions they stressed the individual from different perspectives.

Equality in the classic tradition of natural law suggested that men were equal in the most fundamental sense of having the same generic nature. This nature entails a capacity for more excellence which under the proper conditions all individuals can acquire. Such equality was compatible with economic, political or social inequality.

In the theory of modern natural rights equality is not only an equality in human nature, but also an equality with respect to civil and political rights that include the right to a fair trial, life and freedom (Cranston, 1973, p. 65). Freedom in the older tradition stresses the control of the inclinations and appetites by reason. It was a sort of self-mastery or control which did not deny the satisfaction of legitimate desires (in accordance with man's generic nature), but always achieved it under the rule of reason. Modern natural law considered freedom to be the doing of whatever one wished without restraints from any external source. Such freedom may have had limits set by positive law, but within those limits an individual was free to do what he wills.

Friendship (or fellow feeling) had a significant difference in application in the two traditions of classic and modern natural law. In the classic tradition, the sense of fellowship was natural and entailed the common good of the community. For modern natural law the common good of society was simply the sum total of the separate goods of different individuals. Since his good was private to him, the individual became more isolated from his fellows in the pursuit of his own good, despite modern natural law's avowal of the equality and brotherhood of all men.

These characteristics of freedom, equality and fellow feeling were for the individual's well-being, with, of course, a different interpretation in the two natural law traditions of what was the individual's well-being. The classic natural law view interpreted the individual's well-being as the realization of his generic nature and all that entailed with his moral well-being and happiness both in this life, and (if relevant) in the next life as well. The modern view on the whole considered the individual's well-being to be realized in the satisfaction of whatever desires or appetites he considered worthwhile. The individualism of classic natural law was not to be realized apart from the society as a whole. It included morality as an important aspect of its well being. The individualism of modern natural law, however, was dependent primarily on the individual's own efforts and required only the maintenance of public order and stability. In contrast to this 'policeman' role for the state, the classic natural law tradition viewed the state as the necessary instrument to help the individual achieve his well-being. It was this value of the individual stressed by the classic natural law tradition and by Plato that was retained by the modern natural law, different as its concept of the individual and his rights might have been.

Perhaps the most significant change in modern natural law was in its concept of nature and its application to man. With his reason ('reason' primarily of the sort that comprehends intuitively mathematical truth and demonstrations within the ken of the average man) man can 'read' the book of nature stripped of its metaphysical or theological basis for moral as well as physical laws (Becker, 1959, p. 51). The concept of the state of nature which, for the most part, had only theological implications of a primitive state of man's innocence became a device for assigning to man inalienable rights in his natural condition. Society's primary justification was to protect and enhance the enjoyment of these rights. Initially modern natural law retained something of the generic nature of man as entailing the inalienable rights of life, liberty, equality and property. But it became increasingly difficult to maintain the rational awareness of abstract natural moral rights in the face of the growing trend towards empiricism in European and especially in English thought. Man's nature no longer revealed certain tendencies or inclinations that were the basis of laws of nature and man's comprehension of them as faint reflections of the divine law.

Hobbes (1588–1679) had begun the fragmentation of human nature by his mechanistic behaviorism. No absolute, objective good existed. Whatever the individual had an inclination for was good, whatever he avoided was bad (*Leviathan*, I, 6). In the state of nature the individual could follow his likes and dislikes limited only by his own right of nature to do whatever he wished for his self-preservation. In civil society the individual was free to do whatever he desired as long as the laws did not forbid it. The separation between law and morality was complete.

Hume (1711–76) dealt a death blow to natural law theory in both its classic and modern form by basing moral judgments on sentiment rather than reason. The implications of Hobbes' earlier voluntarism became more widespread. Moral standards either became rooted in feeling or, as later with Burke, in the tradition and established custom of society. Hume's view that the individual had a sentiment for the well-being of others evolved into the utilitarian notion that the good of the whole society could be attained by each individual pursuing his own good in accordance with whatever pleased him. The togetherness of the community of shared experience and of social relationships inherent in the classic natural law tradition was replaced by the 'go it alone' attitude of a 'rugged' individualism intent on procuring one's own interest and well-being.

Rousseau (1712–78) accelerated the decline in the importance of natural law by using it chiefly as a divinely based standard of morality for the exceptional individual (*Emile*, p. 255). The only sanction natural law had in this sense was the remorse of the transgressor (Masters, 1968, pp. 84–5). For most individuals morality could be attained only within the context of society. The influence of Plato and classic natural right on Rousseau's political thought was chiefly through the concept of the unity of morality and law. For Rousseau society based on a social compact is a moral collective body animated by a general will whose manifestation in laws was the basis of society and its political right and justice. The majority of men derived their civil and moral freedom (*Social Contract*, I, 6) from their participation as sovereign in the formulation of the general will and in their obedience to it as subjects of their own will. Laws were valid only if they agreed with the general will in being truly general both in formulation and object. The general will thus performed the function assigned to natural law of distinguishing valid from invalid law. The voluntaristic character of the general will and its lack of a metaphysical basis removed Rousseau's political thought from the mainstream of natural law.

Despite recent interest in presenting Burke (1729-97) as within the tradition of natural law (Stanlis, 1965), the English statesman and writer was more a protagonist of the historical school of society. From experience Burke saw that government and society were natural only in the sense that the world around him was natural, a world which like society developed, matured, declined and renewed (Burke, 1803, vol. 5, pp. 78-81). For Burke rights for the most part were created by convention and their nature and content depended on human circumstances and needs (Burke, 1803, Vol. 5, pp. 121-6), and what was expedient in the larger sense of what was truly good for society both in the present and for the future.

Although Burke does not represent the natural law tradition, his belief that a healthy society such as England was one which incorporated moral, social and especially religious attitudes of the right sort (1803, Vol. 5, pp. 173, 183-4) showed a strong parallel with Plato's political thought, with which he was familiar (Stanlis, p. 36) and which probably influenced him somewhat. Both thinkers agreed that a society based on such a healthy and 'virtuous' tradition reflected a continuity that would allow for necessary social change within the limits of the preservation of that tradition (*Laws*, 793b-d). Plato, however, based the rightness of his society on a metaphysical basis instead of Burke's historical approach to legitimacy through prescription (conventions legitimatized through use and tradition) and inheritance.

The decline in the importance of natural law as a basis for society was completed in Hegel's theory of the state. Natural law as understood by Hobbes and Locke and their contemporaries governed the operation of civil society. But for Hegel civil society was man's social and economic existence as a welter of conflicting and competing interests based on man's natural desires. The institutions of civil society were designed to maintain the necessary order and stability so that individuals could pursue their private ends without internecine conflict. Civil society in this sense would be what Hobbes and Locke considered the state, with its primarily 'policeman' type function. Individuals realized their own private ends, but their true end was the state as the higher and universal ethical end. Civil society was but an aspect of the state; 'Individuals ... do not live as private persons for their own ends alone ... their activity is consciously aimed at none but the universal end' (Hegel, *Phil. of Right*, para. 260). Hegel emphasized that the state has realized its nature or concept only when 'its members have a feeling of their own self-hood' and achieved stability 'only when public and private ends are identical' (*Phil. of Right*, para. 265, add.).

But although Hegel's theory of the state was not totalitarian the individual's ends coalesced with those of the state; 'personal individuality and its particular interests' after achieving their full development and justification 'pass over of their own accord into the interest of the universal' (*Phil. of Right*, para. 260). Hegel did assert the superiority of the state over the individual. Under certain circumstances 'rights and interests of individuals are established as a passing phase' (*Phil. of Right*, para. 324). The true end of the individual was inseparable from the end of the ethical life of the state. For the individual 'rectitude' was the performance of one's duties in the state (*Phil. of Right*, para. 150). The individual can realize himself only insofar as he is aware of the fact that his civic duties constitute his own inner universality.

Hegel agreed with Plato's notion that the individual could achieve his individuality or morality only within the context of the state. But he claimed that Plato denied any distinction between the state and the individual (Hegel, *Hist. of Phil.*, Vol. 2, pp. 110–13; Avineri, 1972, p. 112, n. 78) and subsumed the individual in the universality of the state. Justice of the individual for Plato, however, was quite distinct from that of the individual. Unlike Hegel's own claim that the individual was only a 'passing phase' or a 'nullity' in comparison to the state, for Plato the individual had a reality and value which transcended life in the state. Plato, however, stressed that as a member of the state the individual had his own inward morality which was not finally subsumed in the morality of the state as a whole.

Natural law was eclipsed in the nineteenth century by the historical school of law with its emphasis on the evolutionary and 'folkish' development of legal concepts, and by legal positivism which stressed the validity of all laws enacted in accordance with the duly established norms for legislation operative in the state. Natural law was, however, carefully nurtured within the Catholic tradition. This century has seen something of a revival of natural law (Haines, 1965; Friedrich, 1963, pp. 178–88), particularly in the United States and England. This rekindled interest in natural law was not one of resurrecting the past system of natural law or natural rights based on metaphysics or divine law, but reflected the concern of the Platonic natural law tradition of finding some standard for evaluating the positive laws of a state either as transcendent norm (Friedrich, p. 188) or in terms of the inner integrity or 'morality' of law (Fuller, 1975). Plato, then, as he appeared in our analysis is a significant precursor of the classic natural law, and the Platonic tradition even had some influence on modern natural law. For the value Plato placed on the moral well-being of the individual continued from the Stoic and Christian natural law tradition through modern natural law to the present day (allowing for different interpretations of what it means to be an individual). Surely Plato's focus on the individual and his value has become a part of the heritage of the West.

The concern Plato shared with the natural law tradition for the moral well-being of the individual has been slighted in many contemporary interpretations of his political thought. As a result, Plato's analysis of the relation of the ordinary individual to the state has either received minimal consideration or has been distorted.

The late Leo Strauss places Plato's political thought within the natural law tradition we have just considered. While Strauss contends that according to Plato the state is for the interest of the moral well-being of the individual, the individual turns out to be only the exceptional man, the philosopher. Strauss never admits that the ordinary individual is totally subordinated to the interests of the state. But he seems to think that Plato has left the ordinary individual no other area of activity than the doing of his social function.

Strauss terms Plato's interpretation of natural law as classic natural right. For Strauss there are three types of classic natural right: the Platonic-Stoic; the Aristotelian; and the Thomistic (1953, p. 146). Right is according to nature, especially the true nature of a thing, and not according to convention. According to classic natural right, man's nature determines the importance and hierarchical ordering of human tendencies, needs and inclinations. Man is distinguished from other animals by his capacity for and use of reason and understanding. These characterize his unique function as man (1953, p. 127). The good life is that life in which man's natural requirements are satisfied to their fullest extent. It is life in accordance with nature taken in the familiar Platonic sense of a unity of being and value. The rules prescribing a life in accordance with the requirements of a generic human nature constitute the content of classic natural right.

Man's nature can only be realized in society for he is above all a social being (1953, pp. 130–3). The society must remain small so that its citizens will know each other well enough to develop and retain a sense of trust and comradeship. Only through such trust can genuine freedom exist, according to Strauss' interpretation of classic natural right. To enhance such unity and trust, the good society will not allow visitors or immigrants. The realization of man's nature requires that he live in the best, the ideal society ruled by the true statesman.

Although he admits that according to Plato's version of classic natural right 'all men,' i.e. normal men have the capacity for virtue', Strauss claims that for Plato 'not all men are equally equipped by nature for progress towards perfection' (1953, p. 134). Strauss' contention is that only the philosopher can realize the excellence of the well performance of man's generic function (1953, p. 156; 1963, p. 21). Obviously such a claim clashes with Strauss' admission that all men have a capacity for virtue. For there seems little point of attributing such a capacity to man as such if, in fact, under any conceivable circumstance most men are unable to realize their fundamental natural capacity as human beings.

According to Strauss' interpretation of classic natural right, most men are congenitally unable to achieve virtue under the most appropriate circumstances. The theory of classic natural right is for Strauss unequivocally inegalitarian in this 'decisive respect'. Yet the only texts from those he cites (1953, p. 135, n. 14) from the natural law tradition that support his claim are from Aristotle (esp. *Pol.*, 1254a, 29–31). The others either do not provide adequate evidence for his position or show the opposite. The Stoic view presented in Cicero's *De Officiis*, 1, 107, for example, maintains that mankind is 'invested' with two characters. Reason is 'universal' in all men; from reason 'all morality . . . is derived'. The other character is purely individual and refers to men 'in particular', stressing differences in physical endowment, intelligence, and so on. Nor does the one passage Strauss cites from Aquinas (*ST*, 1a, 96, 3–4) support his view. Aquinas acknowledges that some men in the state of innocence are better able to rule than others. But those with lesser talents and abilities have 'nothing defective or sinful about either soul or body' (*ST*, 1a, 96, 3). Again, Strauss seems to have confused differences 'in particular' among men with a supposed difference in man's fundamental nature.

Strauss I think has confused the capacity for justice as a generic feature of Plato's theory of man with the empirical fact that most men, even some potential philosophers, are unable for one reason or another by their own efforts to acquire justice (1953, p. 134). To admit that most men have a hard time in realizing their excellence in existing societies is not to deny that under proper conditions they can achieve their excellence.

Strauss has further misread the distinction discussed earlier that Plato makes between the function of man as man in a generic sense, 'management, rule, deliberation, and the like' (353e) which resulted in the justice of the individual, and man's social function of doing that job in the state for which he is naturally suited without interfering with the activity of other citizens which resulted in the justice of the state. Men are equal in their capacity for justice of the soul, but unequal in their capacities for performing different social tasks in the state (370a–b). The result of this twofold confusion is that Strauss misinterprets the political analogy between the individual soul and the state. Ignoring the implications of his admission that for Plato all men are equal in their capacity for justice, he allows the difference in social function to harden into the supposed fact that men are unequal 'in regard to human perfection' (1953, p. 135). He identifies the individual's social role with his value as a human being, although in one sense for Plato all roles are equally important for the justice of the state (*Rep.*, 433c–d).

The two senses of function or capacity as we saw are quite distinct and compatible. They refer to different sides of man. Thus there is no reason why, as Strauss says, in terms of social function it should not be that 'some men are by nature superior to others, and therefore, according to natural right, the ruler of others' (1953, p. 135). Plato admitted that some men are naturally more suitable to rule than others. That is perfectly compatible with an egalitarian natural right or law theory. For although such a theory maintains the equality of all men with regard to their distinctive human function, the realization of such a function by men may well require, as in the case of the ideal state of the *Republic*, a strict observance of the natural inequality of social function with only a few men capable of rule. But the purpose of the ideal state is to make it possible so that even with these different and unequal social capabilities or native endowments all men would be able to realize their uniquely human capacity for justice or virtue.

Strauss has totally missed the point of the analogy between the justice of the state and the individual. For by the term 'individual' Strauss really means only the philosopher and not the ordinary individual even though between the discussion of the two kinds of justice in the *Republic* there is an analysis of the three aspects of the soul of any man (435b–41c). As we saw, justice of the individual applied to any citizen of the ideal state. In his analysis of the justice of the state Strauss betrays the fuzziness of his view of the political analogy and its implications.

> a city is just if each of its three parts (the money-makers, the warriors and the rulers) does its own work and only its own work. Justice is then, like moderation, and unlike wisdom and courage, not a preserve of a single part but required of every part. Hence justice, like moderation has a different character in each of the three classes. One must assume for instance, that the justice of the wise rulers is affected by their wisdom, and the justice of the money-makers is affected by their lack of wisdom, for if even the courage of the warriors is only political or civic courage, and not courage pure and simple, it stands to reason that their justice too—to say nothing of the justice of the money-makers—will not be justice pure and simple. In order to discover justice pure and simple, it then becomes necessary to consider justice in the individual man. (1963, pp. 20–1)

Strauss assimilates justice and the other virtues of the state to those of the individual. Only through this sort of assimilation can Strauss conclude that justice as doing one's task is the justice of the individual and applies to individuals in different ways depending on the extent of their wisdom or lack of it. In this fashion he is able to make two classifications of justice (and the other virtues) as they apply to the individual, political or civic justice, and justice 'pure and simple' as the inward ordering for the personal justice of the individual. Only the philosophers have 'justice pure and simple' because their justice only is based on philosophy while the justice of all those who are not philosophers is 'civic', consists only in doing one's social task and is based solely on 'habituation of one kind or another'. Consequently, the non-philosophers 'in the deepest recesses of their souls . . . long for tyranny, for complete injustice' (Strauss, 1963, p. 21).

Strauss has presented this caricature of Plato's political analogy and its significance because he has not kept distinct the function of the individual as a man (with the generic capacity for inward justice) and his social capacity. The inequality of social function which is the basis for the justice of the state becomes a natural inequality of man in a fundamental sense. Members of the appetitive and spirited orders are unable to be ruled by reason, or to attain inward justice. Their only justice is that of doing their social task and obeying laws and apparently they do both unwillingly through the coercion of laws (though Strauss concedes that their justice in this sense is an improvement over what it would be in other states).

In fact, as we have seen, Plato carefully distinguished between the justice of the state and that of the individual. After his definition of the justice of the state and an account of the human soul according to which every man had the three aspects of reason, spirit and appetites, Plato showed that justice of the individual applied to all individuals in the just society. For not only does the very language and context indicate this, but Plato expressly required that an individual have 'justice pure and simple' before he goes about doing his own social function to bring about the justice of the state (*Rep.*, 443e). Nor is it easy to see how the trust Strauss deems so necessary among citizens could be realized if most of them were inwardly longing for injustice. For Plato and for the natural law tradition which he began, although all men can not be philosophers, under the best of circumstances most men could attain the virtue or morality appropriate to human nature.

The second kind of interpretation of Plato's political thought ignores the role of the individual. It focuses on the institutional aspects of Plato's political thought, and seemingly equates the brevity of Plato's discussion of the ordinary man in the *Republic* with the importance he placed on the ordinary individual. Standard treatments of this type with no apparent ideological axe to grind are represented by such scholars as Barker (1960), McIlwain (1932), Sabine (1959), Sinclair (1959) and Wolin (1960). I shall take Sabine's approach as typical of this line of interpretation.

Of Plato's political dialogues the *Republic* is given the most extended treatment despite its admittedly visionary character (Sabine, 1959, pp. 44–69). Full recognition is given to the complexity of the issues discussed there, especially of the nature of the justice of the state. Little attention, however, is paid to the justice of the individual, which precipitated the inquiry. The focus, then, is on a systematic analysis of the political thought and institutions which, on the whole, are treated as a self-contained unit.

The *Republic* is seen by Sabine as Plato's answer to a twofold problem bedevilling and subverting the polis as he would like it to be. Factionalism among the various elements of society, and the ignorance of rulers and ruled, especially of the former, of moral and political standards and the art of rule, promise a continual corruption of man and polis. The *Republic's* ideal state attempts to deal with both of these fundamental social problems.

The realization of the justice of the state ends factional strife and provides for a unity of the state. Such unity is enhanced by the rulers having all things in common to preserve their dedication to the welfare of the whole society from any personal considerations. Statesmanship is an art with the forms, especially the moral and political, as its subject matter which the philosopher ruler knows as a result of his years of education. Ruling as benevolent despots without any significant use of law, the philosopher rulers seemingly use the members of the appetitive order in whatever way best brings about the stability and order of the whole.

Because his primary interest is the political aspect of the *Republic*, Sabine more or less ignores the personal or inward justice of the individual. He virtually identifies the two kinds of justice under the guise of doing one's work in the city (p. 60). 'There is nothing better for a man than to have his work and to be fitted to do it, there is nothing better for other men and for the whole society than that each should thus be filling the station to which he is entitled.'

The third kind of writers on Plato's political thought can hardly be accused of neglecting Plato's view of the relation of the state to the individual. Fite (1934), Crossman (1937), Winspear (1940), Popper (1962) all brand Plato as a totalitarian in his political thought. As they were writing within years of the Nazi rise to power and Germany's subsequently brief but savage mastery of Europe, some of these authors were probably influenced in part by their predecessors' approach to Plato's political thought. The tendency of scholars like Sabine (whose well-known history of political theory was first published in 1937) to identify the justice of the individual with that of the state, combined with the emotional climate created by the German horror, could easily help to bring about an interpretation of Plato as a totalitarian theorist.

The most authoritative, scholarly and influential of these critics is Karl Popper (*The Open Society and its Enemies*, 1962). In contrast to what Popper considers the 'Open Society', a democracy of the Anglo-American kind, Plato is an early advocate of a totalitarian or a 'Closed Society'. Plato's state, Popper believes, is a quasi-tribal society whose members have no existence apart from the society as a whole. They are bound together by feelings of intense loyalty, kinship and commonality of purpose. Together the citizens stand ready to defend themselves against a hostile world.

The rulers of this early version of the 'Closed Society', the philosophers, are like tribal chiefs. The philosophers' knowledge of the forms which Plato thought qualified them for rule for Popper also serves as a magical basis of the society and of its laws (1962, p. 148). The aura of magic and taboo permeating this quasi-tribal society is heightened by the appeal to dread consequences resulting from any infraction of the laws and rules of the society. The retention of rule among those who perpetually form the order of the rulers amounts to 'racialism', according to Popper (1962, pp. 149-52).

Popper believes that Plato is sincerely trying to win happiness for the citizens of his state. He is attempting to provide a therapy or cure for citizens buffeted by the intolerable strain of civilization that was beginning to be felt from the breakdown of the Closed Society and the emergence of a society that at all levels allowed, if not encouraged, a diversity of values (1962, pp. 170-1). Such therapy would require an arresting of all social change and a retention of the Closed Society.

Central to Plato's theory of man and his relation to society is the theory of justice in the *Republic*. Popper's account of the Platonic theory of justice has largely gone unchallenged, leaving the impression that even his severest critics agree with his interpretation of this fundamental issue in Plato's political thought. (Vlastos has recently recognized this lack, 1977, p. 2, but his account of social justice or justice of the state only corrects the error of affirming that justice is the well-being of the state as a super being distinct from its members.)

Popper's attack on Plato's theory of justice stems from his fervent conviction that, above all, it is morally and politically a totalitarian theory.

From the point of view of totalitarian ethics . . . Plato's theory of justice is perfectly correct. To keep one's place *is* a virtue . . . the cogs in the great clockwork of the state can show 'virtue' in two ways. First, they must be fit for their task, by virtue of their size, shape, strength, etc.; and secondly, they must be fitted each into the right place and must retain that place . . . the virtue of keeping to one's own place will be common to all of them; and it will at the same time be a virtue of the whole: that of being properly fitted together—of being in harmony. To this universal virtue Plato gives the name 'justice'. This procedure is perfectly consistent and it is fully justified from the point of view of totalitarian morality. If the individual is nothing but a cog, then, ethics is nothing but the study of how to make him fit into the whole. (pp. 107-8)

Nowhere in the *Republic* does Plato define or describe the justice of the individual as doing one's social task in the state. Yet, this is the account of justice of the individual that Popper would foist on his readers.

Popper's failure to realize the differences as well as the similarities in Plato's analogy between the state and the individual seriously flaws the soundness of his attempt to show a totalitarian ethic in Plato's thought. Without any concern (1962, p. 337) for Plato's analysis of the justice of the individual (441c-5e) Popper immediately applies the justice of the state to that of the individual, so that justice of the individual is 'minding his own business' in the sense of doing his own job in the state. Contrary to Popper's thesis, Plato's theory of justice reveals not totalitarianism, but a deep-rooted concern and interest in the moral well-being of all men as rational individuals.

Popper's distorted interpretation of Plato's political thought has not been uncommon in recent years. Both the Nazis and Communists have considered him as their own (Morrow, 1971, p. 144-5). And today the recently formed Islamic Republic of Iran has been viewed as being shaped after the ideal of the *Republic*. Its actual leader, the Ayatollah Khomeini, who is a keen student of Greek philosophy, especially Plato, is the philosopher king. Far-fetched as these extreme views may be, they have some credence because of the obvious disparity of interpretations mentioned here.

Plato's political thought, according to my analysis, provides both a theoretical framework and a practical means for constructing a state which would embody the traditional values of the Athenian polis, wisdom, unity and fellow feeling, and freedom. Man for Plato displays the capacity for reason and rational self-control and fulfillment of the entire man. These characteristics prescribed how men should act in order to attain their nature as persons endowed with a personality. Although Plato's development of the notion of personality has been realized by scholars it has been limited to the philosophers (de Vogel, 1963, p. 35). Yet the concept of man's distinctive function (*Rep.*, 353d-e) implies a fundamental equality of all individuals to achieve their personalities or justice by living in the right kind of society. The individual transcends his life in the community in the afterlife. The quality of his existence after death depends on his moral characteristics as formed and shaped by his life in the state.

The goal, then, of Plato's political thought marks a significant innovation in Greek and Western thought, the moral personality and well-being of the individual. Hardly a partisan of Plato, Havelock realizes the significance of Plato's theory of justice of the individual when he calls it (1978, p. 322) a 'firm conception . . . the symbol of a purely personal morality which has endured to the days of Marx and Freud'. For Plato the individual has an existence which is apart from, but not in opposition to, the polis. The end of Plato's political thought is not merely the good state, but the moral well-being of the individual.

Bibliography

(Translations of the Platonic dialogues used in the text are marked with an asterisk. Letter paragraph references to the text such as *Laws*, 771e in translations not having them are based on the Loeb (Heinemann) edition.)

Adkins, A. W. H., *Merit and Responsibility* (Oxford: Clarendon Press, 1960).
Anderson, W. D., *Ethos and Education in Greek Music* (Cambridge: Harvard University Press, 1966).
Aquinas, St Thomas, *On Princely Government*, in *Aquinas Selected Political Writings*, ed. A. P. d'Entreves, trans. J. G. Dawson (New York: Washington Square Press, 1960).
Aquinas, St Thomas, *Summa Contra Gentiles*, Vol. 3, pts 1–2, trans. V. J. Bourke (Garden City: Image Books, 1956).
Aquinas, St Thomas, *Summa Theologiae*, Vol. 13, trans. E. Hill (London: Eyre & Spottiswoode, 1963).
Aquinas, St Thomas, *Summa Theologiae*, Vol. 28, trans. T. Gilby (London: Eyre & Spottiswoode, 1963).
Arendt, H., 'What is authority', in *Between Past and Future* (New York: Viking Press, 1968), pp. 91–142.
Aristotle, *The Athenian Constitution, the Eudemian Virtues and Vices*, trans. H. Rackham (London: Heinemann, 1938).
Aristotle, *Politics*, trans. B. Jowett, in *The Basic Works of Aristotle*, ed. R. McKeon (New York: Random House, 1941).
Armstrong, A. H. (ed.), *The Cambridge History of Later Greek and Early Medieval Philosophy* (Cambridge: CUP, 1967).
Augustine, St, *The City of God*, trans. M. Dods (New York: Modern Library, 1950).
Avineri, S., *Hegel's Theory of the Modern State* (Cambridge: CUP, 1972).
Barker, E., 'The law of nature', in O. Gierke, *Natural Law and the Theory of Society 1500–1800*, trans. E. Barker (Boston: Beacon Press, 1951), pp. XXXIV–I.
Barker, E., *Greek Political Theory, Plato and his Predecessors* (London: Methuen, 1960).
Becker, C. L., *The Heavenly City of the Eighteenth Century Philosophers* (New Haven: Yale University Press, 1959), pp. 33–70.
Berlin, E., 'Two concepts of liberty', in *Four Essays on Liberty* (Oxford: OUP, 1970), pp. 118–72.
Bluck, R. E., *Plato's Meno* (Cambridge: CUP, 1961).
Bonner, R. J., *Aspects of Athenian Democracy* (New York: Russell & Russell, 1967).
Bonner, R. J. and Smith, G., *The Administration of Justice from Homer to Aristotle*, Vol. 1 (New York: Greenwood Press, 1968).
Bosanquet, B., *A Companion to Plato's Republic* (London: Rivingtons, 1925).
Bourke, V. J., *The Pocket Aquinas* (New York: Washington Square Press, 1960).
Burke, E., *Works*, Vol. 5 (London: Rivington, 1803).
Bury, J. B. and Meiggs, R., *A History of Greece* (London: Macmillan, 1979).
Cairns, H., *Legal Philosophy from Plato to Hegel* (Baltimore: Johns Hopkins University Press, 1967), pp. 29–76.
Campbell, L., *Sophistes and Politicus of Plato* (Oxford: Clarendon Press, 1867).
Carlyle, Sir R. W. and Carlyle, A. G., *A History of Medieval Political Theory in the West*, Vols 1–6 (New York: Barnes & Noble, n.d.).

Cicero, *De Finibus*, trans. H. Rackham (London: Heinemann, 1921).
Cicero, *De Officiis*, trans. W. Miller (London: Heinemann, 1961).
Cicero, *Republic, Laws*, trans. C. W. Keyes (London: Heinemann, 1948).
Cicero, *Tusculan Disputations*, trans. J. E. King (London: Heinemann, 1927).
Connor, W. R., *The New Politicians of Fifth-Century Athens* (Princeton: Princeton University Press, 1971).
Cooper, J. M., 'The psychology of justice in Plato', *American Philosophical Quarterly*, vol. 14, no. 2 (1977), pp. 151–7.
Copleston, F., *A History of Philosophy*, Vol. 1, pt 2 (New York: Image Books, 1962).
Cranston, M., *What Are Human Rights?* (New York: Taplinger Publishing Co., 1973).
Cross, R. C., and Woozley, A. D., *Plato's Republic* (London: Macmillan, 1964).
Crossman, R. H. S., *Plato Today* (London: Allen & Unwin, 1937).
Deane, H. A., *The Political and Social Ideas of St. Augustine* (New York: Columbia University Press, 1963).
d'Entreves, A. P., *Natural Law* (New York: Harper & Row, 1965).
de Romilly, J., *The Rise and Fall of States According to Greek Authors* (Ann Arbor: University of Michigan Press, 1977).
de Romilly, J., *Thucydides and Athenian Imperialism*, trans. P. Thody (Oxford: Blackwell, 1963).
de Ste Croix, G. E. M., *The Origins of the Peloponnesian War* (Ithaca: Cornell University Press, 1972).
de Vogel, C. J., 'The concept of personality in Greek and Christian thought', in *Studies in Philosophy and the History of Philosophy*, Vol. 2, ed. J. K. Ryan (Washington, D.C.: The Catholic University of America Press, 1963), pp. 20–60.
des Places, E., *Platon Lexique*, vol. 14 (Paris: Societe d'Edition, Les Belles Lettres, 1970).
Diels, H., and Kranz, W., *Die Fragmente Der Vorsokratiker*, sixth ed. (Berlin: Weidmann, 1952).
Diogenes Laertius, *Lives of Eminent Philosophers*, Vol. 1, trans. H. D. Hicks (London: Heinemann, 1925).
Dodds, E. R., *The Greeks and the Irrational* (Boston: Beacon Press, 1957).
Dodds, E. R., *Plato Gorgias* (Oxford: Clarendon Press, 1959).
Dover, K. J., *Greek Popular Morality in the Time of Plato and Aristotle* (Berkeley: University of California Press, 1974).
Ehrenberg, V., *The Greek State* (Oxford: Blackwell, 1960).
Else, G. F., *The Structure and Date of Book 10 of Plato's Republic* (Heidelberg: Winter, 1972).
Ferguson, A. S., 'Plato's simile of light', pt II, *The Classical Quarterly*, vol. 16 (1922), pp. 15–28.
Ferguson, A. S., 'Plato's simile of light again', *The Classical Quarterly*, vol. 28 (1934), pp. 190–210.
Field, G. C., *Plato and his Contemporaries* (London: Methuen, 1930).
Field, G. C., *The Philosophy of Plato* (London: OUP, 1949).
Finnis, J., *Natural Law and Natural Rights* (Oxford: Clarendon Press, 1980).
Fite, W., *The Platonic Legend* (New York: Scribner, 1934).
Forrest, W. G., *The Emergence of Greek Democracy 800–400 B.C.* (New York: McGraw-Hill, 1966).
Foster, M. B., *The Political Philosophies of Plato and Hegel* (Oxford: Clarendon Press, 1935).
Friedrich, C. J., *The Philosophy of Law in Historical Perspective* (Chicago: University of Chicago Press, 1963).
Frisch, H., *The Constitution of the Athenians* (Copenhagen: Nordisk Forlag, 1942).
Fuller, L. L., *The Morality of Law* (New Haven: Yale University Press, 1975).
Gough, J. W., *The Social Contract* (Oxford: Clarendon Press, 1957).
Grene, D., *Greek Political Theory* (Chicago: University of Chicago Press, 1965).

Grotius, H., *De Jure Belli ac Pacis*, Vol. 2, trans. F. W. Kelsey (Oxford: Clarendon Press, 1925).
Grube, G. M. A., *Plato's Thought* (Boston: Beacon Press, 1958).
Gulley, N., *Plato's Theory of Knowledge* (London: Routledge & Kegan Paul, 1962).
Guthrie, W. K. C., *The Greeks and their Gods* (Boston: Beacon Press, 1955).
Guthrie, W. K. C., *In the Beginning* (Ithaca: Cornell University Press, 1957).
Guthrie, W. K. C., *The Sophists* (Cambridge: CUP, 1971).
Guthrie, W. K. C., *A History of Greek Philosophy*, Vol 4, *Plato the Man and his Dialogues: Earlier Period* (Cambridge: CUP, 1975).
Guthrie, W. K. C., *A History of Greek Philosophy*, Vol. 5, *The Later Plato and the Academy* (Cambridge: CUP, 1978).
Haines, C. G., *The Revival of Natural Law Concepts* (New York: Russell & Russell, 1965).
Hall, J., 'Plato's legal philosophy', *Indiana Law Journal*, vol. 31, no. 2 (1956), pp. 171–206.
Hall, R. W., *Plato and the Individual* (The Hague: Nijhoff, 1963).
Hall, R. W., '*Orthe doxa* and *eudoxia* in the *Meno*' *Philologus*, vol. 108, no. 2 (1964), pp. 66–71.
Hall, R. W., 'Plato's just man: thoughts on Strauss' Plato', *The New Scholasticism*, vol. 42, no. 2 (1968), pp. 202–25.
Hall, R. W., 'Techne and morality in the *Gorgias*', in *Essays in Ancient Greek Philosophy*, ed. J. P. Anton and G. L. Kustas (Albany: State University of New York Press, 1971), pp. 208–18.
Hall, R. W., 'Plato's political analogy: fallacy or analogy', *Journal of the History of Philosophy*, vol. XII, no. 4 (1974), pp. 419–35.
Hall, R. W., 'Plato's theory of art: a reassessment', *The Journal of Aesthetics and Art Criticism*, vol. 32, no. 1 (1974), pp. 75–82.
Hammond, N. G. L., *A History of Greece* (Oxford: Clarendon Press, 1959).
Hammond, N. G. L., *The Classical Age of Greece* (New York: Harper & Row, 1976).
Harvey, F. D., 'Two kinds of equality', *Classica et Medievalia*, vol. 26, (1965), pp. 101–46.
Havelock, E. A., *The Liberal Temper in Greek Politics* (New Haven: Yale University Press, 1957).
Havelock, E. A., *The Greek Concept of Justice* (Cambridge: Harvard University Press, 1978).
Hegel, G. W. F., *Lectures on the History of Philosophy*, Vol. 2, trans. E. S. Haldane and F. H. Simson (London: Routledge & Kegan Paul, 1955).
Hegel, G. W. F., *Philosophy of Right*, trans. T. M. Knox (Oxford: Clarendon Press, 1942?)
Heinimann, F., *Nomos und Physis* (Basle: Wissenschaftliche Buchgesellschaft, 1945).
Hignett, C., *A History of the Athenian Constitution* (Oxford: Clarendon Press, 1952).
Hobbes, T., *Leviathan*, ed. M. Oakeshott (Oxford: Blackwell, 1955).
Irwin, T., *Plato's Moral Theory* (Oxford: Clarendon Press, 1977).
Isocrates, Vol. 2, trans. C. Norlin (London: Heinemann, 1929).
Jaeger, 'In praise of law', in *Interpretation of Modern Legal Philosophies*, ed. P. Sayre (New York: OUP, 1947), pp. 352–75.
Jones, A. H. M., *Athenian Democracy* (Oxford: Blackwell, 1957).
Jones, J. W., *The Law and the Legal Theory of the Greeks* (Oxford: Clarendon Press, 1956).
Joseph, H. W. B., *Essays in Ancient and Modern Philosophy* (Oxford: Clarendon Press, 1935).
Justinian/Scott, *Corpus Juris Civilis*, Vols 1, 2, trans. S. P. Scott (New York: AMS Press, 1973).
Kagan, D., *The Great Dialogue* (New York: The Free Press, 1965).
Kerferd, G. B., 'Protagoras' doctrine of justice and virtue in the Protagoras of Plato', *Journal of Hellenic Studies*, vol. 73 (1953), pp. 42–5.
Keuls, E. C., *Plato and Greek Painting* (Leiden: Brill, 1978).
Kirk, G. S., and Raven, J. E., *The Presocratic Philosophers* (Cambridge: CUP, 1957).
Klibansky, R., *The Continuity of the Platonic Tradition* (London: Warburg Institute, 1939).

Köller, H., *Die Mimesis in der Antike* (Berne: Francke, 1954).
Kunkel, W., *An Introduction to Roman Legal and Constitutional History* (Oxford: Clarendon Press, 1973).
Larson, C. W. R., 'The Platonic synonyms, dikaiosyne and sophrosyne, *American Journal of Philogy*, vol. 72 (1951), pp. 395–414.
Levinson, R., *In Defense of Plato* (Cambridge: Harvard University Press, 1953).
Loenen, D., *Protagoras and the Greek Community* (Amsterdam: North Holland Publishing Co., 1940).
Luccioni, J., *La Pensée Politique de Platon* (Paris: Presses Universitaires de France, 1958).
MacDowell, D. M., *The Law in Classical Athens* (Ithaca: Cornell University Press, 1978).
McIlwain, C. H., *The Growth of Political Thought in the West* (New York: Macmillan: 1932).
Maguire, J. P. 'Plato's theory of natural law', *Yale Classical Studies*, vol. X (1947), pp. 151–78.
Marrou, H. I., *A History of Education in Antiquity*, trans. G. Lamb (New York: New American Library, 1964), pp. 95–119.
Masters, R. D., *The Political Philosophy of Rousseau* (Princeton: Princeton University Press, 1968).
Mauer, R., *Platons Staat und die Demokratie* (Berlin: de Gruyter, 1970).
Moreau, J., *La Construction de l'idéalisme platonicien* (Paris: Boivin & Cie, 1939).
Morrall, J. B., *Political Thought in Medieval Times* (New York: Harper, 1962).
Morrall, J. B., *Aristotle* (London: Allen & Unwin, 1977).
Morrow, G. R., 'Plato and the law of nature', in *Essays in Political Theory* (Ithaca: Cornell University Press, 1948), pp. 17–44.
Morrow, G. R., *Plato's Cretan City* (Princeton: Princeton University Press, 1960).
Morrow, G. R., 'Plato and the rule of law', in *Plato*, Vol. 2, ed. G. Vlastos (New York: Anchor Books, 1971), pp. 144–65.
Moser, S., and Kustas, G. L., 'A comment on the "relativism" of Protagoras', *Phoenix* (1966), pp. 111–15.
Mossé, C., *Athens in Decline 404–86 B.C.*, trans. J. Stewart (London: Routledge & Kegan Paul, 1973).
Murphy, N. R., 'The simile of light in Plato's *Republic*', *The Classical Quarterly*, vol. 26 (1932), pp. 93–102.
Murphy, N. R., 'Back to the cave', *The Classical Quarterly*, vol. 28 (1934), pp. 211–13.
Murphy, N. R., *The Interpretation of Plato's Republic* (Oxford: Clarendon Press, 1951).
Nettleship, R. L., *Lectures on the Republic of Plato* (New York: Macmillan, 1961).
North, H. F., *Sophrosyne* (Ithaca: Cornell University Press, 1966).
Pangle, T. L., 'The political psychology of religion in Plato's *Laws*' *American Political Science Review*, vol. 70, no. 4 (1976), pp. 1059–77.
Piérart, M., *Plato et la cité grecque* (Bruxelles: Académie royale de Belgique, 1973).
Plato, *Cratylus, Parmenides, Greater Hippias, Lesser Hippias*, trans. H. N. Fowler (London: Heinemann, 1953).
Plato, *Epistles*, trans. G. R. Morrow (New York: Liberal Arts Press, 1962).
Plato, *Euthyphro, Apology, Crito*, trans. F. J. Church (New York: Liberal Arts Press, 1956).
Plato, *Euthyphro, Crito, Phaedo, Phaedrus*, trans. H. N. Fowler (London: Heinemann, 1926).
*Plato, *Gorgias*, trans. W. C. Hembold (New York: Liberal Arts Press, 1952).
Plato, *Laches, Protagoras, Meno, Euthydemus*, trans. W. R. M. Lamb (London: Heinemann, 1952).
Plato, *The Laws*, Vols. 1, 2, trans. R. G. Bury (London: Heinemann, 1961).
*Plato, *The Laws*, trans. T. J. Saunders (Harmondsworth: Penguin, 1970).
Plato, *The Laws*, trans. A. G. Taylor (London: Dent, 1960).
*Plato, *Meno*, in *Protagoras and Meno*, trans. W. K. C. Guthrie (Harmondsworth: Penguin, 1956).

Plato, *Phaedo*, trans. R. S. Bluck (New York: Liberal Arts Press, n.d.).

Plato, *Phaedo*, trans. R. Hackforth (Cambridge: CUP, 1955).

*Plato, *Phaedo*, trans. H. Tredennick, in *The Collected Dialogues of Plato*, ed. E. Hamilton and H. Cairns (New York: Bollingen, 1961).

*Plato, *Phaedrus*, trans. R. Hackforth (Cambridge: CUP, 1952).

Plato, *Philebus*, trans. R. Hackforth (Cambridge: CUP, 1958).

Plato, *Platonis Opera*, Vols. 1–5, ed. J. Burnet (Oxford: Clarendon Press, 1900–7).

*Plato, *Protagoras*, trans. B. Jowett, ed. G. Vlastos (New York: Liberal Arts Press, 1956).

Plato, *Protagoras and Meno*, trans. W. K. C. Guthrie (Harmondsworth: Penguin, 1968).

Plato, *Republic*, trans. F. M. Cornford (Oxford: OUP, 1978).

*Plato, *Republic*, Vols. 1, 2, trans. P. Shorey (London: Heinemann, 1956).

Plato, *The Sophist and Statesman*, trans. A. E. Taylor (London: Nelson, 1961).

Plato, *Sophist and Theaetetus*, trans. H. N. Fowler (London: Heinemann, 1921).

*Plato, *Statesman (Politicus)*, trans. J. B. Skemp, ed. M. Ostwald (New York: Liberal Arts Press, 1957).

Plato, *The Statesman, Philebus*, trans. H. N. Fowler (London: Heinemann, 1925).

*Plato, *Theaetetus*, trans. F. M. Cornford (New York: Liberal Arts Press, n.d.).

*Plato, *Timaeus*, in *Plato's Cosmology*, trans. F. M. Cornford (New York: Liberal Arts Press, 1957).

Pohlenz, M., *Freedom in Greek Life and Thought*, trans. C. Lofmark (New York: Humanities Press, 1966).

Popper, Karl R., *The Poverty of Historicism* (Boston: Beacon Press, 1957).

Popper, Karl R., *The Open Society and its Enemies*, Vol. 1, *The Spell of Plato* (New York: Harper & Row, 1962).

Pound, R., *An Introduction to the Philosophy of Law* (New Haven: Yale University Press, 1954).

Reverdin, O., *La Religion de la cité platonicienne* (Paris: Boccard, 1945).

Rhodes, P. J., *The Athenian Boule* (Oxford: Clarendon Press, 1972).

Richardson, R. K., 'History and Plato's medicinal lie', *Trans. Wisconsin Academy of Arts and Letters*, vol. 40, pt 2 (1951), pp. 67–76.

Ritchie, D. G., *Natural Rights* (London: Allen & Unwin, 1952).

Rommen, H. A., *The Natural Law*, trans. T. R. Hanley (New York: Arno Press, 1979).

Rousseau, J. J., *Émile*, trans. B. Foxley (London: Dent, 1955).

Rousseau, J. J., *On the Social Contract*, trans. J. R. Masters, ed. R. D. Masters (New York: St Martin's Press, 1978)

Ryder, T. T. B., *Koine Eirene* (London: OUP, 1965).

Sabine, C. H., *A History of Political Theory* (London: Harrap, 1959).

Sandvoss, E., *Soteria* (Göttingen: Musterschmidt, 1971).

Saunders, T. J., 'The structure of the soul and the state in Plato's laws', *Eranos*, vol. 60 (1962), pp. 37–55.

Schlaifer, R., 'Greek theories of slavery from Homer to Aristotle', in *Slavery in Classical Antiquity*, ed. M. I. Finley (Cambridge: Heffer, 1960), pp. 93–132.

Schulz, F., *History of Roman Legal Science* (Oxford: Clarendon Press, 1963).

Sealey, R., *A History of the Greek City States ca 700–338 B.C.* (Berkeley: University of California Press, 1976).

Sinclair, T. A., *A History of Greek Political Thought* (London: Routledge & Kegan Paul, 1959).

Skemp, J. B., 'Comment on communal and individual justice', *Phronesis*, vol. 5, no. 1 (1960), pp. 35–8.

Skemp, J. B., *The Theory of Motion in Plato's Later Dialogues* (Amsterdam: Haknert, 1967).

Solmsen, F., *Plato's Theology* (Ithaca: Cornell University Press, 1942).

Solmsen, F., 'Plato and science', in *Interpretations of Plato*, ed. H. F. North (Leiden: Brill, 1977), pp. 86–106.

Stanlis, P. J., *Edmund Burke and the Natural Law* (Ann Arbor: University of Michigan Press, 1965).

Strauss, L., *Natural Right and History* (Chicago: University of Chicago Press, 1953).
Strauss, L., 'Plato', in *History of Political Philosophy*, ed. L. Strauss and J. Cropsey (Chicago: Rand McNally, 1963), pp. 7–63.
Strauss, L., *The Argument and Action of Plato's Laws* (Chicago: University of Chicago Press, 1975).
Taylor, A. E., 'The decline and fall of the state in *Republic* VIII', *Mind*, n.s., vol. 48 (1939), pp. 23–38.
Thucydides, *History of the Peloponnesian War*, Vols 1–4, trans. C. F. Smith (London: Heinemann, 1965–9).
Troeltsch, E., 'The idea of natural law and humanity in world politics', in O. Gierke, *Natural Law and the Theory of Society 1500–1800*, trans. E. Barker (Boston: Beacon Press, 1957), pp. 201–22.
Vanhoutte, M., *La Philosophie politique de Platon dans les Lois* (Louvain: Publications Universitaires de Louvain, 1954).
Vaughan, C. E., *Studies in the History of Political Philosophy*, Vol. 2, ed. A. G. Little (New York: Russell & Russell, 1960).
Versényi, L., *Socratic Humanism* (New Haven: Yale University Press, 1963).
Vinogradoff, P., *Outlines of Historical Jurisprudence*, Vol. 2 (London: OUP, 1922).
Vlastos, G., 'Slavery in Plato's *Republic*', in *Slavery in Classical Antiquity*, ed. M. I. Finley (Cambridge: Heffer, 1960), pp. 133–49.
Vlastos, G., 'Review symposium: A. W. Gouldner, *Enter Plato*', *American Sociological Review*, vol. 3, no. 4 (1966), pp. 548–9.
Vlastos, G., 'Justice and psychic harmony in the *Republic*', *The Journal of Philosophy*, vol. 66, no. 16 (1969), pp. 505–21.
Vlastos, G., 'Justice and happiness in the *Republic*', in *Plato*, Vol. 2, ed. G. Vlastos (Garden City: Anchor Books, 1971), pp. 65–95.
Vlastos, G., *Plato's Universe* (Seattle: University of Washington Press, 1975).
Vlastos, G., 'The theory of social justice in the *polis* in Plato's *Republic*' in *Interpretations of Plato*, ed. H. F. North (Leiden: Brill, 1977), pp. 1–40.
von Fritz, K., *The Theory of the Mixed Constitution in Antiquity* (New York: Columbia University Press, 1954).
Wild, J. D., *Plato's Modern Enemies and the Theory of Natural Law* (Chicago: University of Chicago Press, 1953).
Williams, B., 'The analogy of city and soul in Plato's *Republic*', in *Exegesis and Argument*, ed. E. N. Lee, A. P. D. Mourelatos and R. M. Rorty (Assen: Van Gorcum, 1973), pp. 196–224.
Winspear, A. D., *The Genesis of Plato's Thought* (New York: Dryden Press, 1940).
Wolin, S., *Politics and Vision* (Boston: Little, Brown, 1960).
Wood, E. M., and Wood, N., *Class Ideology and Ancient Political Theory* (New York: OUP, 1978).
Xenophon, *Hellenica*, Vols. 1, 2, trans. C. L. Brownson (London: Heinemann, 1930–2).

INDEX